WOMEN WITHOUT MEN: MENNONITE REFUGEES OF THE SECOND WORLD WAR

Marlene Epp, who has written extensively on Mennonite history, presents here the story of thousands of Soviet Mennonite women who, having lost their husbands and fathers to Stalinist work camps and the Second World War, made an arduous journey through war-torn Europe. Housed in displaced person camps after the war, many eventually emigrated to Paraguay and Canada.

More than a mere description of the events that led these women from their homes, this work encompasses the culture of women refugees and, in particular, how they 'remembered' the events that marked their lives. The women wove their memories into larger histories that helped them to deal with the horror of the past and contributed to a sense of normalcy in their new and strikingly different homes.

Epp examines the particular difficulties of the emigration experience for women without men. These women often used ingenious strategies to protect themselves and their families, yet they were consistently depicted as weak and helpless by Mennonite refugee boards eager to reimpose traditional gender roles disrupted by the Soviet and war environments.

Epp's study focuses on the intersection of gender, war, and immigration. In her analysis of the relationship of female-headed households with patriarchal, postwar society, she gains access to the personal worlds of these women. In doing so, she offers a better understanding of the culture of postwar immigrants and postwar families, the workings of refugee settlement agencies, and the functioning of postwar ethnic communities in Canada, Germany, and Paraguay.

(Studies in Gender and History)

MARLENE EPP is an instructor of history and Canadian studies at the University of Waterloo and University of Toronto. She has written several articles and lectured on Mennonite women and postwar migration.

STUDIES IN GENDER AND HISTORY
General editors: Franca Iacovetta and Karen Dubinsky

MARLENE EPP

Women without Men: Mennonite Refugees of the Second World War

UNIVERSITY OF TORONTO PRESS
Toronto Buffalo London

© University of Toronto Press Incorporated 2000
Toronto Buffalo London

Printed in Canada

ISBN 0-8020-4491-3 (cloth)
ISBN 0-8020-8268-8 (paper)

Printed on acid-free paper

Canadian Cataloguing in Publication Data

Epp, Marlene, 1958–
  Women without men : Mennonite refugees of the Second World War

  (Studies in gender and history series)
  Includes bibliographical references and index.
  ISBN 0-8020-4491-3 (bound)   ISBN 0-8020-8268-8 (pbk.)

  1. Mennonite women – Canada – History – 20th century.   2. Mennonite
  women – Paraguay – History – 20th century.   3. Women refugees – Canada –
  History.   4. Women refugees – Paraguay – History.   5. World War,
  1939–1945 – Refugees.   6. Mennonites – Canada – History – 20th century.
  7. Mennonites – Paraguay – History – 20th century.   8. Canada – Emigration
  and immigration – History – 20th century.   9. Paraguay – Emigration and
  immigration – History – 20th century.   I. Title.   II. Series.

  BX8128.W64E77 2000   305.48'687'0971   C99-932121-8

University of Toronto Press acknowledges the financial assistance to its
publishing program of the Canada Council for the Arts and the Ontario Arts
Council.

This book has been published with the help of a grant from the Humanities
and Social Sciences Federation of Canada, using funds provided by the Social
Sciences and Humanities Research Council of Canada.

University of Toronto Press acknowledges the financial support for its
publishing activities of the Government of Canada through the Book
Publishing Industry Development Program (BPIDP).

Canadä

Contents

Illustrations follow page 120

Acknowledgments

In the several years after the first draft of this book was completed, I had the opportunity to speak at a variety of events that focused on the lives of post–Second World War Mennonite refugees in Canada. During the 1990s, there were many occasions to both mourn and celebrate at fiftieth anniversaries of pivotal events in the history of this immigrant group: the departure from Ukraine in 1943 and arrival in Canada in 1948 were two significant events to mark.

I always felt humbled and somewhat anxious when I – a second-generation Canadian – faced a group of middle-aged and elderly Mennonites, former refugees whose experiences were so difficult that they almost defied empathy, and analysed their past lives. Few people told me I had the story all wrong. Rather, I was deeply gratified when elderly men, tears in their eyes, would shake my hand vigorously and say, 'Yes, that's exactly how it was,' or, as many women said, 'You finally said publicly what was always secret.' This kind of affirmation ultimately means more than any scholarly appraisal of my research. With that in mind, I offer special gratitude to the postwar Mennonite immigrants who opened their homes and hearts to me and graciously shared their amazing life stories.

In its earliest form, this book was a doctoral thesis at the University of Toronto. My advisor, Ian Radforth, was a pleasure to work with, as were Franca Iacovetta and Harvey Dyck. They all offered criticism and affirmation in good balance and have continued to support me in my post-doctoral life as a scholar. Although she was not closely involved in this project, Wendy Mitchinson first inspired me to explore women's history and was an important mentor as I embarked on graduate studies in history.

Financial support from the Social Sciences and Humanities Research Council of Canada, the University of Toronto, and Quiring-Loewen Trust is gratefully acknowledged. The editorial staff at University of Toronto Press were pleasant and prompt in bringing the book to fruition; for guiding me through the steps of publication, I thank Gerald Hallowell, Emily Andrew, Jill McConkey, and Barbara Tessman.

Archivists and their staff in Canada and the United States shared my enthusiasm for the project and were generous in pointing me to useful sources. I offer specific thanks to Sam Steiner at the Mennonite Archives of Ontario, Waterloo, Ontario; Lawrence Klippenstein, Peter Rempel, Connie Wiebe, and Ken Reddig at the Mennonite Heritage Centre, Winnipeg, Manitoba; Abe Dueck and Alf Redekopp at the Centre for Mennonite Brethren Studies, Winnipeg; Dave Giesbrecht at Columbia Bible College Archives, Abbotsford, British Columbia; Dennis Stoesz at the Archives of the Mennonite Church, Goshen, Indiana; and John Thiesen at the Mennonite Library and Archives, North Newton, Kansas. The library staff at Conrad Grebel College, Waterloo, also deserve mention for their congenial willingness to answer all my queries.

During the years of working on this project, I benefited from specific advice and general encouragement from numerous individuals: in particular I'd like to thank Karen Dubinsky, Frances Early, Helen Epp, Esther Epp-Tiessen, Linda Huebert Hecht, Otto Klassen, Pamela Klassen, Harry Loewen, Royden Loewen, Ted D. Regehr, Agatha Schmidt, Frances Swyripa, and James Urry.

I consider myself blessed to have a community of friends, neighbours, and family who were always enthusiastic about my work, even if they secretly wondered when that book would ever get done. My husband and sons have lived with the writing of this book as long as I have. Paul Born and Lucas and Michael Epp Born have shared my triumphs and anxieties most intimately. For their constant optimism, unconditional support, and love, they have my deepest thanks.

WOMEN WITHOUT MEN:
MENNONITE REFUGEES OF THE
SECOND WORLD WAR

Introduction

On 27 September 1948, Maria Redekop Wall, age forty-seven, arrived in Canada as a refugee, ready to make a new life for herself and her six children. The home left behind was a Mennonite village in Ukraine, which had been evacuated westward with the retreating German occupation forces in the fall of 1943. Maria came to Canada as a widow, although to the day she died, in British Columbia in 1974, she never received any official confirmation of her husband's death. In 1938, as happened in many families living under the Stalin regime, Maria's husband was arrested by Soviet secret police on charges of subversion and was never heard from again. Together with her children, several of whom were young adults on their arrival in Canada, Maria paid off the travel debt owed to her sponsoring relatives and bought a small berry farm in the Fraser Valley of British Columbia. Her children grew up, married, and prospered in the new country they called home.[1]

As refugees from postwar Europe, the Walls were only seven of 125,414 persons who immigrated to Canada in 1948.[2] The first decade and a half following the Second World War, in fact, saw close to two million people come to Canada in response to the nation's increasingly open-door immigration policy. In the five years immediately after the war, most newcomers were war refugees – or displaced persons (DPs), as they were labelled in official policy. Mennonite immigrants were only a very small portion – less than 1 per cent – of the total, yet their experience represents a microcosm of the circumstances surrounding the lives of many postwar newcomers in Canada. At one level then, this book is a case study that offers a glimpse into the lives of displaced persons generally. At another level, it is an examination of a particular community for whom historical circumstances and internal characteristics combined to form a unique experience.

Between 1947 and 1952, approximately eight thousand Mennonites were admitted to Canada as refugees, having been displaced from their homes in the Soviet Union and eastern Europe during the course of the war. An additional four thousand Mennonites went to Paraguay, many of whom then immigrated to Canada during the 1950s. Most notable about postwar Mennonite immigrants – as exemplified by Maria Redekop Wall's family – was a high percentage of female-headed families and an almost universal problem of missing family members. The sex imbalance resulted from the loss of men, teenaged to middle-aged, who had been arrested and exiled in the Soviet Union or were killed or lost in action as soldiers conscripted into either Soviet or German armed forces.[3] Beyond the fact that many immigrant households had few or no adult males in them, family units almost without exception had experienced separation and fragmentation and could name many missing members from either the nuclear or extended circle.

One of the purposes of this study is to record and analyse the stories of individuals and families like the Maria Wall family, whose tragic tales and amazing narratives of survival have received little public attention. As 'ordinary' people living very extraordinary lives, Mennonite refugees of the Second World War deserve to have their stories told to add a rich layer of individual experience to the broader narrative of the era. The absence of adult men in many families is the most startling feature of the Mennonite refugees described here, but female predominance does not make this group unique historically. What makes their story deserving of attention is the intersection of multiple identities – those of woman, of widow, of Soviet, of ethnic German, of Mennonite. Throughout the refugee sojourn, these identities combined and conflicted to produce unique choices and experiences. These layers of identity unfold by means of several major themes addressed in this study.

The first theme, which overlays the entire book, concerns the intersection of gender, war, and immigration. This study intends to contribute to, complement, and challenge the hitherto dominant modes of historical writing on immigrants in which single males, or indeed single females, or father-headed family groups, whether extended or nuclear, have characterized the flow of migrants globally. As a female-headed refugee family, the Walls and others like them were part of a special category of immigrants rarely given much attention in historical study. It is my contention that because of both the life experiences that propelled them into refugee identities and the predominant femaleness of the group, these Mennonite immigrants represented a discomforting aberration to the Mennonite communities that received them and to postwar society generally. Part of this discomfort lay in the altered gender roles that these women without men assumed as they led their families through the terrain of war to a new land. Although the women at the heart of this study, like the 'gold rush widows' of the American midwest described by Linda Peavy and Ursula Smith, interpreted their changing roles as 'something to be endured, not relished,'[4] the responsibilities they carried and opportunities they found changed them as women and at times put them in direct conflict with the norms of the communities that received them in Canada and Paraguay.

In historical writing, the immigrant experience has frequently been defined by male norms.[5] In such depictions, the typical immigrant is a temporary male sojourner or permanent migrant taking advantage of labour opportunities to earn money for his family of the future or the family left behind in his homeland. Where families did accompany the adult male to a new country, women and children are often grouped together as 'dependants' while the active decision-making and breadwinning roles are represented as the domain of the male head of household.[6] Critics of male-oriented writing on immigration point to the fact that women, in this scenario, are typically 'non-migrants who wait in the sending areas for their spouses to return or ... passive reactors who simply follow a male migrant.'[7]

There is, nevertheless, a growing body of literature that focuses on the female experience of immigration.[8] Much of the published research has described the lives of single, female immigrants who, like the more familiar male sojourner, were proactive in seeking adventure and wage-earning opportunities.[9] Women who immigrated with their husbands within a family unit were also active participants in the decisions surrounding migration and settlement.[10] Most of the historical writing on women immigrants has emphasized women's paid labour, as well as their roles within families and communities to resist or accommodate to the host society. The assumption underlying this emphasis is that women willingly left their homeland, motivated by the pull factors of chain migration and economic opportunities in the receiving country as well as by a variety of economic and social factors that limited their options at home.

Little attention has been paid to the meaning of immigration for women who were dislocated unwillingly from their homes and for whom migration represented an escape from tragedy and despair more than hope for future betterment. While official definitions of the refugee immigrant vary, for the purposes of this study a refugee is an individual who has fled her or his country due to fears of persecution or to intolerable political and social disruptions and violence.[11] A large portion of refugees include family units that are composed of women with children or other dependants but without adult men as spouses or fathers. It has been reported that women and children constitute 80 per cent of the world's contemporary refugee population.[12] Given this fact, anthropologist Doreen Indra has called for the study of gender as central to the refugee experience, pointing out that most research concerning refugees begins with primarily a 'male paradigm.'[13] While there has been little historical study of refugees as a unique category among Canadian immigrants, there is even less analysis that considers gender as a central factor in organizing the lives of those refugees.[14] As refugees whose families and communities had been drastically altered by the loss of men, the Mennonites who emigrated from the Soviet Union in the 1940s and 1950s had experiences of uprooting, sojourn, settlement, and assimilation that were all mediated by gender.

An important question raised throughout the present study relates to the manner in which gender roles were transformed, or not, throughout the process of flight and resettlement. Studies of female migrants in other national contexts have reached a variety of conclusions on this question. Janice Potter-MacKinnon, in her study of Loyalist refugee women, describes the challenges that women, in the absence of their menfolk, surmounted in support of the Loyalist war effort. But once in exile on British territory, these women were placed into a 'patriarchal, paternalistic power structure as burdens – mouths to be fed, bodies to be clothed and housed – whose own accomplishments were irrelevant.'[15] A study of Turkish guestworkers in West Germany notes that in cases where women migrated without their husbands to take up jobs in Germany, an almost complete reversal of traditional sex roles occurred when they were later joined by their husbands. Having already established themselves, wives were frequently the main or sole providers, were responsible for finances and housing, and also had to teach their husbands how to adapt in the new society. Husbands, for their part, often remained home and were responsible for childcare, at least initially.[16]

On the other hand, studies of Algerian immigrants in France and East African Sikh women in Britain found that, in response to the disruptive effects of immigration, women often helped to reinforce the status quo with regard to traditional gender roles, rather than seize opportunities for autonomy or model the independence exhibited by Western women.[17] Therapists working with Cambodian refugees in the United States have similarly observed that new familial and gender roles of some men and women have produced a 'backlash' in which individuals cling to traditional gender patterns as a way of ordering the chaos in their lives.[18]

With respect to Mennonite women, one might ask whether the disruption of family life and the difficult and often tragic circumstances in which women assumed non-traditional roles influenced the later arrangement of gender roles. The observation of historian Royden Loewen that 'migration ... often gave women the occasion to exert high degrees of power and influence' may well apply here, although he is writing about a different group of Mennonite migrants.[19] The way in which Mennonite women's roles were deconstructed prior to and during the war and then reconstructed after immigration was shaped by a range of factors, including the values of the Soviet, Paraguayan, and Canadian Mennonite communities, the societal discourse that surrounded the refugee community during a given era, and by the individual personalities of the women themselves. At the level of the individual it is difficult to draw conclusions that can be broadly applied, since each woman acted and thought about her gender in ways unique to herself. Some women responded to their situations with bravery, strength, and spirit; others were resigned, selfish, or bitter. In the context of the communities that they related to, there are more obvious contradictions between women's behaviour, choices, and self-perceptions, and what was expected of them and imposed upon them.

My analysis is complicated by the fact that the context in which women stepped out of traditional gender roles was also one of great personal pain and tragedy. Annemarie Tröger, in analysing the war memories of German women, observes that many women displayed a psychological ambiguity between their need to be 'strong, brave and tough' and take on unconventional leadership and management roles, and their need for warmth and security, often epitomized in a 'male saviour figure.'[20] It is difficult for women themselves, and for the interpreters of their experience, to assess the refugee experience as wholly 'liberating,' even though women took on tasks and responsibilities that would otherwise have been barred to them. Achieving a balance of interpretation between refugee women as 'agents' or 'victims' in the shaping of their gender identity has been one of the challenges of this study.[21]

The story of Mennonite refugee families is also intrinsically shaped by ethnicity, a second theme of this book. While the experience of postwar Mennonite immigrants is comparable to that of other displaced persons of the era, their strategies, decisions, and interpretation of situations were – like other immigrants belonging to ethnic and national groups – influenced, often determined, by the cultural norms of their distinctive society. Simply put, they lived out their lives within the interpretive framework of Mennonitism as defined for and by them at a particular time and place.

The Mennonites, often characterized as an ethno-religious group, have historical roots in the radical Reformation of the sixteenth century. Originally called Anabaptists due to their practice of rebaptizing adults, in opposition to the prevailing norm of infant baptism, they were persecuted by both Catholic and Protestant authorities for over a century. In addition to their belief in voluntary church membership, symbolized in adult baptism, they rejected the use of the sword and became pacifists. Mennonites further emphasized the importance of a pure church that separated itself from the evils of the world, and accordingly, in varying degrees, they exercised discipline toward members who deviated from the standards of the church. At the same time, they developed a strong community orientation and practised forms of mutual aid that were based on biblical ideals of Christians helping one another.

Early in their history, Mennonites were located mainly in Switzerland, the Netherlands, and Germany, but a tradition of migration quickly developed in response to persecution and the search for religious freedom and economic opportunity. Beginning near the end of the seventeenth century, the migratory path of Mennonites in Switzerland and southern Germany was mainly westward, across the Atlantic to North America. This strand of Mennonitism is not central to the present study. From the Netherlands, other Mennonites migrated east to Prussia and, beginning in the late eighteenth century, settled in southern Russia, where they established semi-isolated communities. Many of their cultural forms, such as foods, crafts, architecture, and dialect have origins in Dutch tradition, yet Mennonites in Russia were identified by their German cultural heritage, having adopted the German language during their sojourn in Prussia. A small ethno-religious minority in a large empire, these Mennonites nevertheless carved out a thriving economic and cultural niche for themselves in imperial society.[22] Although there was disparity within their settlements, Mennonites, in comparison with their Russian neighbours at the end of the nineteenth century, were wealthy, well educated, and at the helm of some of the most important agricultural and commercial enterprises in the southern part of the empire.

Following the Bolshevik Revolution, the fortunes of the Mennonites began to diminish, and during the 1920s approximately 25,000 left the Soviet Union for North and South America. The majority, about 21,000, immigrated to Canada. By 1930, however, opportunities to emigrate had disappeared. In that year there were roughly 100,000 Mennonites living in the Soviet Union, approximately two-thirds of whom lived in southern Ukraine, the remainder living in settlements in the trans-Volga region and further east in Asiatic Russia.

This study is concerned with the Soviet Mennonite population that experienced the full impact of Stalinist oppression during the 1930s and the resultant disintegration of Mennonite community life, at least at the institutional level. More particularly, I follow the history of those who fled the Soviet Union during the Second World War and later emigrated to Canada and Paraguay. A smaller Mennonite population resident in eastern Europe – Poland, Prussia, and Danzig – was similarly displaced during the war and became part of the same migration.

Within the canon of Mennonite historiography, the postwar immigration has been described in various ways. In scholarly works, the stories of the refugees themselves tend to be subsumed beneath parochial analyses of the institutions that facilitated the relief and migration process,[23] with a focus on the inter-organizational and governmental negotiations that dealt with the identity of displaced persons,[24] and by narratives written by or about North American relief workers who encountered the refugees in Europe.[25] Popular accounts of this dramatic era of history abound and include the personal memoirs of postwar immigrants as well as fictional and semi-fictional accounts.[26]

Many of the accounts about wartime experiences make mention of the imbalanced sex ratio among adult Mennonite refugees and the hardships women shouldered as a result, but there has been no attempt to analyse this striking disturbance in traditional family life. Until quite recently, this lacuna reflected a general disregard for, or more honestly unfamiliarity with, gender as a category of analysis in the writing of Mennonite history. While women refugees of the Second World War are described in heroic terms, their amazing lives are for the most part placed in a framework of abnormality, which obviates the need to inte-grate their choices and actions into the overall history of either the Soviet, Canadian, or Paraguayan Mennonite experience.[27] The fact that the 'women without men' at the heart of this study were not just immigrants or refugees but were women living out their lives in the context of a community with distinctive religious beliefs and cultural practices is significant in understanding how they responded to situations, how they adapted to their various post-migration settings, and how they processed their experiences in memory.

In addition to their identities as refugee immigrants and as Mennonites, the women examined here are distinctive because of the nature of their families. The theme of family fragmentation and reconfiguration is thus a third theme that runs through this study. The intact, nuclear family was such a rarity among postwar Mennonite immigrants that an early study contained a photograph of 'one of the few complete family units.'[28] The practical, if not ideological, definition of 'family' had become fluid throughout the Soviet period of Mennonite history as each individual nuclear family lost members and as family remnants came together to form new supportive units. Throughout the war, living units were varied in form, composed of individuals with an assortment of kinship relationships, or connections based on neighbourhoods and friendship, or simply alliances based on circumstance. Many families fit Sheila Fitzpatrick's definition of a 'grab bag family' or Annemarie Tröger's notion of a 'war family' – one in which individuals with or without a blood relationship come together to share housing, food, and other resources for the purpose of survival under wartime or comparable conditions.[29]

The group of people that an individual looked to as 'family' might go through a number of alterations over time. Daniel Bertaux and Paul Thompson's definition of a family as a 'collectivity constituted from an individual standpoint' seems particularly apt when applied to some immigrant families, who, when examined from the perspective of one individual's life story, were continually being remodelled, depending on the manner in which that person identified with the people close to her or him at any one time.[30] The life histories of refugees, and immigrants generally, provide a vivid illustration of Diana Gittins's thesis that families are 'infinitely variable and in a constant state of flux.'[31]

By examining family fragmentation and reconfiguration within the Mennonite refugee community, this study seeks to contribute to the historical understanding of families in 'their various configurations' and to an awareness of their 'diversity of form and function.'[32] When juxtaposed against the discourse surrounding 'the family' in postwar Canada, the refugee family in its multiplicity of forms represented an anomaly. Even though the idea of family was of crucial importance in the lives of most refugees, for whom security was equated primarily with loved ones close at hand, the roles that individuals played within their families and how duties and responsibilities were allocated was often at variance with Canadian and Mennonite norms. The way in which refugee families and their host communities attempted to create normative families out of fragmented ones was part of the process of integration. This process also worked to remove from the social consciousness, as much as was possible, the realities of the refugee experience.

Within the broader theme of changing family structures, the specific roles of and attitudes toward widows are important issues. Given the demographic composition of the postwar Mennonite migration, a key aspect of the anomalous nature of family structure was the meaning and place of widowhood in Mennonite communities and families. Ida Blom, in a useful survey of literature on the history of widowhood, observes that 'the growth of the widowed population as a result of wars and the possible effects this may have had on the situation of widows and widowers have been little explored.'[33] There has been limited historical writing on widows generally, perhaps, as Arlene Scadron suggests, because of 'an underlying aversion to women alone, especially older women.'[34] The women at the heart of the present study do not easily fit into most interpretive frameworks applied to widows. First of all, many were not 'old' women, and some in fact were quite young – in their late twenties and early thirties. A further qualification to their experience is that many were not technically widows; that is, most had never received any official confirmation of their husband's death. Therefore, although they functioned and were treated as though they were widowed, the ambiguity of their marital status complicated their lives, particularly with respect to remarriage.

For women who lost their husbands, strategies to overcome their economic vulnerability were central, as several historians of widowhood have observed.[35] Economic factors were also central to a widow's decision whether or not to remarry. But for Mennonite widows, the impulse toward remarriage also related to issues of respectability and to the familial norms of their community. Widowhood had characteristics that were both liberating and debilitating, but for the women without men in this study, outcomes were rarely simply one or the other.

It should be stated that while this is a study about gender, it is primarily about women, who after all outnumbered men in the postwar Mennonite migration by about two to one. Men's experiences are referred to, but the ways in which they experienced the war and subsequent emigration are not central to this analysis and remain for future study. While the women described here experienced much tragedy, loss, and violence in their lives, some of which was gendered in nature, my chosen focus is not meant to suggest that men did not also endure much pain and carry extraordinary burdens. In a sense, men were victimized in a more obvious way than women; thousands were arrested, exiled, or shot even prior to the war, and countless more died during the war itself. They were considered martyrs of Soviet oppression and, as such, their tragedy could be understood within a theological construct familiar to Mennonites, one that eased the integration of men's stories into a known history. The experience of men also differed from that of women in that many were conscripted (some volunteered) for service in either the Soviet or German armed forces. Despite Mennonites' traditional adherence to pacifism, or non-resistance, even such wartime experiences presented an intellectual and theological dilemma that fitted into accepted categories.

In attempting to uncover historical experience and to address the themes and questions outlined above, I have adopted a variety of research tools and methodologies. First of all, there is a wealth of archival material that offers data and interpretation from the perspective of organizations and individuals who facilitated the process of immigration and settlement. Most notable are the records of the Canadian Mennonite Board of Colonization (CMBC), which, together with the Mennonite Central Committee (MCC) and the Canadian government, arranged for the sponsorship and migration of some 12,000 Mennonites to Canada and Paraguay in the first decade after the war, and to a certain extent followed up on their settlement. The CMBC records, along with those of a sampling of Canadian Mennonite churches that received immigrants, provide both demographic data on the postwar immigrants and also qualitative material from the perspective of individuals and institutions looking in on the immigrant experience. For the most part, however, an 'insider' perspective – that of the refugee herself – is absent from these archival sources.

To obtain that insider viewpoint, I listened to and tape-recorded the stories of thirty-four individuals from the postwar immigration, who, by that time, were living in Ontario, Manitoba, Alberta, and British Columbia. The individuals represented a cross-section of refugees, in terms of age, sex, and place of origin. Some narrators were adults with children when they arrived in Canada; others were children or young adults arriving with widowed mothers; still others were teenagers or adults arriving on their own. Some came directly to Canada from Europe, while others emigrated first to Paraguay, and then to Canada up to ten years later. Because the majority of individuals interviewed preferred anonymity, I have created first-name pseudonyms in conveying their stories.

Although my own research has been informed by feminist approaches to oral history, life stories, and ethnography, my interviews do not fit the 'collaborative' model adopted by some scholars who attempt to maintain a reciprocal relationship between interviewer and subject.[36] Because I wanted to obtain a reasonably large sample of personal stories, a collaborative approach, in which the ongoing relationship between narrator/subject and listener/researcher is central to the oral 'text,' was quite simply not possible. I do not believe that the one-time encounter between storyteller and researcher necessarily represents an appropriation by the latter of the former's life story. The collector of stories holds the power of synthesis and interpretation, but the narrator inevitably maintains power over her own story to the extent that she can withhold, emphasize, and indeed fabricate aspects of her life at her own choosing. Like Susan Geiger, I believe that 'doing oral history within a feminist methodological framework is about intellectual work and its processes, not about the potential for or realization of a relationship beyond or outside that framework.'[37]

Recognizing that a narrator is actively creating her life story even while telling it in retrospect, I have found interpretive methods that examine the meaning and manner in which individuals tell their life stories particularly helpful for this study. James Fentress and Chris Wickham suggest that what many oral historians fail to emphasize is the fact that an oral interview is not 'a set of documents that happen to be in people's heads' as opposed to an archive, but is a source based on memory.[38] Concerned with the ways of deriving meaning from oral histories and narratives, Luisa Passerini has argued that 'meaning lies in the silences and contradictions contained in a life story just as certainly as it lies in what is said.'[39] The role of memory in the presentation of historical events and the way in which individuals and societies – in this case the Mennonites – process recollections of their past is thus a fourth theme that recurs in varying degrees throughout the book.

Although oral interviews are most obviously sources based on memory, written memoirs are also reconstructions by an individual of her or his life based on a retrospective examination at the time of writing. Some theorists suggest that because of the potentially more public nature of written memoirs, they are in fact more likely to reproduce myths than are oral narratives.[40] At any rate, the increasing number of personal narratives written by postwar immigrants, together with oral sources, provides a rich 'insider' perspective based on personal and collective remembering.

Several kinds of memory sources,[41] as I shall call them, have been used in this study: oral interviews (several done in 1951 with recent Mennonite immigrants to Canada, and more done with the same population in the early 1990s); published and unpublished autobiographies and memoirs; and semi-autobiographical historical fiction. Although these particular sources are created through the process of remembering, and are therefore highly subjective, substantial objective information is not absent. As Fentress and Wickham observe, memory is often 'selective, distorted, and inaccurate,' yet 'it is not necessarily any of these; it can be extremely exact.'[42] Rather than setting up a dichotomy between the 'true' or 'false' aspects of memory, I think it more helpful to examine the societal and cultural constraints that shape particular memories and to recognize that 'we are what we remember.'[43] The 'truths' revealed by life histories are invariably shaped by context and worldview. In this study, I have used memory sources in a traditional sense, to provide anecdotal and qualitative evidence from the lives of refugee immigrants themselves, but also to explore the creation of patterns and myths in the process of remembering. The latter approach is especially useful when examining certain wartime topics such as rape, violence, escape, and morality, experiences that rarely receive a straightforward narrative.

What is evident in the use of memory sources for this study is not only the unique character of individuals and their corresponding memories, but also the existence of a 'social memory' or a master narrative that can either parallel or contradict the memory of an individual.[44] The idea of a shared memory is particularly relevant for a society or ethnic group such as the Mennonites, one that imbues history with religious significance and for whom, as has been said about the Jews, 'the memory of history is a religious duty.'[45] Individual memories of personal experience that do not fit into the accepted Mennonite narrative of the war, the trek out of the Soviet Union, and the subsequent immigration, may become submerged and even lost in the effort to preserve the social memory of the group. Or, as Joan Ringelheim argues with respect to Holocaust studies, a 'split memory' occurs, whereby women's gender-specific experiences are ignored and hidden, while memories of genocide are not.[46] For the Mennonites, the split is evident when, for example, women's memories of wartime rape are subsumed beneath the communal recollection of the victims of Stalinist oppression in the 1930s. The way in which Mennonite women tell their life stories is directly related to the way in which they understand the cultural and religious dynamics of their community and the way in which they view themselves as women with gender-specific roles within that community. That the existence of a social or collective memory may be especially relevant to a study of women is suggested by Billie Melman, who argues that the recognition that women are active agents of historical change is directly related to their inclusion within the collective and national memory. The 'cultivation of a female memory,' she observes, can 'de-unify the past and subvert sanctioned historical myths and narratives.'[47] In undertaking this analysis, I am juxtaposing the history and the memory of female refugees against the accepted historical narrative about the immigrant and, at another level, against the popular myths of ethnic historiography.

The themes and methodologies described above are present in varying degrees in the chapters that follow. Although this is a study of migration to Canada and Paraguay, the first three chapters are set in the Soviet Union and Europe. After all, the self-identity of immigrants and the manner in which they negotiate their lives in a new country are intrinsically shaped by their identities prior to migration. Chapter 1 describes and explains the loss of males and the resulting sex imbalance in the Mennonite communities of southern Ukraine during the decades prior to the Second World War. In chapter 2 the Mennonites of Ukraine and eastern Europe are followed through the war as they become refugees accommodated in camps for displaced persons in postwar Europe. Chapter 3 deals with the process of finding new homes for Mennonite refugee families by government and Mennonite church organizations and how the potential immigrants negotiated their new identities. Chapter 4 focuses on the migrant group that went to Paraguay and details the problems confronting female-headed families in pioneering in a virtual wilderness. Chapters 5 through 7 describe the experiences of those refugees that immigrated to Canada: their economic situation; their circumstances as mothers, widows, and marriageable women; and the dilemmas and opportunities that postwar immigrant women faced within Canadian Mennonite church congregations.

A brief note about spelling is in order: where applicable I have used Library of Congress spellings for Russian place names, except in the case of the two Mennonite settlements most relevant to this study, Molotschna and Chortitza, where I have maintained the traditional German spelling used by Mennonites themselves.

Individuals who migrate from one country to another can frequently divide their life stories into two separate and distinct parts. This was certainly true for postwar Mennonite refugee women. Their comparatively settled and stable existence in Canada belied the tragedy and dislocation that characterized their pre-migration lives. Yet their identity as refugee women remained part of them for the rest of their lives. It shaped their experience of integration into Mennonite communities in Canada and Paraguay, and also shaped their understandings of themselves as women and members of families. Giving their stories the place they merit in this particular episode of international migration is the main purpose of this study.

1

When the Men Went Away

On a fall evening in 1937, in the village of Paulsheim in the Ukrainian Mennonite settlement of Molotschna, there was a knock at the door of the Wiebe family's home. Katie Wiebe, then eight years old, recalls that the family members were preparing to eat their evening meal and were awaiting the arrival of Katie's father. The caller informed them that her father had been summoned to the village office. There he was arrested by the NKVD,* the secret police, and he was never again seen by his family. He was given no opportunity to say good-bye to his family nor was his wife allowed to send anything along with him or to him in prison. In subsequent years the family received no letters nor were they able to confirm his death, although there were rumours that he died in a labour camp in Siberia in 1945. Katie Wiebe's mother, then a relatively young woman in her thirties, was left with four children, Katie being the second youngest. Her two sons had been evacuated eastward in 1941 and thus were also left behind when the family fled their home in Ukraine in the fall of 1943.[1]

Stories similar to that of Katie Wiebe and her family were repeated over and over again in the Mennonite villages of Ukraine, especially in 1937 and 1938. During these years, the 'Great Purges' of the Stalin era reached their height, arrests and disappearances were frequent and expected, and half of Mennonite families lost the head of the family, namely the father. The fragmentation of families had begun much earlier, but by the late 1930s Mennonite families and villages came to be characterized as communities of 'women without men.' This chapter, set in Ukraine,

---

*NKVD is an abbreviation for the Soviet secret police during the years 1934–46. They are also referred to as the GPU prior to 1934, the MVD (1946–54), and the KGB (1954–).

provides a context for the disintegration of Mennonite family and community life in the decade prior to the Second World War. It describes the events that precipitated the loss of men and the struggles that families experienced as a result. It also suggests that, beyond the demographic shift that occurred, Mennonite families began to create an idealized place in their memories for departed husbands and fathers, even while witnessing the deconstruction of gender roles within their communities.

Russian Mennonite society – often referred to in Mennonite literature as a 'paradise' or 'commonwealth' – was radically transformed by the Bolshevik Revolution of 1917, the First World War, and the subsequent Civil War that was fought in the environs of Mennonite settlements in Ukraine. Prior to the upheavals of war and revolution, Mennonite communities were characterized by self-sufficiency (though not complete isolation) and prosperity in comparison with their neighbours. As German colonists who first arrived on the Russian steppe in 1789, Mennonites were set apart as an ethnic minority in Russian society; such separation was enhanced by an earlier history of religious persecution and migration in search of religious freedom. Their settlements, of which Chortitza and Molotschna were the first and largest, were politically self-governing and had a strong religious orientation. The civil and religious structures in fact operated as parallel and frequently overlapping systems in communal life. Membership in the Mennonite community, or *Gemeinschaft*, as it was called, demanded conformity to norms of both belief and behaviour. Yet conformity did not mean uniformity, and Mennonite society was characterized by a strong social hierarchy based on the possession of land, wealth, and political power.[2]

Within the context of the community, the Mennonite family was central. According to Harvey L. Dyck, the family was 'the primary economic, social, and welfare unit of Mennonite society' in the nineteenth century.[3] Mennonite families, which tended to be large, were oriented around the nuclear household, yet extended kinship ties were also crucial to an individual's identity and welfare. Gender roles were clearly defined within a patriarchal framework that assigned headship to fathers and in which wives deferred to their husbands. Like other families, Russian Mennonites were accustomed to losing loved ones in childbirth and through disease.[4] High infant and child mortality rates were one of the reasons women bore many children.

Although there was continuity in the importance of family, both nuclear and extended, the structure and size of most Mennonite families changed drastically in the first half of the twentieth century. For Mennonites living in Ukraine, war, famine, murder, and exile all became significant factors in family losses. Already during the First World War, Mennonite families bade a temporary farewell to sons and husbands who were compelled to perform various forms of labour as an alternative to military service, in keeping with Mennonite pacifist beliefs. Many men spent several years in the medical corps or as forestry workers far from home. During this time, women stepped out of traditional roles by doing much of the heavy farm labour. As well, mothers performed the roles of both parents, even if only for a short time.

A much more serious catastrophe befell Mennonite families in the years after the war. The Civil War between Red and White Armies, fought in Ukraine, was accompanied by terror and destruction by anarchist bands. Mennonites were viewed with hostility by Red Army forces and unorganized terrorists for their affluence, social status, and counter-revolutionary sentiments. Numerous families were victims of robbery, rape, and murder. An outbreak of typhus, as well as a severe famine in Ukraine in 1921–2 added to the already significant death toll.[5]

For many Mennonites, the civil war, famine, and violence of anarchy in the years following the revolution offset any optimism for the future promised by the new order. The mass emigration of Mennonites from the Soviet Union during the 1920s was a response to the ever increasing pressure on their cultural and religious institutions by communist authorities. During this migration, which saw close to 25,000 Mennonites leave for North and South America in the years 1922 to 1930, extended families and villages were split up as some family units chose to go while others elected to remain and hope for an improvement in their situation. These separations were painful, but in most cases resulted from decisions made by Mennonites themselves, unlike the family fragmentation that would follow.

For Soviet Mennonites who remained, the decade of the 1930s saw two significant waves of arrests, executions, and deportations of families and individuals. These abrupt ruptures within households altered family structure markedly. The first wave, often referred to as de-kulakization, followed the implementation in the late 1920s of collectivization, inaugurated as an official agricultural policy with Stalin's first Five Year Plan. The kulaks, loosely defined as the more well-to-do farmers, saw their property confiscated and sold, and themselves exiled. Unrealistic grain quotas and significant increases in taxes on income and property were part of the strategy to liquidate kulaks. Individuals and families who resisted or were unable to meet the demands on them usually faced arrest.[6] For Mennonites and other German-speaking colonists, de-kulakization was especially dramatic given their relative prosperity. According to Benjamin Pinkus, Germans represented about 14 per cent of kulaks in the Soviet Union, although they represented only 1 per cent of the total population. Furthermore, while Soviet Germans were prosperous compared with the general population, Mennonite Germans, concentrated in Ukraine, represented the most successful stratum of that group in the 1920s.[7]

While kulaks were targeted as an economic class, other groups were also subject to arrest and deportation during this first wave. When churches were closed beginning in 1929, religious clergy were exiled, particularly in the early 1930s. In addition, teachers and bureaucrats – in short anyone who was suspected of being a traitor to the regime – might be imprisoned for weeks, months, or years, or might even be shot. Adult men experienced the highest rate of exile during the years of de-kulakization, but it was not uncommon for entire families to be sent to labour camps in the distant regions of the Soviet Union. In the predominantly Mennonite settlement of Chortitza, with a population of 13,000, approximately 500 individuals were exiled during the period of de-kulakization from 1929 through 1935.[8] The most intense period of deportations occurred up to 1931, after which there was a decline.

In some cases, individuals or parts of families who were exiled returned to their homes. Margaret, a woman interviewed for this study, spent four years (1930–3) in Siberia with her family, who was exiled because her father was a minister. Margaret's father died of a heart attack in the second year, and her mother starved to death shortly thereafter. Margaret, who was fourteen at the time of her parents' deaths, and her sister escaped from the camp and spent several weeks travelling – on foot, by truck, and by train – back to their home in Ukraine. The conditions in exile, confirmed in other reports and memoirs, were so bad that Margaret could hardly talk about them sixty years later.[9]

The fear of being labelled a kulak and exiled was one of the hardships of the period. Living conditions worsened during 1932–3 when a severe famine occurred in Ukraine.[10] Although individuals had not enough food to meet the delivery quotas placed on them, many were accused of withholding foodstuffs from the collective and were subject to imprisonment. The famine and the fears of retribution for unmet production brought hardship to families already on the brink of starvation. For example, in 1933 the father of Mary, another woman interviewed for this study, was given a five-year sentence for withholding grain from the collective (he was released after serving two years). In the meantime her mother was responsible for milking the collective's fifty cows both morning and evening. The family's pig died of starvation and was taken away by beggars, but Mary's mother was able to bring home a little bit of milk, which kept her three young daughters alive.[11]

During the famine, the quest for food was uppermost, and in desperation people ate horse manure, cats, and dogs, and dug for acorns under the snow.[12] Recollections of this time include stories of eating acacia flowers, going begging, and sweeping out granaries and silos to salvage whatever kernels of corn or grain might be left behind.[13] Bread was scarce and, when it was available, costly. In 1932, Maria Martens Bargen wrote to her children in Canada and reported that they had lived through the winter without any bread; this was particularly hard for her as she had only one tooth and could eat nothing hard.[14] Children were frequently sent to neighbouring villages to beg. In one case a young girl and her brother, too humiliated to continue, returned home empty-handed after knocking on only a few doors. Yet their hunger drove them to join others in cutting meat from a horse that had drowned in a nearby river.[15]

One man related the story of communist officials searching his family's house for flour or grain in 1933. His father stated that they had nothing but a small container of sorghum, and since he had a reputation for being truthful, they believed him. When the family managed to survive the winter, the mother quizzed the father as to why he had never asked how she could cook sorghum the way she did. She then admitted that she had hidden thirty kilograms of flour and each day had mixed in a little with the sorghum to make it stick together. To explain her deception of the authorities while her husband had told the truth, she said, 'I had to save my children ... my truth is my children.'[16] As would occur repeatedly for many women refugees in years to come, for this woman, difficult moral and ethical choices were made within a framework of identity that ranked maternalism high as a motivating factor.

The famine caused widespread malnutrition, illness, and death, especially among the Ukrainian peasantry. Mennonite families experienced lower losses, partly due to care packages sent by relatives in Canada and the United States. This outside aid contributed to suspicions that the Mennonites were spies and traitors and thus increased the levels of arrest and exile in later years.

After a brief lull toward the mid-1930s, a second wave of arrests, executions, and exiles descended on the Mennonite settlements from 1936 to 1938. These years are considered the climax of the purges, during which arrests were frequent and entire truckloads of men were taken from a village at a time. Some men exiled in the late 1920s or early 1930s returned home only to be taken again during the purges of 1937–8. The period described as the Great Terror began at the highest levels of the Communist Party bureaucracy, in which state and military officials considered counter-revolutionary were arrested, jailed, and often executed. The purge worked its way down through the party cadres and eventually 'blanketed the whole country.'[17] The reasons behind this time of terror are varied, but included the increasingly unstable international situation as a significant factor. With a German invasion already threatening, Stalin's government adopted a policy of eliminating all potential disloyalty to the regime should war break out.

The Mennonites quickly fell into a suspect category because of their identity as a religious sect and their connections with Germany. Mennonite families came to expect and dread the recognizable knock on the door, followed by the arrest of the adult men in the household. Various estimates state that by the time the purges came to an end in 1938, 50 per cent of Mennonite families had lost fathers. In some villages the percentage was as high as 70.[18] Although German-speaking settlements experienced higher rates of disappearance overall, the sex imbalance in Mennonite families was reflected in the larger Soviet population. As Sheila Fitzpatrick notes, according to the 1937 census, women outnumbered men by two-to-one in the working population of agricultural collective farms in the Soviet Union.[19]

With the loss of men from their families and villages, the hardships of daily life were compounded, and women had to assume full responsibility for the material sustenance of their families while coping with the emotional trauma caused by the sudden loss of a father, spouse, or son. The experience of Anny Penner Klassen was representative of the stories of many women whose husbands were arrested. A young woman of twenty-nine when her husband, Johann, was arrested on 12 June 1938, she had one son, almost two years old, and was pregnant with a second child. After her daughter was born, Anny found work doing the laundry for the local kindergarten. The job was arduous, but necessary because it allowed her to purchase bread.

It truly was hard work, for I had to walk two kilometers and carry the heavy bundles of bedding and towels for forty people – children and workers. It required a lot of water which had to be carried from the well which was several building sites away. This water had to be heated so it required a lot of wood. I ordered loads of wood for a fee, but I had to saw and split it myself. Naturally, all the laundry had to be scrubbed on the scrub board, wrung out by hand and hung out to dry ... I did this every two weeks, and it usually took four days to get it all done.[20]

Anny later supplemented her laundry income by knitting kerchiefs while her children slept – from five to seven o'clock in the morning, during their noon nap, and in the evening from eight o'clock until midnight.

The mother of Justina was left with three little girls when her husband was arrested and so she went to work cooking for the tractor operators of the collective. Justina recalls, 'How my mother managed I don't know. She sold my father's clothes, she sold his drafting tools, and she somehow managed to get us a little house.'[21] Like many other women, Justina's mother did handwork to earn some money. In her case, she knit stockings in exchange for peas and made house slippers out of fabric and glue. Justina expressed great regret that at age seven she had been too young to be of much help to her mother.

Recollections of other individuals who were of similar age at the time suggest that children did indeed contribute much to the family economy. At the young age of eight, one girl stayed home to care for three younger siblings while her mother and two older sisters worked on the collective from early in the morning until late at night. With unusually heavy responsibilities for a child of her age, she also lost the opportunity to attend school.[22] Sometimes children had to move in with relatives when their mother could not feed them or was unable to look after them. This was the case for Lena and her brother, whose mother was responsible for milking and caring for twenty cows as well as the other animals on the collective. At night she would wash, card, and spin wool to sell in order to feed the three children still at home.[23] That the struggle for sheer physical sustenance could offset some of the time and energy given to emotional suffering is suggested by one widow and mother of six children aged eleven months to sixteen years, who said, 'We didn't even have time to worry, we had no time for nothing except to survive.'[24]

Their husbands having been publicly branded as traitors or subversives, women also experienced a loss of their already limited rights and privileges. Anny Penner Klassen recalls that women whose husbands were arrested and thus no longer contributing to the economy lost their rights and were not entitled to buy bread.[25] In some cases, families were expelled from the collective and left with no source of income except what they earned as day labourers.[26] One woman with four young children to support was forced to leave her teaching position in the local school and instead go to work on the collective when her husband was taken in 1937.[27] Children whose fathers had been labelled 'enemy of the people' also experienced harassment from their Soviet classmates.

While working to sustain their own households, women also made attempts to provision their husbands in prison. Prior to being exiled to labour camps in the east, most arrested men spent several months at a nearby prison, where, depending on the benevolence of the guards, they were able to receive clothing, food, and sometimes money from their families.[28] Some women spent several days travelling by train in the hope that they might obtain a brief visit or at least a glimpse of their imprisoned husband, brother, or father. A woman's worry that her husband be warm and well fed was compounded by the knowledge that he was also subject to torture. Anny Penner Klassen's husband, Johann, suffered various tortures that included squeezing thirty prisoners into a cell meant for fifteen and being alternately exposed to extremes of heat and cold. He also told of being dragged by rope through mud holes and being physically beaten during interrogations.[29] Maria Unger, whose husband was arrested in 1937, wrote that nails were forced under his fingernails and his genitals were squeezed in the doorway.[30]

The emotional stress women experienced in worrying about their husbands was compounded by fear for their own safety. Women clearly felt the painful loss of physical intimacy with a spouse, but also became vulnerable to sexual advances and abuse. One woman recalled that after her father was arrested in 1937 they were compelled to share their large house with a Russian communist family. Her mother then had to endure frequent 'passes' from the man. When drunk he became violent and persistent, threatening to have her arrested like her husband. Children then lived with the constant fear that their mother would also be taken.[31] This fear was real: some women too were arrested, though not nearly in numbers comparable to men. As well, women were more likely to be released to return home. In February 1938 Marie Regehr was accused of causing the death of seventy head of cattle and was imprisoned for a year. She was released after signing a confession following torture during her interrogation.[32] In another case, a woman was accused of sabotaging the pig farm on the collective where she worked after some of the pigs became ill. She was let go after two of her Ukrainian co-workers spoke up on her behalf.[33] In the rare case where both parents were taken, children might be distributed to orphanages with the hope of being found by relatives or returning mothers.[34] The problem of providing for orphaned or dependent children was in fact one deterrent to any widespread deportation of women.

As nuclear families lost members, other family and village remnants came together to form new supportive units, thus creating new family structures altogether. The story of 'Anna,' as told by Gerhard Lohrenz, typifies the reorganization of family life that occurred following the arrest and disappearance of men. Anna was a young woman whose husband was arrested by the NKVD, presumably in the late 1930s. The next day she miscarried her first child and went to live with her mother, her father having died. Of four brothers, only one was still at home; one was overseas and two others had been arrested. The young families of these latter two came to live with them, as did Anna's sister with her two children who had also lost their father. They were thus a family of five women, one young brother, and an unknown number of children. Anna's extended family eventually became known as the 'family with a tablecloth' because, throughout the events that transpired over the next few years, one of the few possessions they managed to keep with them was a tablecloth.[35]

Living units composed of individuals with extended family relationships became common. As well, neighbours looked to one another for mutual help, which might include taking in an orphaned child, either temporarily or permanently. Many families fit the 'grab bag' description offered by Sheila Fitzpatrick or the 'war family' portrayed by Annemarie Tröger, in which related and non-related individuals created households for the sake of physical and emotional survival.[36] The close kinship ties and the strong community orientation of Mennonite society did much to facilitate the creation of new family units.

The common experience of women without men also drew them together in supportive ways. One young Mennonite woman observed that the 'common burden' shared by women whose husbands were taken drew them together for support. She went on: 'They would constantly talk about this ... especially that summer of 1938, getting the men ready to go for a life in Siberia, sending them money to the prison, and clothes and things like that. Whenever they were together, that's what they talked about.'[37] The formal institutions of mutual aid that had operated through the church were no longer active, but the principles of helping one another that imbued Mennonite culture continued to function. Barriers of social status that had been eroded through the forced equalization of wealth may have also drawn families together with greater ease. Sharing limited material resources, caring for each other's children, even working side by side on the collective farm, brought women closer together and reinforced a sense of community.

The seizure of men from their families cast a cloud of sorrow and despair over households, but the extra physical and emotional demands placed on women also meant the development of new skills, ingenuity, and adaptability. In memories of the times, emotions of pride, stemming from personal accomplishment against all odds, coexisted with sadness and exhaustion. Agatha Loewen Schmidt describes how, when another family came to share their house, her mother tore down the centre wall, which contained the oven separating the two families, and remodelled the house. Arrangements for stoking the fire jointly by the two families proved unsatisfactory, so she built a new dividing wall and a separate oven for her own family. In doing this, she had to reuse the old bricks as no others were available. Not stopping there, she used leftover bricks to make additional improvements to the barn area. Agatha recalled, 'Our new oven worked wonderfully well and was very economical. Mother was very pleased. In fact, some people even came to her and asked if she would do the same thing in their homes! ... Our mother was not an average person. Nothing could overwhelm her spirit, and necessity only spurred her inventiveness.'[38]

Working from early morning until late at night, women had little time to ponder the future; quite possibly they deliberately avoided any contemplation of future misfortune. Hopes that they would be reunited with their menfolk never dissipated, but there was little optimism. Even deeper despair may have set in had the Soviet Mennonite population known what was in store for them over the next decade.

Following the signing of the Molotov–Ribbentrop Pact between Germany and the Soviet Union in August 1939, arrests and deportations let up. But a new wave began in the summer of 1941 following Hitler's declaration of war against the Soviet Union. Soviet authorities feared, and German officials expected, that many Soviet Germans would act as collaborators with the advancing German forces. Following the evacuation eastward of men and youth with machinery and livestock during the summer of 1941, many of the remaining villagers were drafted to join the Soviet work army, or *Trudarmee*, as it was known. At first this work involved digging trenches near the Dnieper River to halt German tanks. For some families, enlistment in the work army meant further separation and uncertainty about the possibility of being reunited at this critical point in the war.

In one family, remarkably still intact in 1941, the father and two eldest daughters were sent into the *Trudarmee* for several weeks, leaving the mother and three younger children at home in their village of Liebenau in the Molotschna settlement. Fortunately for them, Liebenau had not yet been evacuated east when the Germans arrived, and the family was reunited.[39] In another family, both father and mother were conscripted into the *Trudarmee*, leaving three daughters – aged fifteen, twelve, and five – to fend for themselves for several weeks.[40] Over the summer of 1941 the burden of labour on the collective farms intensified with the loss of more able-bodied workers to the trench-digging crews and the loss of machinery that had already been sent east. As well, women who were working long days attempting to bring in the fall harvest without tractors or horses were then called upon to take their turn assuming duty as night watch in their villages.[41]

On 16 August 1941, in response to the relentless advance of Hitler's troops, orders were issued for the evacuation of all German villages west of the Dnieper River. The seventy Mennonite villages of the Crimean peninsula were successfully evacuated east by train on that day.[42] The settlement of Chortitza, on the immediate west bank of the Dnieper across from the Ukrainian city of Zaporozhe, began its evacuation on 16 August as well. The movement of thousands of people with horses and wagons was hindered by a bottleneck created at the bridge crossing the Dnieper, which was also the site of the huge hydroelectric dam, Dnieprostroi. While Soviet personnel anxiously tried to expedite the civilian crossing, German villagers moved as slowly as possible, hoping to be overtaken by the rapidly advancing German army. Recollections of the evacuation include stories of elderly women refusing to cross while others purposefully caused wagon breakdowns at the bridge, thus slowing down the Soviets and allowing more time for the German takeover.[43] Some individuals and families escaped deportation by hiding.

Just prior to the German takeover of the city of Zaporozhe on the east bank of the river, the retreating Soviets dynamited and partially destroyed the dam on 20 August, adding to the confusion and terror. Helga Hildebrand recalled, 'Our family had barely crossed over, we were a few thousand feet past the bridge, when it blew up, killing many women and children. It was horrible.'[44] In the midst of the chaos, women performed acts of desperate heroism as they struggled to protect their remaining family members. Anna and her two children, mother, and sister were evacuated from their Chortitza village, had crossed one arm of the Dnieper, and were hiding in ditches on the Island of Chortitza situated in the river, while German–Soviet gunfire flew over their heads. Anna's small daughter was very ill at the time, so Anna begged that she might return a short distance to retrieve their cow and obtain milk. With permission from the soldiers, she retrieved the cow. Normally a ten-minute walk, it took her over an hour because she was forced frequently to drop to the ground to avoid being hit.[45] The family hid for hours while the war front moved east, leaving them in German-occupied territory and free to return home. As a result of Soviet disorganization and the swiftness of the German advance, the deportations west of the Dnieper were relatively unsuccessful.

The story was different on the east side of the river, where German forces did not arrive until early October. With more time to organize and carry out the evacuation of villages, the Soviets were able to move out most of the remaining men and youth between the ages of sixteen and sixty and about half of the women and children as well. The southern half of the largest Mennonite settlement of Molotschna was almost completely depleted, although the northern half suffered lesser losses; of fifty-six villages, twenty-three were evacuated prior to the arrival of the German army.[46]

It was in the northern villages that a dramatic change of power occurred, literally over the heads of the German and Mennonite residents. In the first days of October, following Soviet orders to deport all remaining Germans in the Molotschna colony, crowds of women, children, and the elderly were gathered at five railway stations to await transport eastward. Although the evacuees at the first two stations were successfully loaded onto freight trains and sent out, the lack of Soviet trains and the quick advance of German forces allowed the five thousand or more civilians gathered at each of the other three stations to escape the same fate. Numerous memoirs describe the drama that occurred over several days as families hid in open fields, in nearby forest clumps, or in empty granaries while Soviet and German planes fought an air battle over their heads. Katie Dirks Friesen describes the scene at Stulnevo, where six thousand to eight thousand civilians waited to be transported east. Katie herself was alone, her father having died in 1934 and her mother and brother having recently been sent to the front near the Dnieper River to dig trenches.

Sunday, October 5, dawned and we still had not been put on the train and sent east. In fact we had been moved farther and farther away from the train tracks ... Then all of a sudden an airplane came flying toward us like a bolt of lightning. At about the same time two other planes appeared out of nowhere and fired at the first. They downed it right near our camp, killing the pilot and totally destroying the aircraft. The meaning of what had just transpired quickly became clear to us. Since we had not been sent to the east the Russians had decided to do away with us by bombing us ... That's when all hell broke loose. The Germans launched an artillery attack, billowing clouds of smoke sprang up all around us, the cannon shots became clearer and louder, the railroad tracks were blown up by the Russians and pieces were sent hurtling throughout the camp and people were screaming and shouting instructions to get down on one's stomach. Russian artillery retreated right through our camp and then regrouped behind a row of trees to the east of us. That put us between the fighting forces, right in the middle of the battle.[47]

By the next morning the battle front was quiet, and Katie with her aunt and cousins returned to her home village where they were met by Rumanian soldiers serving the German occupation forces.

By the time that the German forces had established the occupation boundaries, an estimated fifty-five thousand of an entire Soviet Mennonite population of about a hundred thousand had been deported eastward or otherwise removed from their homes, a ratio comparable to that of the German-speaking Soviet population generally.[48] The Mennonite population in the settlements of Crimea, Caucasus, and Memrik and about half the residents of the Molotschna were deported to Siberia and central Asia. Mennonites who had earlier established settlements in Siberia and the Trans-Volga region were never deported. Most of the remaining population that came under German occupation was living in Chortitza, parts of the Molotschna, and smaller settlements on the west side of the Dnieper River.

The two years of German occupation of Ukraine have been described by one Mennonite historian as 'years of grace for the Mennonite church in the fullest sense of that word.'[49] While religious practice was indeed revived to a certain extent and some churches opened, the years of occupation represented mixed blessings for the Mennonites who remained in Ukraine. A common sentiment was that the greater happiness during the German occupation was not due to better conditions so much as the hope that things would get better should Germany win the war, an outcome expected by most Soviet Germans.[50] The initial response to the uniforms of the German *Wehrmacht* was relief and excitement. Indeed, in some recollections, the German soldiers seemed akin to lost family members, as in the description of a woman's return to her home in Gnadenfeld, Molotschna, after the German takeover: 'The whole house was lit up and German soldiers occupied it and had made themselves comfortable. They cheerfully emptied half of the house for us to move back in and tried to make us welcome, serving us tea and biscuits.'[51] Naturally, the German language and culture shared by the occupiers and the occupied made them seem like kinfolk, and some Mennonites in fact viewed their later trek to Germany as a return to the homeland.

The freedom of Christian religious expression that the Germans brought with them was a positive change for Mennonites who had grown up in a cultural community with a strong religious self-identity. While permitted to reopen church buildings that had been converted to granaries and clubhouses, Mennonites had few ordained ministers left who could perform the official rituals and functions that went along with sanctioned church leadership. In the Russian Mennonite Church tradition, women could not serve in leadership positions, nor did they have an official voice in church decision-making. Although a few ministers had been released from prison and resumed their duties during the occupation, and several mass baptisms took place, there were not enough clergymen to serve all the Mennonite villages with regularity.[52] Nor were there many adult men who, because of their gender, could have acceptably stepped into the role of minister. As a result, women came to dominate the church during this period and attempted to re-create the institutions as they remembered them. Most church choirs, long a significant part of Mennonite worship, were all-female, some women learning to sing tenor and even bass. Again challenging conventionality, most such choirs were directed by a woman.[53] The church buildings themselves had to be restored. One woman recalled, 'Women were seen on the roofs of buildings, on high ladders, anywhere, doing men's jobs because it HAD to be done, and they were not afraid to do it.'[54]

Where men were available to serve more strictly gendered functions such as preaching, it was expected that they would be called on to do so, although the descriptions of the two men in the following memory suggests that they may not have been fully up to the task. In the Gnadenfeld area, sermons were sometimes given by 'old Mr Penner the teacher' or '80 year old Rev Boldt,' but 'most of the time women read a sermon from a book.'[55] One woman recalled that several men would go from village to village giving sermons, but that often 'we would just have a lady read to us out of the Bible, that was it. We gathered together and would sing spiritual songs.'[56]

While officially sanctioning the religious revival that occurred for Mennonites from 1941 to 1943, the German forces did little to assist in the organization of churches. Traditional Christian celebrations were frequently secularized by the Nazis, and religion in many ways became a form of German nationalist expression. Nor did religious instruction become part of the school curriculum during the occupation, much to the chagrin of the Mennonites. There was generally more interest on the part of the German command in establishing new educational institutions and reorganizing agricultural production than there was in promoting religious practice.

With crops such as sunflowers, beets, potatoes, and corn still in the fields when the Germans occupied the Ukraine, one of the first priorities was to organize the fall harvest. The extent to which the agricultural production was reorganized according to pre-collectivization custom varied. For the most part, privatizing the farmland was not really feasible after over a decade of collectivized agriculture, especially with limited labour and machinery. Instead, families were organized into groups of about ten to bring in the harvest with the limited machinery and livestock available.[57] One young woman recalled that her group consisted of her grandfather, his daughters, and their children. They adopted antiquated methods to harvest the grain: '[we] got out the old heavy threshing stone, hitched a horse to it, and going round and round threshed our wheat or oats. Just like it was done in the olden days.'[58] In some areas there seemed to have been more of an effort to privatize land. For instance, in the Baratov-Shlakhtin colonies, northwest of Chortitza, each family received a parcel of land; in the village of Gruenfeld, widows received fourteen hectares of land while couples received twenty-one. In addition, each family received a horse, although farm equipment had to be shared because of the shortage.[59]

As with religious institutions, village reorganization looked to the few adult men, whether qualified or not, to take official leadership. Katharina's father, one of the few men left in their village, was immediately elected mayor, and in general took a supervisory role in a variety of situations. 'He sort of ran the village,' she said.[60] One woman recalled with some irony that of the men given supervisory roles over the work groups in her village, 'three of them were sort of healthy' while 'two were at home and crippled.' The women in this case continued to perform the heaviest labour.[61]

For the many all-female households, the presence of German soldiers was ambiguous, offering the kind of protection that an occupation of the Reich gave to its own ethnics, while simultaneously representing a sexual threat. As one woman said, 'We got the feeling of being taken care of, although we soon noticed that the behaviour of some of the men left much to be desired. Most of their efforts concentrated on creating a comfortable life for themselves, far exceeding their necessities.'[62] For some women the threat of physical molestation was very real. In the following recollection, a young woman with her two sisters and mother had just returned to their village in the Molotschna after narrowly escaping deportation to the east in the fall of 1941. Several trips back and forth to the train station at Tokmak were required to bring all their belongings home:

Mother had gone to the station to fetch more belongings and I was left in our home to look after my two younger sisters. I went outside to get some straw for us to sleep on, and when I came back, the house was full of soldiers. They had had the same idea and were sleeping soundly on the floor already. I was able to find a space for us three to make our beds. Actually I had never been alone with so many soldiers and the two young girls and I were afraid. The house was full of them. Luckily, they did nothing serious. Big hands were grabbing me and touching me all over in the dark. Early in the morning, before they got up, I grabbed my two sisters and moved over to my grandfather's where we stayed until the army moved. Mother was upset when she came back and heard my story.[63]

In one case, a complaint was submitted to German occupation officials that a Miss Thiessen had been raped by a German officer.[64] The evidence of one rape does not point to widespread sexual abuse on the part of German soldiers, but it does suggest that the occupation forces posed a sexual threat. At any rate, given the presence of an all-male army in a mostly female community, it would have been unusual had there not been sexual relations, coerced or voluntary.

Because of their language facility in both Russian and German, young Mennonite women were frequently called to jobs as interpreters, translators, and clerical staff for the occupation forces. As well, some women were recruited as *Ostarbeiter* (eastern worker), a program whereby mostly young women from the German occupied territories were sent to Germany to replace the labour losses in factories there. Anna, sent to Germany in 1942 together with another woman from her village, worked as a translator at an underground aircraft factory until the winter of 1944, when she was reunited with her family, who had left Ukraine.[65] Women who worked as translators found they were in a position to receive special favours or make special requests. But job opportunities also demanded reciprocal favours. One woman who applied for a position as an interpreter for the German command in her district, turned down the opportunity when she discovered that she was expected to serve as the officer's mistress.[66] Some women took on the job but successfully rebuffed the sexual advances made toward them.[67] Other recollections confirm that some Mennonite women did indeed enter into such alliances.

Yet not all of the relationships were of a coercive nature. For young, unattached women, the presence of German soldiers represented better times culturally and also offered companionship and romance. Given the dearth of Mennonite, or other Soviet German, men, it is not surprising that intimate relationships developed and that mention is made of the 'German soldier and his Mennonite girlfriend.' One woman recalled that in her village, at least two Mennonite women became engaged to German soldiers during the occupation, engagements that were broken off when the Germans moved out. Confirming the fact that many such liaisons were mutual, even between soldiers and widows, she said, 'There were things going on all the time like that ... I would not say that they would do it forcefully, not with German women.'[68] Her statement sets up a contrast with the violent rape and coercive relationships that Mennonite women experienced from Red Army soldiers under Soviet occupation later in the war. The behaviour of occupation forces thus might have been viewed as more benign simply because they were German and not Soviet.

The 'widows' who entered into relationships with German soldiers were not always widows in the real sense. Some were women whose husbands had been arrested and exiled sometime during the 1930s. In her historical novel, Ingrid Rimland describes an affair, resulting in pregnancy, between a German soldier and a young Mennonite woman whose husband was taken away.[69] However, relationships between soldiers and Mennonite women whose husbands were possibly still alive were generally not viewed kindly by their relatives and community. Under the occupation, Tina was invited to work as a cook at an agricultural training station established by the Germans. Her husband had been arrested in 1937 with no subsequent word about him, so she moved with her two children to a Russian village to take up her new post. A romance developed between Tina and a German officer, and they were married in an unofficial ceremony. Since the fate of her husband was unconfirmed, Tina was shunned by most of her Mennonite relatives. Her daughter recalled, 'Some people were so rude that they would have thrown stones at my mother.' The girl was quite happy with her new stepfather who was a 'most gentle person.' The couple legalized their marriage in Germany, but Tina's second husband was killed in action toward the end of the war.[70]

It is difficult to conclude, based on isolated memories, the extent to which intimate relationships developed between German soldiers or officers and Mennonite women. The remarriage of Tina was a rare case but points to the loneliness faced particularly by young 'widows' who had barely tasted the intimacy and companionship of a marriage relationship. For unmarried women who were already kindly disposed toward the arrival of German forces, the soldiers offered romance and pleasure in otherwise difficult times.

In other respects, the presence of German soldiers may have been disappointing to German ethnic minorities who had come to anticipate and idealize a German takeover with the same intensity that they had come to despise their Soviet rulers. Although the 'Gott mit uns' (God with us) inscribed on the belt buckles of German soldiers was a sign that public religious practice would be tolerated, the activities and behaviour of the occupation forces at times seemed anything but godly. The initial enthusiasm for the German occupying forces also began to wane when their treatment of the Ukrainian and Jewish population became apparent. The German forces viewed Ukrainians as second-class citizens and treated them as such, even though the Ukrainians, also disenchanted with the Soviet regime, anticipated the German advance with almost the same eagerness as the ethnic German population.[71] Some Mennonites felt torn in their loyalties. Although their dominant feeling was pro-German, most Mennonites, while despising the Soviet regime, bore no animosity toward their Ukrainian and Russian neighbours. In fact, in many villages, Mennonites and non-Mennonites lived as neighbours. Anna, a Mennonite woman employed in the kitchen of a German camp for Russian prisoners of war, 'sympathized with our Russian fellow citizens deeply,' and risked severe punishment by secretly preparing food parcels for the prisoners.[72]

As for the Jews, Mennonite memories about their awareness of the Final Solution are strangely mixed. Ingeborg Fleischhauer observes that the reaction of ethnic Germans to the execution of Soviet Jews ranged from 'embarrassment to deep moral distress' and that local Germans in fact had to dispose of the bodies and in some cases actually participated in the killings.[73] While some Mennonite memoirs deny any knowledge of Hitler's policy toward the Jewish people, others contain stories of Ukrainian Jews being shot by occupation soldiers.[74] Most would not know until later about the extent of the atrocities at concentration camps such as Auschwitz, yet Soviet Germans did witness the way in which Jews were targeted for persecution.

There were also isolated incidents of Mennonites interceding on behalf of Jewish individuals as best they could. For instance, Mary Fast, while in the hospital with malaria, was saved from deportation by the Soviets when a Jewish doctor hid her records. Later, when German authorities were rounding up the Jews of the Ukraine, she tried in vain to speak up on his behalf.[75] The response of most Mennonites fell somewhere in between extreme acts of participation in eliminating Jews and clear gestures of helping them. The awareness that their protectors were also murderers was discomforting for some Mennonites, but it seems there was little outward resistance to the manner in which the Nazis dealt with the Jews. One Mennonite woman, who discovered that clothing she received from the German army had been taken from the Jews, had a typical comment. She said, 'That did not make us feel so good, but at the time we received the clothing, we thought that the Germans were doing their best to take care of us.'[76] Some Mennonites, having not seen atrocities, or perhaps refusing to believe what they had seen, adopted an attitude of denial concerning the extermination of the Jews, partly out of a need to maintain faith in Germany as their fatherland and liberator. The Mennonites' affinity for the Germans, combined with not uncommon anti-Semitic feelings, resulted in no overt opposition to what was happening to the Jews.

The German occupation also meant the loss of more young Mennonite men from the villages as they were drawn into self-defence leagues organized by the German army to protect the zone of occupation and, in particular, the German settlements. Some were killed in battle in the winter of 1942–3 and more were divided into other military units after the German retreat into Poland in the fall of 1943. From the large village of Gnadenfeld, Molotschna, alone, of fifty-one men thus conscripted, thirty fell or were still missing in battle in 1949.[77] Thus, by the end of the German occupation in autumn 1943, the demographics of the Mennonite settlements in Ukraine were radically altered. Women, children, and the elderly were all that remained in most families, while the family unit itself had been reconfigured, if not consciously redefined. The absence of adult men and the fragmentation of families came to be the defining characteristic of Soviet Mennonites living in Ukraine.

The collective memory of this group of Mennonites focuses on the departure and absence of men as a pivotal and transitional event. One woman's written memoir of the departure of men following evacuation orders in September 1941 conjures up a visual impression that is central to the social memory of these events:

Hundreds of men and boys, fifteen and up, walking in formation, flanked on both sides by policemen fully armed. A wagon, pulled by two horses, went in front of them. Weaker older men sat on the wagon and some baggage or feed for the horses. The walking created quite a cloud of dust, for the road was not paved. They walked in the middle of the road, and on both sides of the sidewalk large groups of women and children followed them. Some for miles. So they could see the faces of their loved ones a bit longer. Almost all of them used their handkerchiefs quite freely, for waving, as a sign language or wiping their tears. That's how our men and boys disappeared.[78]

A painting by artist Agatha Schmidt, titled *Off to Siberia, September 1941*, is a visual archetype for the stories that are central to personal narratives and published histories about this era in Mennonite history.[79] This painting depicts a group of Mennonite men – clad in black, heads down – walking down a village street while women and children stand to the side watching them depart.

Personal narratives about these events create an impression that literally all the men were gone from the villages. Narrators frequently state that 'almost all' the men in their village were exiled during the deportations of the 1930s or evacuated eastward at the outset of the war in 1941. Katie Friesen recalls that after the last group of eastern evacuees left her village of Gnadenfeld in September 1941, there were 'only the very young and old, and a few middle-aged women were left behind.'[80] That there were at least 'some' or 'a few' men in each village is attested to by statistics gathered by German occupation forces as well as in the stories of individuals who did not lose their fathers. Data collected from German villages mainly on the west side of the Dnieper River in 1942–3 generally confirm the commonly cited statistic that 50 per cent of Mennonite families were without a male head by 1941 (see Appendix, Table 1). Of course, this average obscured broad variations. For instance, in the relatively small village of Hochfeld in the Yazykovo settlement, 79 per cent of families lacked a male head in 1942, and in Altonau in Zagra-dovka, that number was as high as 85 per cent. Thus, some villages were indeed composed mainly of women without men. In the village of Neu-horst in the Chortitza settlement, on the other hand, only 16 per cent of households were without a male head. The corresponding ratios of women to men also varied from a high of four to one to a more general-ized ratio of two to one. Unfortunately, the village reports do not ana-lyse the population according to age as well as sex. Consequently, one cannot know with precision whether the male population that was left consisted mainly of men who were over the age of sixty, or in their late teens, as one might suspect was the case.

Those families whose fathers, husbands, and sons were not taken dur-ing the waves of arrests and deportations, or had been released or escaped to return home, considered themselves fortunate. This feeling was driven home when they witnessed the suffering experienced by widows who had no means of support other than their own labour power and possible help from extended family and the community. Such suffering bred jealousy and even resentment toward families that were still intact. Mary recalled that a neighbouring household was much better off than her own fatherless family because their father was still at home and able to earn more wages on the collective farm. While they had 'ham, fried eggs, and nice white bread,' Mary's mother had only enough flour to make bread that was more like a pancake.[81] Another woman, who was age twelve at the time of the occupation, when asked if life were easier for her family because her father had been released from prison, replied, 'Well, at the time I didn't see it that way, but of course it was, of course it was.'[82] Even women fortunate enough to have their husbands spared the fate of exile sometimes had to man-age on their own, given that the remaining men had to spread them-selves thin in terms of roles and responsibilities in their communities. One woman whose husband was still with her when they evacuated Ukraine westward in 1943, observed that 'he didn't have much time for us since he was the trek leader and it was his duty to see that no one in that long [line] was left behind.'[83]

Men who were arrested and later returned home, some with little rea-son to account for their good fortune, were also viewed with some sus-picion by those families who remained without their menfolk. There were well-grounded suspicions that certain individuals had acted as informants, providing names for communist officials of individuals who could be labelled as 'enemies of the people.' Most recollections confirm that a few Mennonites were Communist Party members and were known to have betrayed neighbours and, in some cases, even relatives.[84] Denunciations that labelled a fellow villager as a kulak or a conspirator were in fact 'standard practice' in the 1930s, according to Sheila Fitzpatrick.[85] Knowledge and suspicion of such cases continued to cause hostility and distrust in Mennonite communities long after the war.

One unusual interpretation of the immediate prewar years adds to the sense that those who remained were somehow suspect. In writing his family's story, Alden Braul says, 'grandmother and her children made out much better in 1938 since all the essential needs were met. Mom remembers how the men who were not deported sat on the fence and smoked while the women brought their children to the day care as they went to work in the fields.'[86] In this anecdote, laziness rather than collaboration was grounds for distrust of men who remained. The story also serves to highlight the extra burdens that women carried during these years.

In oral narratives that chronicle the war, the flight from Ukraine, and the subsequent years as refugees, events surrounding the loss of fathers and husbands commonly elicit heart-rending emotions, story-tellers often pausing to gain control over their sobbing and tears. It is at this point in the life story of an individual that the father figure took on completely new meaning. From being a flesh-and-blood everyday part of the family and its struggles, the father/husband became fixed in memory as a symbol of better times past and hope for the future. This was so particularly because the time of the father's departure coincided chronologically and psychologically with the onset of increased hardship, uprooting, and uncertainty. The date on which fathers and husbands were taken frequently correlates, in memory, to a transition from a happy life to an existence filled with sorrow. In one interview, a woman described with animation the musical evenings held in their home under her father's leadership. Then abruptly she shifted emotional gears and stated that, after he was arrested, there was nothing but 'eating and working and crying.'[87] Similarly, another woman, born in 1932, commented decidedly that her life to the age of five was 'very happy'; the final moment with her father prior to his arrest in 1937 was the last bright spot in a narrative that followed her family through many subsequent tragedies.[88]

The men who disappeared through arrest, exile, and death are often idealized in the memories of their wives and especially their children. Negative memories are almost nonexistent. Fathers in particular are recalled with reference to their kindness and love, their strength, and also their accomplishments. One woman, only five years old when her father was arrested, nevertheless continued to have very intense feelings for him sixty years later: 'I had a longing to go back to Russia. That was such a strong pull. I was such a lover of my father. I loved him so much. He was such a genuine person in my life. I wanted to go once more to that place and go the steps towards the house where they took him away from.'[89] For her, a return trip to the former Soviet Union later in life helped bring completion to her relationship with her father, given that no confirmation of his death had ever been received.

One man, pausing to analyse the telling of his own story, recognized that his father's absence had had a significant effect on the way in which he was remembered. He said: 'Sometimes I think maybe it was not that bad to have grown up without a father. I remember only good things about my father. He was loving. He was very, very good to me.'[90] Others who were too young to have any real memories of their fathers created mythic images based on the memories of others. One individual who was only three when his father was seized continued to hear how other people held his father the teacher in high esteem. The man created an image of his father as a 'tremendous human being' who had been loved by everyone.[91]

At the same time, memoirs portray men who remained with their families as heroic. A young woman who was the eldest child in a family that remarkably remained intact throughout the war says very little about her mother in her oral narrative, but a great deal about her father. In describing the responsibility given to her by her father, she remarks: 'Actually, he always treated me like a son.'[92] Maria Parrino, in her analysis of women's autobiography, notes a pattern whereby women substitute their father's story for their own. In so doing, they not only deny their own experiences, in order that their stories might be read, but they represent the rapport between father and daughter as an idyll, rather than as the complex relationship that was more likely closer to the truth.[93] The young woman, recognizing her own fortune at having a father that stayed with the family, placed him at the centre of her narrative.

The idealization of departed men is made especially apparent by the way in which images of martyrdom are attached to the exiled and executed. The Mennonite veneration of the martyr is an historical paradigm that dates back to the persecution of their Anabaptist ancestors during the sixteenth-century Reformation.[94] In 1949 a Canadian Mennonite minister published a collection of short biographies mainly of men he considered martyrs of the religious repression in the Soviet Union during the 1920s and 1930s. The original German book, titled *Mennonitische Maertyrer der juengsten vergangenheit und der Gegenwart* (Mennonite martyrs of the recent past and present), contains several stories of women, but the English translation, published in 1990, profiles no women except a few together with their husbands.[95]

The centrality of martyr stories in the Mennonite tradition provides a ready-made pattern within which the memory sources of the postwar immigrants could fit. In fact, Katharina (Dyck) Ediger, the wife of one of the men profiled in *Mennonite Martyrs,* published her autobiography in 1994, but misleadingly titled it *Under His Wings: Events in the Lives of Elder Alexander Ediger and His Family.* The title page includes a photograph of Alexander alone; however, the three main parts of the book are subtitled: 'My [that is, Katharina's] Life,' 'Events in the Lives of My Children,' and 'Friends Who Helped Me.' Separated from her husband in 1938, Katharina Ediger nevertheless subsumes her own life story under that of her husband Alexander, the minister/martyr.[96]

The victims of the Stalin purges were not martyrs akin to the early Christians or radical Anabaptists who endured torture and witnessed to their religious beliefs to the point of death. Their arrests and deaths arose from multiple factors, mostly political, and not from particular beliefs that they could choose to renounce in order to save their lives.[97] As such, the loss of men was meaningless unless memories of them were constructed to fit the image of heroes dying 'for a cause.'

Given the patriarchal family ideology that existed in Mennonite communities, the loss of the father was viewed not only as a physical absence but also as a loss to the moral fibre and, indeed, the integrity of the family itself. Secondary historical accounts of the era express this image as much as – perhaps more than – first-person memoirs do. Historian Cornelius J. Dyck, author of a standard text in Mennonite history, describes family fragmentation in Soviet Mennonite communities during the 1930s in these words: 'Many wives whose husbands had been deported had all they could do to provide daily bread for their children. The children grew up without proper parental attention and without Christian training.'[98] Another historian comments: 'the Mennonite family, traditionally the promoter of Mennonite culture and faith, was weakened by the removal of the male adult and loss of independence.'[99] The author of this statement does not explain what he means by 'loss of independence,' and one is left wondering whether he is referring to the loss of economic freedom under collectivization or suggesting that a female-headed family by nature became dependent. Most likely the latter. At any rate, such statements clearly associate the absence of the father with a weakening of the family unit.

As German forces advanced further east into the Soviet Union through the end of 1941 and into 1942, occupying territory and setting up military governments, Mennonite families held onto the hope that their fragmented families would be reunited. Many felt that should Germany win the war, husbands, fathers, and other exiled family members would be returned. At that point, normative family life would be restored, husbands and wives could resume their proper gender roles, and children could once again be children. The role that women assumed as heads of their families after the departure of husband/father and adult sons was not to that point viewed as a permanent alteration to family structure. Like collectivization, famine, the purges, and war, the fragmentation of nuclear families and the creation of female-headed families with their modified gender roles were, in the memories of individuals who experienced these events, tragic aberrations to normal times. The loss of fathers became a symbol for all the tragedy that Soviet Mennonites weathered during the 1930s. But as the war progressed and the Soviet forces began to push back the German advance, hopes for the return of the missing men began to wane. Families realized that their life in Ukraine was coming to an end and that life itself would never be the same. The hardships that women experienced prior to the war and during its first two years would soon pale in comparison to what lay ahead for them as widowed refugees leading their families through the changing fronts of war.

2

Leaving Home, Becoming Refugees

In the second week of September 1943, Katie Wiebe's family, together with the rest of their village, received instructions from German occupation officials that they had three days to pack their possessions in preparation for a westward evacuation. In that short amount of time, the Wiebes butchered and preserved their pig and chickens, baked and roasted buns, and packed their wagon with as many possessions as it would hold. Before leaving their house for the last time, they filled it with straw in preparation for torching by the German army. On 12 September, Katie, her mother, younger sister, elderly grandfather, aunt, and three cousins climbed on top of their overloaded wagon and joined a trek of thousands of people leaving their homes in the Molotschna. The next four months they spent slowly moving westward, challenged by endless rain and mud, increasing cold as winter approached, wagon breakdowns, and continual exhaustion, hunger, and fear.

This chapter will chronicle the westward evacuation of Mennonites as they left their homes in Ukraine and became refugees finding their way through war-torn Europe. It will demonstrate the ongoing shifts in gender roles and breaking apart of families provoked by a war environment. In this context, women were at once innocent victims of violence and protagonists of survival as they devised strategies to see their families to safety.

With the defeat of the German forces at Stalingrad in the winter of 1942–3, the tide of war had shifted and the Red Army was advancing rapidly westward to reclaim territory that had been occupied by Germany for the previous two years. In response, the German army retreated, accompanied by approximately 350,000 Soviet Germans, including some

35,000 Mennonites from Ukraine. Until the summer of 1943, Mennonites had generally clung to the conviction that Germany would win the war, and many women hoped and expected that their husbands and sons would be freed once the Germans had advanced far enough. Not until the westward trek began did families realize they would likely never see their menfolk again. It was with a deep sadness that Katie Wiebe's family and many others like them said goodbye to their homes.

Villagers from the Molotschna, situated closest to the eastern front, were the first to be evacuated. After a treacherous crossing of the Dnieper River, over temporary and unstable pontoon bridges constructed to expedite the movement, the Molotschna residents reached the Mennonite settlement of Zagradovka. They remained there several weeks, hoping that German armies could maintain their hold on territory west of the river. Such expectations soon proved futile. In October 1943 the residents of the Chortitza settlement on the west bank of the Dnieper were evacuated, and on 16 October, Dnieprostroi, the hydroelectric dam spanning the river, was once again dynamited, this time by the retreating Germans. Although about 1,200 Chortitza Mennonites fled west by train, most joined the caravan of wagons and horses from the Molotschna, which by November had grown to include the inhabitants of Zagradovka and other smaller settlements. The westward trek also included thousands of other Soviet ethnic Germans and units of retreating German military. The immensity of the wagon train was overwhelming; the two thousand wagons of the Molotschna settlement alone made a slow-moving ribbon twenty kilometres long.

The trek itself has been mythologized in Mennonite memory through stories and photographs. Numerous photographs reproduced in Mennonite books and periodicals as well as a 1991 film entitled *The Great Trek*, produced by a former refugee, provide graphic visual images of the hardships of the trek.[1] Deep mud and bone-chilling cold are recurring images in memory and in visual depictions. Helene Dueck's recollection, typical of the refugees, vividly portrays the physical conditions experienced by the trekkers:

Winter was coming, and with it never ending rains. The main roads, paved ones, were as much as possible reserved for the army. We used the others. They were a sea of mud. It is impossible to describe them and the hardships they caused to the trekers [sic]. Often up to the axles in mud. The horses would slip and fall. Often even the whip would not get them up. We would push the wagon, walking deep in mud ourselves. Faces, hands, clothing, shoes – everything full of mud and wet. We were cold and wet, hungry and had little strength left. No men to help us.[2]

After several days of travel, continuous rain and overburdened wagons made travel treacherous, and most families had to dispose of heavier belongings, thus leaving sewing machines, bicycles, butter churns, chests, and even sacks of dried fruit by the roadside. Travelling on open wagons through steady rain in unusually intense late autumn cold, the refugees were soaked to the skin and bitterly cold, and many people became sick.[3] Many deaths occurred along the way, most from illness, but there were also killings by attacking partisan groups and roaming bandits in the Ukrainian countryside. Burials were hurried and unceremonious; bodies were simply rolled in blankets and laid in hastily dug, shallow graves. Sometimes families would carry their dead in the wagon for a full day until they stopped long enough for a burial. Births, sometimes prematurely induced by the hardships of travel, took place in and under wagons. Infants were often the ones who succumbed, vulnerable as they were to inadequate nutrition and harsh elements. With few resources to provide care, mothers with small children were particularly burdened. They could do little to remedy the illness caused by the elements and lack of proper food. One woman years later marvelled at how mothers of babies managed with only a few diapers that needed constant washing along the way.[4] At the same time, children also provided women with the necessary motivation to keep going when giving in seemed easier.

Train travel presented similar challenges as refugees fought for limited places on traincars that were scarce, particularly toward the end of the war. Travel by train, while somewhat faster and offering slightly more protection from the elements than travel by horse and wagon, nevertheless had its own discomforts. The refugees were packed tightly together in closed freight cars or on open coal cars. Toilet facilities were primitive, and lice became a major problem. Furthermore, train travel was not necessarily safer. Several memory sources relate how a train carrying refugees was hit at full speed from behind by an army train in Poland. A number of people were killed, including a Mennonite woman's three children, and many were injured.[5]

That the westward trek was composed primarily of women, children, and the elderly had significant implications for the kind of difficulties encountered and the ways in which obstacles were overcome and resources were allocated. The 'strong gender implications' of refugees' flight, noted by Doreen Indra, was especially apparent for the Mennonites when it came to the handling of horses and wagons.[6] That men may have been at an advantage is suggested by some participants in the trek, particularly when it came to the distribution and management of horses. Helene Dueck recalled, 'the few men we had in the village, got the best horses and the best wagons, one family to a wagon. The women, usually the mild-mannered, not aggressive ones, had to be satisfied with what they were given. And two families to a wagon and two horses.' Helene, with her mother and two sisters, shared a wagon with her aunt, who had four children all under the age of ten. Helene's mother held the reins of the two horses pulling the wagon, 'because she knew best how to do it,' while Helene walked in knee-deep mud beside the young stallion. She held tightly to its halter since the horse had never before been hitched to a wagon and was 'very unruly.' The difficulty was compounded by the fact that the stallion was paired with an old horse that was 'almost blind [and] had hardly any teeth at all.'[7] Many of the horses used on the trek were not fit for such travel. They were mainly unshod draft horses, to be used in the fields but not able to travel long distances on asphalt or gravel roads. Since there was no time to shoe all the horses, many of them became incapacitated as their hooves began to wear down with travel.

For another family of women, receiving 'good' horses only added to their difficulties. Frieda's sister had worked for the German occupation forces at the district agricultural offices, where she had been in a favoured position, and thus received two strong horses to pull the family's wagon on the trek. But the horses proved difficult to manage because the stallion was so spirited. After crossing the Dnieper River, the family requested permission to continue by train and handed the horses to their cousins. Frieda recalled that for her male cousin the powerful horses were a real advantage, whereas for the family of women they had been nothing but trouble.[8]

Families like Helene's were also disadvantaged because their slower rate of travel meant they often were the last to arrive at the care and feeding stations set up by the German military along the way. Helene recalled that her family never reached the stations in time: 'Only the strong ones did, usually those were men, who had the best horses and the strongest wagons. Those that eventually reached the nightcamp, those that were late, often came to empty wells and tables.'[9] In this reflection, as in others, women are characterized as weak vis-à-vis men.

A converse perspective is described in the historical novel *The Wanderers*, which tells the story of three generations of Mennonite women who left the Soviet Union on the trek in 1943 and eventually migrated to Paraguay. The three female heroines are strong and independent while the one adult male accompanying the family on the trek is a pathetic, comic figure, portrayed mainly as a good-for-nothing. Yet even in this reversal of the gendered traits of strength and weakness, one of the heroines 'had to admit with reluctance that a man was useful when wheels broke down or a new horse had to be obtained by someone who knew how to bargain.'[10] Women used their gender to obtain necessary male assistance but were disappointed when men did not rise to the occasion as saviour figures. They also recognized that in surmounting the obstacles that faced them daily, they were by necessity undertaking tasks that in other circumstances they would have left to their menfolk.

The hardships faced by the travellers meant that each member of a family had a role – whether large or small – to play in the day-to-day survival of the unit as a whole. One woman's memory of how her family negotiated their wagon up and down steep hills demonstrates how they all worked together to avoid disaster. 'Going down, one woman, usually a mother, would hold the reigns [sic] and the others, including children, would hang on to the wagon and pull it back with all their little strengths, while we older ones would put a piece of wood through the wheel spikes and push down.'[11] Families worked together, as did neighbours and friends. The difficulties of the trek were, to a degree, lessened by the comforting knowledge that families were part of a larger community experience. Many individuals and families travelled as village groups, bonds that were maintained sometimes right through the process of migration. As an example, Jacob A. Neufeld's chronicle of the trek is full of references to his 'fellow Gnadenfelders,' Gnadenfeld being his home village in Molotschna. Neufeld takes care to recount in detail the fate of various Gnadenfeld families and their repeated separations and reunifications during the trek and subsequent flight across Germany.[12] Few families were isolated and completely self-reliant, at least not until the refugees were dispersed on arrival in Germany.

While family groups worked together in the context of a larger Mennonite community, there is memoir evidence to suggest that a 'survival of the fittest' mentality also existed among the trekkers and that help from others was often not forthcoming. Two middle-aged sisters had trouble obtaining assistance when they experienced their second wagon wheel breakdown, as one of them relates:

Our trek leader went ahead with about half of the vehicles. We were left behind with ten other vehicles. Then a wheel on our wagon broke another time. The others drove on and we were left all alone. My sister and I were helpless as we had no tools to repair the damage. We were frightened at the thought of robber bands and of being all alone on the road with no village nearby ... Forty more wagons of our trek arrived. We begged for help to repair our wagon. Love for one's neighbors seemed to have grown cold in many hearts. Thirty wagons passed before someone took pity on us.[13]

In another case, a family whose horse dropped dead on the road were shouted at to 'get out of the way. The trek must go on.'[14]

While not all the refugees interpreted the allocation of resources or ability to surmount obstacles in a gendered way, most were well aware that women were having to assume new and unasked-for roles. As Katie Friesen stated simply, 'We women had to endure innumerable difficulties and assume many new responsibilities' on the trek.[15] Adult women travelling together shared and exchanged the roles required to feed, shelter, and care for their children and also manage the wagon and relate to the military officials in charge of the trek. Agnes and her sister-in-law, with seven children as well as a grandmother between them, shared duties much as a husband and wife would have in a family that was intact. Rather than remain fixed in their roles of driver and caregiver as a husband and wife might have, however, these two women shifted roles on a daily basis. According to Agnes: 'My sister-in-law and I took turns in our special duties. One day she would do the driving while I would look after the needs of the children and the next day we reversed our positions.'[16]

Women who were especially competent in managing a team of horses were described as driving 'like a man.' Their actions were thus seen as abnormal in a framework in which altered gender roles were a matter of temporary expediency. Jacob A. Neufeld, who chronicled the trek in a diary, offers a typical characterization of these events, portraying the heroic acts of women as outside of the normative abilities of their gender. 'The fact that the trek can be viewed in any kind of favourable light at all is attributable to the services and hard work of the women. One can become lyrical in praise of their practical work, courage and tough endurance. Quietly and heroically, they "stood as men" while discharging all their duties.'[17] That women are described as 'standing as men' points to the irregularity of their situation, as interpreted by the writer. Furthermore, that they performed their services 'quietly' suggests that even while doing men's duties, women were behaving in a properly gendered manner.

While women stepped out of traditional gender roles, boys and girls took on tasks and responsibilities well beyond what would normally be expected of their age. Each child had a job to do, whether it was to scavenge for food in farmers' fields, gather wood for fires, care for the horses, or watch younger siblings. Even a small boy of three was expected to carry a water kettle in one hand and a potty in the other after his family was forced to proceed on foot.[18] About expectations placed on her during the trek, one woman remarked: 'I was fourteen but had to act like another adult.'[19] Recalling his boyhood years as a refugee, one man said it was a time he should have been learning 'reading, writing and arithmetic,' but instead he was learning how to 'beg for food and find edible berries, leaves and mushrooms in their natural setting,' as well as repair shoes and 'make something out of little.'[20] Children of the trek had to assume roles far beyond their age, and many recall regret over lost childhoods. Yet, they also carried less emotional burdens than their elders and found ways of experiencing the trek and unknown future events as adventures. One woman, a teenager at the time, recalled that when their train broke down in western Ukraine, she and her friends went dancing and to the cinema in a nearby town.[21]

Most families had begun the trek with an ample supply of food – dried fruit, roasted bread and zwieback, and sometimes preserved meat. As weeks of travel lengthened into months, however, food stocks ran out, and the refugees often had to scavenge for meals. Mary Krueger, who was ten at the time, recalled that on arrival in Poland in late 1943 her family's food supply had completely run out. One evening her mother gave each of the three children a spoonful of syrup with a little sugar on top; this was to be their last meal from their own resources.[22] When the food shortage became crucial, children were sent ahead into villages to beg for food or to dig up whatever grain or root vegetables remained in the near-frozen ground. Cows, brought along for their precious milk supply, were butchered. Cooking was also a challenge. Camp fires had to be doused when air raids threatened, sometimes before the meal was prepared.

By early 1944 the westward trek had reached the region of central Poland occupied by Germany since early in the war and then known as Warthegau. Germany's plan was to settle the Mennonites and other Soviet Germans in territory from which resident Poles had been expelled earlier that year. To further strengthen Germany's claim to the

Warthegau, Soviet Germans were naturalized as German citizens shortly after arriving. Most Mennonites received their new citizenship without question, and in many cases quite eagerly. In the Warthegau, the Mennonites came under the administration of the *Volksdeutsche Mittelstelle* (German Ethnic Liaison Office), which organized housing and work placements and also recruited refugees into various military and non-military wartime services.[23] Germany's plummeting fortunes in the war as well as a severe labour shortage meant that the influx of ethnic Germans offered a new source for workers and soldiers.

Young men in their late teens as well as older men who had escaped deportation in the Soviet Union were conscripted into various departments of the Nazi military. Although non-participation in war was a central tenet of Mennonite religious doctrine, the forced recruitment undertaken by the German army did not allow Mennonite men the option of refusal. To do so would have meant certain imprisonment or perhaps death. At any rate, for young men who had grown up during years of religious suppression, teachings of non-resistance during wartime had little meaning, particularly in light of the hard political realities of the day. Most Mennonite men, full of hatred for the Soviet regime, donned a German uniform without protest, and in some cases did so quite willingly. The enlistment of these men on a losing warfront, however, meant further separation for families and, for women, the painful knowledge that sending one's father, son, or brother into the German army could mean good-bye forever.

Ethnic German families, like the Mennonites who were settled in the Warthegau, occupied homes that had been forcibly vacated by Poles earlier in the war or were given rooms in homes, where resentful Polish owners had little choice but to share their accommodation. Some were settled in country summer homes formerly owned by Polish Jews.[24] Women found work on Polish farms and in factories and offices. Because of their language facility in Russian and German, Soviet German women were valued as interpreters for the military effort. Similar work placements were found for families that had made the trek by train and thus ended up further west, in Germany proper, or in occupied Yugoslavia, where there was also a labour shortage. The feeling of temporary stability was such that some young women were able to enter school for training as teachers and to establish or upgrade skills in nursing and midwifery.

While the Mennonite population of Ukraine was on the trek to Poland, another settlement of Mennonites in eastern Europe was also experiencing the full force of the war. Not all of the Mennonites of Dutch ancestry who lived in Poland and Prussia during the sixteenth and seventeenth century had migrated to Russia. Many had remained in their old settlements. Unlike their Russian cousins, who had developed semi-isolated and self-governing colonies, Mennonites in eastern Europe were thoroughly integrated into the economic order and administrative structure of the nations in which they lived. In September 1939, there were approximately 665 Mennonites in East Prussia, 3,000 in West Prussia, 6,000 in the Free City of Danzig, and 2,000 in Poland. Those living in Prussia were citizens of Germany, while residents of Danzig and Poland became citizens of the Reich during the early part of the war.[25]

From the outset of the war, Prussian Mennonite women coped with a sex imbalance in their families, not because of deportation and exile, but because the majority of draft-age men were conscripted into the German armed forces. The male losses among the Mennonites of eastern Europe were enormous. For instance, in the Prussian community of Heubuden, of 250 men in the German military, 100 had been killed before the end of 1944.[26] Unlike Soviet Mennonite women, who had already experienced a decade of prewar hardship, Prussian women experienced the war as a sudden upset of what had been a long-established and prosperous lifestyle. During the war, Prussian Mennonite women assumed responsibility for sustaining their families economically and emotionally. One account of the Prussian experience states: 'Since the men were in the war, the women were now in charge of the farms and farmworkers. It meant that they also had to make all the decisions about when and where to plant what.'[27] One young woman operated the family business, a bakery, on her own after her husband was drafted in the first year of the war. She saw him only sporadically over the next five years, and eventually he went missing in action. When the Soviet front advanced on their home in West Prussia in January 1945, she had three young children aged two, four, and six.[28] Her situation was common.

Mennonites living in Poland, Prussia, and Danzig experienced little direct destruction of property during the first years of the war. But with the advance of the Soviet army into East Prussia in October 1944, life changed forever for Mennonites and other Germans living in the eastern territories of Europe.[29] In its devastation, the 'cataclysmic campaign' of the Red Army in eastern German territory has been described as 'possibly without parallel in European history.'[30] News of the atrocities that followed the first thrust of Soviet troops into East Prussia prompted a panicked flight of Germans from the eastern territories of Germany,

Danzig, and central and western Poland. Although a counter-offensive on the part of German forces delayed the Soviet takeover, by January 1945 the residents of Danzig and West Prussia found themselves desperately trying to flee Soviet tanks. Since the Soviet westward advance had been more rapid further south, Germans in Danzig and in the northern portions of East and West Prussia had little choice but to attempt an escape by sea. Thousands of evacuees died trying to reach German rescue ships in the Gulf of Danzig and Baltic Sea, where the dangers of crossing treacherous ice-covered lagoons were compounded by strafing from Soviet bombers from above and the threat of Soviet submarines and mines below.[31]

At the same time, Soviet Germans, including Mennonites from Ukraine, became part of the same flight. A large portion of the Mennonite refugees had remained in the Warthegau for close to a year until the Soviet advance in late 1944. Most were Mennonites from the Molotschna who had made the trek from Ukraine by horse and wagon. Villagers from Chortitza and other colonies west of the Dnieper, many of whom had been evacuated by train, had been settled mainly further west in Germany. News of the rapid advance prompted another hurried packing of possessions for further flight westward. The departure this time was more panicked than that from Ukraine, and fear was certainly heightened by the knowledge that the consequences would be dire should the refugees fall into the hands of the Soviets. Some refugees were able to secure places on scarce German trains or other forms of military transport in retreat. German officials, trying to bring some order to the evacuation, requisitioned Polish drivers to carry German civilians and refugees west by horse and wagon. In many cases, these drivers abandoned their charges after a day of travel, with or without horse and wagon. Individuals and families who were unable to obtain transport by train, truck, or wagon simply fled on foot in a direction that would take them away from the sounds of approaching Soviet tanks and aircraft. In the flight ahead of the Red Army, the only desire was to keep moving westward. Few had any more specific destination.

Once again, the refugees were travelling in the bitter cold of mid-winter. Many narratives describe frostbitten limbs, bread too frozen to eat, and blinding snowstorms that obscured any sense of direction.[32] Elizabeth Wiens described the horrendous travel conditions, six days after fleeing her home in West Prussia:

The morning was clear with an icy wind from the east. I stuffed all the cracks in the wagon with blankets as much as possible so that the children wouldn't be so cold. Then we continued further on the main road. But what use was good asphalt, when the snow was knee-deep and snowbanks lay across the road ... On one stretch the road was higher and there the snow blew down. But instead the wind blew harder and went right through the bones. Afterwards we came into the woods. There the snow lay so thick that one couldn't move forward at all ... I estimated the cold at 18 to 20 degrees below zero. Later I heard that it was 25 to 30 degrees.

Soon it became necessary to unhitch the four-horse team and lead them further one by one, and then for everyone to push the wagon wheels to get them started. This arduous travel occurred with the sounds of canon-fire and aircraft approaching from the east. 'It was a dreadful struggle for people and beasts,' she said.[33]

Thousands of people were overtaken by Soviet troops and killed in the ensuing flight. Memoirs recall Soviet tanks rolling over everything in their path, leaving behind a wasteland of human and animal carnage, and property destruction. Some Mennonite refugees were among the 100,000 killed in the firestorm that destroyed the city of Dresden in February 1945. Others found themselves in Berlin during the Soviet take-over. They experienced some of the most brutal violence of the war. This was the case for Marga Siemens and her son Heinz. She reported the following: 'I lived through the heaviest bomb attacks over Berlin that I thought the world was coming to an end. I carried away bodies, which in the heat were becoming small like dolls, in my arms. Heinz and I were buried under for three days. I lay in the middle of the front lines, then crawled until my knees were sore but fell into Russian hands anyway. Then I lost all my things. But I thank God that I was allowed to keep my Heinz.'[34]

Many other families, despite the odds, had managed to stay together. Now they too were separated in the chaos of the Soviet advance. A number of young women and girls attending boarding school some distance from their families in Poland fled west with their teachers and schoolmates without knowing the route taken by their mothers. While the girls successfully reached the West, often in fragmented groups or even alone, some of their families were taken prisoner by Soviets. Others were fortunate to be reunited with family members along the way.[35] Katie Friesen describes her flight with her schoolmates and teachers. She was woken at four in the morning of 19 January 1945 with orders to evacuate; the Russians were very close. 'Before leaving we took time to carry all the textbooks into the basement, just in case we would return. We wrote messages on the chalkboards, played one last song on the piano, bade farewell to our classrooms and then assembled in the school-yard with tears streaming down our cheeks.' In the days that followed, the girls and their teachers travelled by wagon, bicycle, foot, and finally by train, barely stopping to eat or sleep. On more than one occasion they had to abandon a hastily cooked pot of unpeeled potatoes. During a three-day stretch by train, they were lucky to receive one piece of bread per day; to quench their thirst, they ate handfuls of snow when the train stopped long enough for them to disembark. After about a week of flight, the group stumbled upon a group of refugees; miraculously, Friesen's mother was among them.[36]

Sometimes, when not all family members were equally able to travel, difficult decisions were made about who would be left behind in the interest of the long-term safety of other members. In one case, a Mennonite woman joined the flight west, leaving her elderly mother, blind brother, and a cousin behind, thus choosing to separate her family group in order that her four daughters not fall into the hands of Soviet soldiers, which was her greatest fear.[37] Irene Peters chose to leave her mother and sister behind while she fled west with her employer, a German woman with three children; Irene said she could not leave the latter, nor did she want to, since the woman was ill and one of the children was paralyzed. Later she was separated from this family as well when their train was destroyed in a phosphorous bomb attack that killed one of the children. Irene then continued on foot with a group of soldiers.[38]

Some families, for whatever reason, chose not to join the hurried and chaotic flight west. Anna Heide Retzlaff chose to remain in the Warthegau rather than risk further separation from the people close to her. In her words, 'I was very glad that I had all three of my children with me. I did not know the where-abouts of my husband Willy. I could have escaped to the West with my children at first, but there were the other women, my friends and relatives with their small children, they would not be able to run. So we decided to stay together.'[39] Anna was sent back to the Soviet Union but later was able to immigrate to Canada to join her husband, who had gone there after the war. Another woman remained in Poland because her midwifery and other medical skills were in great demand and because she had begun a refresher course there. She too was repatriated with her mother and young children.[40]

Most Soviet Mennonites who had been unable to escape the rapid Soviet advance into the German-occupied lands of eastern Europe were quickly taken prisoner and sent back to their country of birth. According to Ingeborg Fleischhauer, at least 200,000 (about 57 per cent of those who escaped) Soviet Germans were overtaken by the Red Army as it swept toward Berlin and were sent to the trans-Ural region. Another 80,000 were similarly repatriated from Germany proper by Allied forces. By contrast, only about 70,000 Soviet Germans escaped repatriation and either remained on German soil or emigrated elsewhere.[41] Individuals who had been born in the Soviet Union but who found themselves at war's end on Allied soil were subject to repatriation according to the terms of the Yalta Agreement. Even though Soviet Germans had been naturalized as German citizens soon after their arrival in the Warthegau, their citizenship in 1939 was the date on which their status was determined. From May through September 1945, Allied forces fulfilled their obligations and rounded up Soviet citizens and placed them in guarded camps to await transport east. As it became clear that many displaced persons from the Soviet Union were being returned against their will, repatriation efforts by British, French, and American authorities eased off. By the end of 1945 over two million Soviet citizens had been repatriated from Western occupation zones.[42] Of the 35,000 Mennonites who had left the Soviet Union in 1943, approximately 23,000 were in fact repatriated or were dead or missing, and only 12,000 remained in Europe or emigrated to North and South America.[43]

Situations in which families found themselves on the brink of being sent back are recalled with references to individual courage or, conversely, to providential and fortuitous intervention. Sometimes families escaped repatriation by the sheer determination of their mothers. Elsie Pauls recounted how she, her two sisters, brother, and mother were in a transit camp in the Russian zone at the end of the war, waiting to be sent back. 'But our mothers dug in their heels, and went to the American Embassy, and simply refused to return to Russia.'[44] Another woman similarly attributed her family's fortune at not being sent back to the outspokenness of her great-aunt, who was 'a very aggressive woman.'[45] Two sisters recalled how their mother, with three other women, successfully persuaded repatriation officers that they were of German, not Russian, background, even while their uncle had packed his bags and was ready to return to the Soviet Union.[46] Two young Mennonite women in the western zone decided ahead of time that, if they were threatened with repatriation, they would immediately marry their new, German soldier boyfriends and thereby hopefully receive permission to remain in Germany.[47]

While some women successfully resisted, or planned strategies to resist, a forced return to their country of birth, others faced repatriation with a certain fatalism. One woman's letter, written to relatives in North America seemingly the day before she was sent back, exhibits a weariness and lack of resistance that characterized some refugees.

Dear Parents, Brothers and Sisters: ... My five children and I are in Germany. Would very much like to know who of you are still living ... My daughter Helena who is 18 years of age, disappeared while on flight to Germany. We do not know whether or not she is still alive. My husband has been missing for seven years now. I have four sons, 16, 14, 12, and 10 years of age. Agnes is 8 years of age ... I have experienced much sorrow in my life. I have become old in my youth. No one would believe that I am still young. We have been on flight now for two years ... Dear Father: This is our last evening in Germany. Tomorrow we will be on our way back to Russia. Oh mother, mother! Pray for your children! I find no words today to write to you. I shall remember you all until death.[48]

The letter, poignant in its matter-of-factness, expresses a marked interest in knowing who is living among family in North America, as if the writer is desperately trying to recreate living family to compensate for her losses. Other refugees, particularly those who were alone, offered no initial resistance to repatriation officers because they were unaware of the repatriation agreement that had been signed at Yalta.

Although the threat of repatriation diminished in the Allied zones of occupation by late 1945, for Soviet-born displaced persons in the Russian zone, the possibility of being discovered and 'sent back' was a daily reality for years. The fear was especially acute for women who were assigned to work for Soviet occupation officials, many as housekeepers. These women had to be constantly vigilant that neither they nor their children betray the fact that they could understand the Russian language. Knowing the language could also work to the advantage of Soviet Germans. A Mennonite woman working in an office of Soviet occupation authorities overheard several officers talking about the plan to repatriate Soviet Germans. That night she, with her mother, siblings, and several uncles, escaped to the West using a bottle of liquor as a bribe. Until that day, the possibility of being sent back to the Soviet Union had not occurred to them.[49]

The fear of being repatriated only added to the difficulties that all Germans experienced under Soviet occupation in the immediate postwar years. All sectors of postwar Germany were characterized by what

Eve Kolinsky has called a 'culture of physical survival.' Shortages of food, heating materials, clothing, and household goods meant that most Germans had to develop pre-industrial methods for meeting daily needs. Poor health and malnutrition were common, and some individuals in fact 'lived close to starvation levels.'[50] For Mennonites and other Germans living in Soviet-occupied Poland, daily hardships were exacerbated by the hatred that Poles felt for Germans. One young Mennonite girl, only thirteen at the time and on her own, was 'mistreated very, very badly' by the Polish estate owners where she was employed and, on one occasion, came close to being shot simply because she was German.[51] Edna Schroeder Thiessen, a Mennonite who had grown up in Poland and remained there at war's end, was imprisoned by Polish soldiers in 1945. In prison, she was tortured and interrogated by her captors. Later, when she was assigned to work at an estate formerly owned by a wealthy landowner, Thiessen went without food for over a week on several occasions.[52]

The main goal for Mennonites and others living in the Russian zone was to cross the border to the West. Memory sources contain stories that range from dangerous, night-time border crossings to cases where individuals simply bought tickets and passed across the border with no questions asked. In all cases, ingenuity and courage were required. Again, mothers carried most of the responsibility for planning and executing the escape of their families. In one recollection, tribute is given to a mother's 'intelligence and daring' in leading her family out of the Russian zone.[53] Some women planned their strategies very carefully. Aware that she had a brother-in-law living in western Germany, Helene Hildebrand addressed a letter to herself purportedly from this relative, inviting her and her family to come live with him because he had plenty of room and work for them all. In actual fact he was a struggling refugee like themselves. At the border crossing, Helene showed the letter to the commanding officer, gave him a bottle of vodka, and received the necessary papers to proceed.[54] Bribery with alcohol and cigarettes was a common and successful device to ensure uncontested passage.

Many families crossed the border without tickets or papers, instead making furtive night-time escapes across rivers and fences, trying to avoid the Soviet border patrols. Susan made such an escape with her three young children, her brother, and her disabled sister. As they approached the intended place of crossing, they were confronted by Soviet soldiers who had detected them despite heavy fog. The soldiers offered to let them go if they left Susan's twelve-year-old daughter, but

Susan was able to bribe them with her watch and wedding band. The story continues in the daughter's words:

So we went, pulling the carriage, a mucky beet field, very cold. My aunt said don't go so fast, I'm losing my galoshes. I said just leave them. Our baby he didn't make a sound, he did not cry. My mother and my uncle were pulling the carriage with the baby and our few belongings. I had a knapsack and my brother had a knapsack. That was all we had. And pulling the aunt. We stood by a stream of muddy water. We were caught [by Soviets] again. We didn't have much to give anymore. They were really threatening, they were threatening very hard. But ... I guess something distracted them and my uncle checked the water and said we could make it. They just let us go.[55]

Despite the presence of an adult male, Susan's uncle, it is her mother who negotiates with the soldiers, all the while pretending that she cannot understand the Russian language.

Men, of necessity, had to be inconspicuous because of the likelihood that they would have served in the German military and would thus be arrested as prisoners of war. Because women aroused less suspicion from a military point of view, they were able to pass more easily through dangerous areas without hindrance. In another story of escape, Irmgard and her mother returned to the Russian zone by bicycle twice after settling the rest of the family in the American zone. They did so to retrieve some valued items, including a sewing machine! Irmgard recalled, 'At that time we didn't have anything ... so our things were very important.' Even though her family group included two uncles, 'they didn't dare' go back. 'Young women had much more pull in those times,' she said.[56]

In at least one daring escape, the stereotypical gender roles of man as rescuer and woman as captive were quite obviously reversed. Mary was a young woman in her early twenties who, together with her family and group of villagers, was living about eight kilometres from an American prisoner-of-war camp near Munich. Camp security at that point was fairly lax, allowing local people to enter the camp to trade goods with the prisoners. One day when Mary and a friend entered the camp, they discovered a number of Mennonite men from Ukraine who had been drafted into the German army and were now destined for repatriation and imprisonment. As it happened, one of the men was Mary's boyfriend. A plan was then launched whereby Mary and some others would bring civilian clothes into the camp for these men who might then walk out undetected. When others backed out of their involvement in this rescue mission, Mary made several trips into the camp on her own, eventually bringing out three men, including her boyfriend.[57] Her narrative of these events is lengthy and detailed – though somewhat confusing and inconsistent in chronology – but what stands out is her self-perception as a woman of bravery and cunning.

Isolated incidents of ingenuity and courage, such as Mary's story of rescue, or strategies to avoid repatriation, or escapes across the East–West border, revealed women's strength and leadership. However, the militarized and violent atmosphere that was a daily reality for refugees was also a constant reminder to women of their vulnerability as civilians and as women.

For women, the worst fear of falling into Soviet hands was of being raped or murdered. Various sources have produced documentation of widespread raping of German women by Soviet soldiers, beginning with the occupation and continuing well into the aftermath of the war. Although much of the savagery can be attributed to spontaneous retribution for German atrocities during Hitler's occupation of Soviet territory, there is also evidence of systematic incitement, if not actual military policy, of Soviet soldiers to rape women as they occupied territory.[58] Estimates of the number of German women raped range from twenty thousand to two million.[59]

Wartime rape of Mennonite refugee women fleeing the Soviet army warrants close examination for a number of reasons. As a wartime atrocity experienced almost exclusively by women, rape is particularly salient to a study that focuses on gender. Widespread rape of German women by Soviet soldiers was the most obviously gendered aspect of wartime violence inflicted on civilians. Aside from the physical and emotional pain that it inflicts on women, wartime rape has a societal function that, as Ruth Seifert explains, 'regulates unequal power relationships between the sexes: it serves to maintain a cultural order between the sexes or – when this order becomes fragile – to restore it.'[60] For women without men, forced by circumstance to step out of traditional gender roles, the fear and reality of rape reinforced a gender hierarchy in which women were vulnerable in the face of male violence and also dependent on male protection.

The incidence of rape has received little attention from chroniclers of the story of Mennonites in the Second World War, partly because women's stories have not been central to most published narratives, and because of the sensitive nature of rape itself.[61] While mass rape is recognized as part of the litany of horror that accompanied the Soviet occupation of eastern Germany, the personal trauma of individual women is rarely examined. In oral and written memoirs, references to rape reveal a variety of narrative patterns. These are especially striking in memories that are personally traumatic and difficult to process through a literal telling. A common story-telling device is to sum up the particular historical period or event in question as too enormous to begin to describe, and thus the narrator is free to move on without having dealt specifically with it. One woman's description is typical: 'On January 18, 1945, when I was in college, Soviet tanks rolled into the countryside. It would take pages to describe the cruel inhumanity of their soldiers to innocent women, the old and the disabled.'[62] Another witness to a brutal rape says of the Soviet soldiers, 'They were terrible, just like animals. You can't explain.'[63] In a 1949 letter to a friend, a postwar Canadian immigrant woman writes: 'We ... reached Brandenburg before the Russians overtook us. How they tormented us! Words cannot describe how horrible that was.'[64] Another woman brought closure to the topic by saying, 'I cannot describe this time adequately to you, it was too terrible.'[65] Such statements of closure by Mennonite women starkly contrast with their descriptions of events such as the trek out of Ukraine in late 1943, which is chronicled in great detail.

Another common pattern for dealing with rape in memory is to deny it or depersonalize it and place it within an impersonal historical narrative. Most often, rapes by Soviet soldiers are woven into the overall narrative of the Mennonite refugee story and become part of a factual chronology. In these cases, highly emotional events are dealt with as history outside of oneself, as opposed to personal experience. Rape thus becomes one of many themes in a litany of tragedy that shapes the total Mennonite story, rather than a singular event in the life of a woman, or a form of wartime violence that was gender specific. The following written account follows this pattern:

From 1938 to 1939 I worked as a teacher in the Volga Republic. In 1939 Hans Wiens and I were married and moved to Chortitza. My brother David was arrested in 1940. In October 1943 we left Chortitza and fled with the Germans westwards. Hans was conscripted in Poland, while mother and I with our daughter Erika fled to Oberschlesien to join Hans' mother and sisters. There I had to have an operation. Before I came out of the anaesthesia I was loaded onto a train to flee to Niederschlesien, since the city was being bombed heavily. Now I not only had lost my husband, but also my mother and my daughter. The Russians overtook us. A terrible time of rapes and plundering started. Fear would not let us come out of hiding.[66]

Referring to the consequences of rape, rather than the assault itself, was another way for women to describe it indirectly. Angela Showalter describes how a Polish Mennonite woman acknowledged the frequency of rape, yet often spoke of the pregnancies that resulted, rather than the act itself: 'We saw so much of that, young girls with babies, older women with babies in the war time. Horrible.'[67]

Stories are often related in the third person, even though it is hard to believe that the narrator did not also experience that which she is describing. Such accounts are frequently detached from the narrator, giving the impression that the teller of the story was invisible. Yet while the context makes it obvious that the narrator was present, she often depersonalizes the story, providing third-person details of another's fate without revealing any about her own, even though she may be personally forthcoming on another topic. In doing so, a woman might thus protect her own fragile memories by more objectively describing the experience of others. In 1951, a recent immigrant to Canada described in lurid detail the brutal attack by Soviet soldiers on a group of women. Although the narrator fits the profile of the women who were victims, she tells the episode apart from herself. She switches abruptly from 'they' to 'we,' however, when she moves on to the more benign subject of food rations.[68] Whether this woman was herself raped is not evident from her story, though it is highly likely given the circumstances. Yet, even if she were not raped, it is possible that as an observer she was affected psychologically to almost the same degree.[69]

In her moving account written shortly after the war, Johanna Dueck describes in detail the rape and murder of Helene Hamm, the supervisor of a home for the elderly in West Prussia. Johanna mentions that she also responded to the familiar demand of the Soviet soldiers – 'Woman, come here!' – but in her narrative focuses on the story of Helene, who she obviously held in high esteem. Though her own experience was equally traumatic, she is later full of reproach for herself and cites her lack of courage in taking actions, which she feels could have prevented the shooting of Helene.[70] The story of Helene Hamm, told also in the memoir of another woman present during the same events,[71] may be easier to tell exactly because she did not live to tell it herself. Helene's story of rape had closure and finality, and thus found a fixed place in the memories of other Mennonite refugees, even if memories of their own circumstances remained fluid.

Women in Soviet-occupied territory at the end of the war continued to fear random and brutal rape attacks by individual or groups of Soviet soldiers well into 1947, according to Norman Naimark.[72] As time went on, and flight was no longer an option, women devised strategies to cope with living as a German woman under Soviet occupation. One Mennonite woman recalled that she and the daughter of her farmer-employer hid each night in a concealed closet in the horse barn. During the day, when it was necessary to work in the fields, all the young girls and women would disguise themselves as boys or elderly people as a deterrent to rape.[73]

After experiencing successive rapes, or threats of rape, some women sought out a protector, usually a Soviet officer. In that way, they could escape ongoing brutal attacks from numerous soldiers in favour of 'voluntary rapes' by the same man. Similar scenarios saw women submit to sexual acts in order to avoid other forms of violence against herself and her children, or to obtain assistance in crossing tightly guarded borders. While the phrase 'voluntary rape' seems a grotesque oxymoron, it suggests the extreme ways in which women could have an active will in a context that threatened to dehumanize them completely and render them only as victims. Annemarie Tröger has suggested that in such instances the difference between rape and prostitution became slight; and Atina Grossmann observes that women themselves were sometimes confused over the meaning of what she describes as 'instrumental sex.'[74] In these cases, the term rape hardly even applies to sexual relations that were at times coercive, at times mutual, but always resulting from the limited, difficult choices women had during war.

Such alliances occurred for Mennonite refugee women. One woman, who found herself doing housework for Soviet officers in the Russian zone following the war, said, 'it was better ... if you had a friend, then the others would leave you alone.' As food was increasingly scarce, her motivation for submitting to the sexual demands of an officer became the desperate need to feed her three young children. In later years she categorized her actions as sinful, yet felt justified in her choices because of her maternal responsibility.[75] Such openness is rare in first-person memoirs. More often, sexual alliances are recounted in semi-fictional memory sources. The Mennonite heroine in *The Wanderers* offers herself to a Soviet commanding officer after being repeatedly raped by soldiers. The decision to prostitute herself was made after her family was threatened with death. She counters her mother's protests with the following: 'seven, eight, ten brutes used me every day. Now it's only one. And we have shelter. And food. And protection. Don't talk to me about honour, mother.'[76]

For Soviet-born Mennonite refugees, sexual services were also the price women paid to win their release from Soviet repatriation camps or to receive permission to cross the border to the West. The story of Tina Enns is suggestive of the choices that some Mennonite women faced. Tina, with her two children, was taken into the employ of a Russian major as seamstress and housekeeper to his wife. Soon, she was forced to provide sexual compensation in exchange for the major's promise to help her and her children reach the West. Her sessions with the officer continued twice a week for about two months, when he was transferred and Tina given documents declaring her German citizenship.[77]

In first-person memoirs, possible cases of sexual coercion are rarely spoken of directly but instead place the reader/listener in the realm of speculation. Cases of children born out of wedlock or in the absence of the mother's husband suggest rape, or sexual liaisons that were either coercive or mutual. One woman's memoir about her widowed mother's experience curiously places the birth of her 'illegitimate' sister immediately following the threat of repatriation: 'All immigrants were to return to their homeland. Could two women and children hide, especially after the children were registered in school? Was it a miracle? Although two [Soviet] soldiers appeared at the door one day demanding full names of all living there, an order to leave never followed. That unit of soldiers was transferred and our names were probably lost in the red tape involved. No-one knows for sure. In July B—— was added to our family.'[78] Given the otherwise well-ordered sense of the woman's narrative, the reader is left with the stark impression that the birth of the child was related to the family's fortuitous escape from repatriation. Information that came later to this woman (who was twelve at the time) would reveal that her sister was conceived when her mother entered into a sexual relationship with a Soviet officer.[79] It is nevertheless revealing that her earlier, written memory source placed the birth together with the question of repatriation, suggesting that if not for their family, then possibly for others there was in fact a link between sexual favours and threats of repatriation. Other narrators, especially those who were children or teenagers at the time, recall vague suspicions about what had transpired between their own mothers and persistent Soviet soldiers.

That rape and repatriation are so closely linked in memory and also in historical chronology demonstrates another pattern in the development of social memory. The life histories of many Mennonite refugees are shaped by 'master narratives' – stories of myths that structure meaning and that can in fact mask the particularities of an individual's situation.[80] In this case, the threat of repatriation by Soviet authorities becomes a master narrative, subsuming stories of rape by Red Army soldiers. One young chronicler of his grandmother's story in fact adopts his family's memory of the war years, although he himself did not experience them. He describes the postwar scenario in the Soviet zone as follows: 'The German Mennonite refugees had every right to fear the invading Russian soldiers. At night the soldiers would enter the camp, usually inebriated, and proceed to destroy everything and rape the girls. The greatest panic, however, set in when the thought of being shipped back to Russia and to Siberia started to become a reality.'[81] One might rightly ask, was repatriation really a worse fate than rape? Given that the narrator here is male, the juxtaposition might indicate a stronger and gendered identification with stories of male imprisonment in the Soviet Union prior to the war than with women's stories of rape, which at any rate were much less part of the Mennonite historical record. Grossmann's suggestion that German men actually pressured women to go with Russian soldiers in order to protect themselves from the worse fate of Siberia or getting shot may have been an extreme reaction on the part of a few.[82] Yet it does set up a hierarchy of wartime experience based on gender that contributed to the silencing of women's stories.

It is furthermore helpful to consider the importance of contextualizing memory and to understand a narrative both for the evidence it provides about historical experience but also for what it reveals about the development of group historical consciousness, or social memory, over time. Experiences of rape were not universal for Mennonite refugees; the threat of repatriation was. However, while memory sources refer to repatriation as an overwhelming fear, at the time (1945–6) it is possible that most Mennonite refugees would not have fully known the fate that awaited them should they be discovered by Soviet agents and 'sent back.' Although few, if any, would have wanted to return to their lives under a communist regime, not everyone expected a sentence to severe hardship in labour camps scattered across the far eastern and northern expanse of the Soviet Union.[83] Some Mennonites expected to be returned to their former homes in Ukraine or even hoped to be reunited with husbands, fathers, and sons.[84] Jacob A. Neufeld writes that a 'great number' of Mennonites, feeling hopeless over the situation in Germany, were 'bewitched' by Soviet promises of returning home.[85] The fact that some of the repatriations were voluntary is not often acknowledged in the literature. The stories of extreme suffering – cold, starvation, punishing labour – experienced by those who were repatriated began to surface only about a decade later, when communication between separated family members became possible. They were increasingly told as Mennonites began to emigrate from the Soviet Union in the 1970s.

The narratives of those who escaped repatriation are informed, and emotionally charged, with the knowledge of the more difficult postwar lives of their families and neighbours who were 'sent back.' A pattern of anxiety and guilt about loved ones left behind is evident in the stories of Mennonites who successfully emigrated. It could be that their own experiences of suffering, including rape, are minimized by the threat and reality of repatriation, which has become a central theme in the social memory of this generation of Mennonites.

The difficult moral choices faced by refugees and the consequent reconstructions of morality that took place with respect to wartime rape have extreme manifestations in the issues of suicide and abortion. According to several general sources about this historical period, suicide was a common occurrence among rape victims or to avoid rape.[86] It is difficult to know whether the number of Mennonites who committed suicide was comparable in proportion to the German population generally. Most memory sources and some first-hand accounts acknowledge that some Mennonites did choose to end their own lives in response to rape.[87] One Mennonite woman who knew she would be 'mistreated' if captured by the Russians, said she 'would rather die than fall into their hands,' although she was spared from rape.[88] Margaret L. Dick writes in her memoir that after her three friends were raped, 'There were days that [they] didn't care to go on with their lives.'[89] Some German women carried cyanide capsules with them at all times, so that they would be prepared if faced with the choice between rape and death. One story tells of a Mennonite woman who was also offered cyanide but, after being repeatedly raped, chose to live. She was admonished not to take the capsule by an adult male, who reminded her that, for Mennonites, the taking of life, including one's own, was a sin. However, the lifetime of psychological and emotional depression that followed prompted moments of regret over her decision.[90] Narratives of the Soviet advance into eastern Germany speak of suicide dispassionately and factually, as if there is no category of analysis that will help to give meaning to this course of action. A woman who was a child during the war described the experience of her mother.

The worst thing was molesting women and girls. My mother hid me under coal and she herself had to suffer. The grandparents had a very big house right beside a fresh water lake. Women and girls ran into the lake, drowning themselves. Bodies were just coming to the shore. I saw all that. It was, I could almost think, hell. There was a family from Berlin staying at my grandparents' place. Every year they would come there for their holidays. This young lady was my mother's friend. She was on her way to drown herself. She said I don't want to live after [being raped]. My mother just didn't let her go. No, you can't do this, you will get through this, you have two children, don't do it. She kept her back.[91]

For these two accounts, the memory of suicide as an option is contextualized as problematic first because it is sin, and second because it represented a rejection of maternal responsibility. If Mennonites dismissed suicide because it went against their religious principles or because it meant abandoning their children, choices that favoured life may have also been undergirded by the strength they received from families, friends, and community.

Abortion in the aftermath of rape, like the assault itself, is rarely spoken about in the memory sources of Mennonite refugees. In terms of numbers it is difficult to compare Mennonites with the German population generally, among whom abortion was widespread in the years immediately following war's end.[92] That memory itself can bring greater clarity to experience is suggested by the narrative of an adult woman who as a child in postwar Germany accompanied her friends to transport their sick mother home in a wagon. At the time the children realized only that the woman was seriously ill. It was some years later before they concluded that 'Auntie K. had an abortion from a back alley butcher [and] just about bled to death.'[93] One Mennonite refugee, a nurse and midwife, performed abortions on numerous German women who had been raped by Soviets. She recalled how the hospital in which she worked was filled with rape victims, some as young as eight years old, and that Soviet soldiers even raped sick people in the hospital. She shuddered at the reversal in her medical task: 'After a while, the expectant mothers who were raped, pregnant women and girls, there were no more normal births anymore. Only abortions, abortions, abortions. From morning till late.'[94] There were in fact many children born as a result of rape, although exact numbers are unknown.[95] Yet this woman's statement that there were 'no more normal births' is curious. It bears a similarity to accounts of suicide that depict a scenario in which 'all' the women were drowning themselves in the aftermath of or to avoid being raped. In remembering such disturbing events, it could be that narrators are again following the pattern of generalizing situations to avoid the specific and the personal.

Moral issues of suicide, abortion, and sex were likely the most drastic, but not the only, ethical dilemmas facing some Mennonite refugee women struggling to survive the war. Lying about one's country of birth and citizenship was a common device to avoid detection by Soviet and Allied repatriation officials. Some Mennonites sidestepped Soviet inquiries as to their place of birth by simply stating the name of their village in Ukraine. Since most villages founded by Mennonites in Ukraine had German names, the interrogator would often assume that the village was in Germany. Others took the more drastic step of assuming new identities altogether. Justina and her family group consisting of about twenty women and children found themselves in the British zone at the end of the war. During the early months, when the British were cooperating fully with the Soviets in their repatriation efforts, Justina and her family several times narrowly avoided detection as Soviet-born. When they finally came to a refugee camp, Justina declared that they had just escaped from the Russian zone and required identity papers. Filling out the forms, she said they were evangelical Protestants from Poland, and gave the entire group new names. Over the next months their new names caused alternately instances of tension and humour as both adults and children momentarily forgot their new identities.[96] For Justina, tactics of deceit were simply survival strategies and provoked no personal moral crisis.

Smuggling or stealing food was also common, particularly for refugees in the Russian zone, where food shortages were severe immediately after the war. Two women who worked in the kitchen of a Soviet headquarters received their noon meal free. Their seven children survived on the watery soup made of ground-up grain, potato peels, or any other scraps that their mothers could smuggle home past the guards. In one instance, one of the women hid a small roast in a pail full of water that had been used for washing the floor. She laughed when recalling how, to her horror, the roast floated to the top as she was exiting past the guard and how she quickly threw a dirty rag over the meat to conceal it. For this family, the meal that resulted was an unheard of treat. In the same manner, the two women smuggled out pieces of coal, stale bread, and anything else that would supplement their meagre existence. In recalling her family's strategies of survival, the daughter of the woman who took the roast said: 'Some people would likely say, "you were stealing" ... sure it's stealing, [but] we would never do it under ordinary circumstances. Mom didn't become a thief because of it.'[97] Such rationalizations are common in memory sources that look back to a context in which morality and ethics were structured differently than in the stable communities to which refugees immigrated. For most refugees, falsifying information, bribing border officials, and stealing food from farmers' fields were necessary, if regrettable, actions taken for personal survival and for the protection of one's children. Such behaviour is frequently related, in memory, to ingenuity, courage, resourcefulness, and a certain amount of bravado. Conduct based on wartime necessity would, however, come back to haunt some refugees after emigrating to North and South America.

The personal struggles with and reconstructions of morality, and the avoidance of sensitive issues like rape, have been cited as narrative patterns in recollections of war and the refugee experience. Other common themes emerge in women's memories of their experiences as refugees. Many women (and indeed men as well) viewed their survival as miraculous and providential, attributing their own courage and ingenuity to forces outside of themselves, most often to God. The following comment by Katie Friesen, describing the westward trek in September 1943, is typical: 'We had done fairly well considering the difficulties we had encountered at our departure, the heavy loads our horses had had to pull and the muddy roads. The courage and heroism of the women involved had to be admired, and yet we knew that without God's help we could not have proceeded.'[98]

Stories of providence are plentiful in accounts of escape and rescue through the refugee years. This is most apparent in the well-documented and oft-told story of the escape of about one thousand Mennonite refugees from Berlin in January 1947. These events, in which a group of Soviet-born refugees received fortuitous and last-minute permission to leave the American sector of Berlin and travel through Russian-occupied 'East' Germany to the West, has been described by Mennonite chroniclers as 'a miracle in our day and age.'[99] The emphasis on the providential and miraculous aspect of this rescue has given the story the status of myth in Mennonite history. One consequence of this is that attention has been directed toward the North American relief workers facilitating the escape and away from the Berlin refugees, who were mostly women and children.

For narrators recalling their own experiences as refugees, stories of providence help to bring religious meaning to people from a religious culture but who find themselves in settings where faith in God is severely challenged. Such stories also provide moments of hope in otherwise hopeless situations. One woman recalled a vision that she had while on the trek from the Ukraine near Christmas 1943. It was nighttime and very cold, and she describes seeing a castle built of ice, with Russian Orthodox priests carrying torches and candles and singing music reminiscent of the opera *Tosca*. She interpreted this as a vision of salvation during a time of despair.[100] In other stories, unknown persons function as angels, appearing with a loaf of bread after the last crumb has been eaten or giving words of guidance to a refugee uncertain of which direction to follow.[101] Thus, as a rhetorical device, stories of fortune allow both the narrator and audience (this can be true for both written and oral memory sources) a brief reprieve from an ongoing spiral of disaster, fear, and tragedy.

Focusing on divine intervention also removes attention from the individual's role in altering events and making choices at difficult moments. This is evident in situations in which women narrowly escaped rape. These incidents of escape are often told in the first person, yet women generally attribute their good fortune to forces outside of themselves – to other individuals, to curious twists of fate, or to God. One woman who was literally in the hands of Soviet soldiers gives no explanation for her release, but focuses on the divine intervention that she believes induced a religious transformation in her at that point. In her words: 'the Russian guerrillas surrounded me. And I had no chance of being rescued, or [of] surviv[ing] even. And all of a sudden they dropped ... and let me go. That time I think is the first time that I really prayed, whoever you are up there, thank you for helping me.'[102] In another situation, Irmgard Kriese 'had managed to hide herself from the monster [Russian soldiers] in some city, and when his hoped-for sacrifice disappeared from view he took off in pursuit of her daughter, who suddenly caught his eye. When Sister Kriese saw this she ran after her daughter in order to rescue her, and the Lord performed a miracle and helped them both to escape.'[103] Presumably Irmgard Kriese's actions contributed, at least in part, to her daughter's rescue and their escape, but the reader is given no details as to how the situation unfolded.

Despite the impersonal forces of war that swept them and their families along, women were indeed making choices and devising strategies to accomplish the immediate goals of obtaining food, shelter, and safety for their families. In the absence of adult men, who would normally be expected to undertake the heavy physical tasks and take leadership in family decision-making, women were compelled to take on roles traditionally allocated to both genders. They had to be brave and strong – physically, emotionally, and intellectually – and also be nurturing and care for their families. As wartime refugees, these women were sometimes disadvantaged by their sex when it came to allocation of the resources needed to survive. At the same time, groups of women and children travelling with few or no men were less likely to be objects of suspicion and might, as a result, more easily climb onto trains, scavenge for food, and pass through border crossings. Women's actions as protagonists of survival were offset, however, by their vulnerability as targets of rape, molestation, and murder.

The experience of no two women was exactly alike, although there were many commonalities in the losses and tragedy of their lives. Some women were outspoken, daring, and undaunted by the obstacles confronting them as refugees. Others were more resigned and fatalistic in the midst of the overwhelming sadness they felt and in the face of forces over which they had no control. Most women, with a few understated exceptions, do not interpret their wartime experience in a gendered way. Nevertheless, in a climate in which their stories as women are being uncovered and acclaimed, the memory sources of women refugees reveal a pride and awareness of the unique responsibilities that they carried and the heroism of the acts that they performed. The environment of war temporarily eliminated most normative standards of how people behaved, and thus women are most inclined to interpret their gender roles in a context of necessity and survival. As the war ended, and as women found safety in refugee camps awaiting a new future in the West, they came into an environment where they were dependent on the benevolence and instruction of relief workers and immigration officials. At this point, the paradoxical adjective of 'weak' came to be applied to these women without men.

3

New Identities, New Homes

In 1949 Agatha Wiebe and her two daughters escaped from the Soviet-occupied zone of Germany, where they had been living since the end of the war. They crossed the border to the British zone and travelled to the north German town of Gronau, where a North American agency called the Mennonite Central Committee had established a camp for Mennonite refugees. Agatha was all but penniless after trading her virtually useless East German marks for a much smaller amount in West German currency. Nevertheless, a priority for Agatha was to purchase nightgowns for herself and her daughters in order to 'be decent' while housed at the refugee camp.[1]

At one level, the desire to buy nightgowns was an obvious and common-sense response to the lack of privacy that characterized the accommodation at most displaced persons camps. At another level, Agatha's desire to be decent symbolized a transition from her wartime identity as a wanderer through an environment of chaos, brutality, and ambiguous morality, to her postwar identity as a Mennonite refugee widow. Although she was leaving behind years of terror and insecurity, the safety and security that she was moving toward was accompanied by the norms, expectations, and hierarchies of Mennonite churches in North and South America. Having made her one-way passage out of the Soviet zone, Agatha was also taking final leave of her former home in Ukraine, and was setting her sights on finding a new home for herself and her family in the West. In order to be eligible for immigration, she had to demonstrate both to Canadian immigration authorities and to Mennonite officials that she was acceptable as a potential citizen and a decent Mennonite.

In this chapter, I will discuss the circumstances under which Soviet and eastern European Mennonite refugees migrated to Canada and South America in the decade following the war. In the process of relating to Mennonite relief workers from North America and negotiating government immigration regulations, Mennonite refugees confronted their own identities, at the national, religious, and personal levels. The immediate postwar years in Europe represented a transition period, as refugees were drawn into the norms of Mennonite religious practice and gender relations.

By the end of the war in Europe in May 1945, millions of people had been displaced from their homes, estimates ranging widely from twenty to forty million. As the apogee of forced migrations in European history, the years 1939–49 have been called the 'black decade.'[2] Mennonites represented only a small portion – perhaps fifteen thousand – of the millions of displaced persons in central and western Europe who could not, or would not, return to their former homes.[3] The Mennonite relief agency in Europe was the Mennonite Central Committee (MCC), an organization based in Akron, Pennsylvania, with Canadian headquarters that opened in Kitchener, Ontario, in 1944. MCC had been established in 1920 with the initial purpose of providing material aid to Mennonites in the Soviet Union in the wake of civil war and famine.[4] During the Second World War, MCC coordinated a variety of relief efforts in England, the areas of the continent under German occupation being off limits. With the end of the war, MCC, along with other private relief organizations, entered the four Allied military zones of Germany as a member of the Council of Relief Agencies Licensed for Operation in Germany (CRALOG). In addition to sending food and clothing to war sufferers in Europe, MCC also sent over a hundred workers from North America to manage relief operations and make contact with Mennonite refugees scattered across the continent.

After having its credentials confirmed with the International Refugee Organization (IRO), the Mennonite Central Committee established and operated two refugee camps in western Germany and one in the American zone of Berlin. The largest camp was set up in February 1947 at Gronau in the British zone of Germany on the Dutch border. About 80 per cent of Mennonite refugees were in the British zone in northwest Germany. Equipped to feed and shelter five hundred to nine hundred refugees, the camp at some points held as many as two thousand people. It became a small, nearly self-sufficient community with its own hospital, carpenter and shoemaker shops, kitchen and laundry facilities, school and kindergarten, church services, library, and newspaper.[5] The second of MCC's refugee camps was established in June 1947 at Backnang, near Stuttgart in the American zone. In addition to the camps in occupied Germany, MCC set up a centre in Holland for the purpose of relief distribution and immigration processing, and sent workers to Denmark where over a thousand Mennonites were in government-run camps. MCC found many other refugees in DP camps operated by the United Nations Relief and Rehabilitation Administration (UNRRA). Another significant locale for prospective immigrants was the IRO-operated camp at Fallingbostel in northern Germany, which served as a processing centre and transit camp. But not all Mennonite refugees were housed in camps; the majority found work and housing on farms and in villages and used the MCC camps for the purposes of receiving relief packages and preparing for emigration.

The MCC workers from North America, brimming with enthusiasm, energy, and a sense that they were called by God, were unprepared for what they saw when they encountered Mennonite refugees. Most workers were quite young, in their early twenties, and although some had been born in the Soviet Union, they had for the most part grown up in the secure environment of North America. Workers were repeatedly struck by the small number of adult men among the refugees. Indeed, when the Mennonites were gathered together in close quarters in refugee camps, the sex imbalance among the migrants became even more obvious. Among the 1,500 Mennonites in DP camps in Denmark, there were 300 men and 750 women sixteen years of age and over, the remainder being children of both sexes.[6] The sex ratio in the MCC refugee camp in Berlin was especially striking. Of the approximately 1,000 Mennonites in that city, only 126 were men over the age of sixteen, and many of these were old men.[7] The comment of Walter Gering, who wrote about Mennonite DPs in Denmark, is typical in its description of the refugee family from the perspective of a worker: 'There are any number of young mothers with 4–5 small children looking out into the future with apprehension. They have no money, no home and no able-bodied husband and father to provide a living.'[8] Peter Dyck observed that Mennonite refugee women of thirty-six years looked to be more like fifty.[9] And Cornelia Lehn commented about a refugee woman who had just escaped from the Soviet zone: 'She didn't look like women in America. I can't describe the difference, but it is nevertheless there.'[10]

The refugees in turn viewed the MCC workers as 'angels of mercy' and held them in reverence. On Gronau camp director Siegfried Janzen's birthday, the smaller children of the camp sang for him early in the morning, then 'flowers and birthday greetings came in all day,' and celebrations continued until eleven o'clock that evening.[11] Cornelius F. Klassen, the first MCC worker to enter Germany after the war, is mentioned in many first-person accounts and has attained almost mythic stature in both the historiography of MCC's postwar work and also in the memories of refugees who met him.[12] For many refugees, the initial meeting with Klassen was a first step away from their identity as homeless refugees and toward a connection with a new land and a new community.

A paternalistic relationship developed between workers and the refugees. The latter are frequently described in childlike terms, despite Peter Dyck's comment that the women looked much older than their years. Cornelius Wall, a Canadian Mennonite minister undertaking religious work among the refugees in Europe, and his wife, Agnes, were called *Onkel* and *Tante* (uncle and aunt) although they were close in age to many of the adult refugees.[13] Given the large number of women and children among the refugees, female workers had a special role to play. While male workers tended to assume fatherly roles, their female counterparts were able to enter into the more intimate circumstances of women's lives. One female worker was lauded by the director of the Gronau camp for her efficiency and dedication, and also her 'very keen understanding of the individual family affairs.'[14] It is noteworthy that in a report on the work at the MCC hospital at Gronau, the head nurse, Elise Schwarz, made a point of mentioning that of the forty-three patients currently there, eight were women who, 'following cruel and great misfortune in the East,' required constant care. One can gather from her statement that these women were likely victims of rape who required, not only nursing care for their physical condition, but also emotional support that only female caregivers could have provided.[15] Cornelius Wall wrote in a 1948 report: 'It is evident that the presence of Mrs. Wall is decidedly an advantage. She has a definite mission to fulfil with the women and children. Repeatedly joy is being expressed over her presence and visits.'[16] Agnes Wall herself wrote that praying with refugee women 'paves the way to confidential, frank discussions of situations.'[17]

There were also commonalities that refugee women shared with female workers. Aside from their sex, marital status may have fostered a shared sense of independence between refugees and workers. While many refugee women were widows or single, most female MCC workers were unmarried as well. The independent nature of one worker is evident in her response to news that many of her friends at home were getting married. Susan B. Peters, who worked for MCC in Europe for three years, wrote to a Canadian friend in 1946, 'I just can't see, why people want to work so hard to get a ring. For so many it does not last so very long either.'[18] Her latter comment suggests that Peters' personal renunciation of marriage – 'I am a confirmed old maid' – may have been reinforced by her exposure to many young widows among the refugees. Their experience demonstrated that marriage, expected to be a life-long relationship, could be very transitory indeed.

Camp life introduced an orderliness and regimentation that had been non-existent in the lives of most refugees during the previous few years. The presence of leadership, regular meals, a bed to sleep in, and daily tasks to perform was comforting after years of upheaval. At the same time, as Martha Bohachevsky-Chomiak observes about Ukrainian DP camps, life in the camps was a 'combination of routine and instability in which the quick-witted, the resourceful, and the enterprising did better than those who were used to settled patterns of behaviour.'[19] The atmosphere of instability resulted from the constant arrival and departure of families and individuals, the unknown future that loomed before all refugees, the ongoing fear of repatriation, and the emotional fragility that afflicted most persons surviving the war.

The combination of regimentation and instability was perhaps most evident and tested most severely in the limited living space and lack of privacy within the camps. Most memory sources related to camp life include a description of the small cubicles assigned to each family unit, separated only by grey army blankets hung from string. The very crowded surroundings were described as 'unwholesome,' and stretched relationships to the limit.[20] In describing the close living quarters at Gronau, camp director Siegfried Janzen vaguely implied that problematic sexual relations resulted from the lack of privacy. In his words: 'We have families consisting of parents and grown sons and daughters living together in one small cubicle without any separate walls or rooms to serve the purpose of separate bedrooms. The tragedies arising out of such circumstances are alarming.'[21]

The lack of privacy also encouraged intimacy between adult men and women, some of whom had missing spouses. The existence of sexual relations outside of marriage, or common-law marriages as some of them became, was perhaps the greatest moral problem that concerned Mennonite relief and church workers. In May 1948, a Mennonite 'brotherhood' meeting was convened at the Fallingbostel camp to deal with two questions: the first related to the training and upbringing of the refugee youth; the second concerned the promotion of a moral way of life based on Christian-Mennonite norms. The thirty-seven men participating in the consultation were distressed by the 'pernicious and wicked' example set by individuals who had no certain word that their first spouse had died, yet engaged in affairs with others. The group passed a resolution that denounced such relationships as adultery and whoring, according to the Bible. They further agreed that anyone persisting in such behaviour would be barred from serving in any public way within the refugee community, such as teaching children and youth, as preacher or deacon, or in the church choir.[22] The conclusions arrived at by this body could only be expected given the biblical literalism of Mennonite ethics and doctrine. Yet the quick condemnation belied the insecurity of refugee life, the fact that many Mennonite refugees from Ukraine had been separated from their spouses for ten years already and assumed them dead, and the intimacy that was fostered by the cramped living within camps. A converse issue, cited by one worker as 'a difficult social and moral problem,' was the many young women of marriageable age with no prospects of finding a partner within their own group, given the limited number of males above age twenty.[23] One consequence of this was the tendency of young Mennonite women to befriend, and sometimes marry, non-Mennonite German men.

The predominance of women and children in the camps also highlighted the gendered nature of camp administration. Doreen Indra has argued that the 'emphasis on males as family spokespersons and as brokers between refugees and (primarily male) camp functionaries guarantees the close identity of public camp discourse on "family" or "refugee" concerns with the concerns of men.'[24] Given that many Mennonite families did not have male spokespersons and that many camp functionaries were also female, women's opinions and priorities might have had greater weight. However, early in the organizing process MCC appointed *Vertrauensmaenner* (representatives) and *Gruppenmaenner* (group leaders) as representatives to act as intermediaries between MCC and the refugees outside the camps. These persons were mainly former ministers or others that had carried a leadership role among the refugees. Most were probably men, although Jacob A. Neufeld, himself a *Vertrauensmann*, refers to women in this capacity as well. Yet Neufeld's own list of eleven *Vertrauens-* and thirteen *Gruppenmaenner* names only men.[25] The twenty-five *Vertrauensmaenner* were each responsible

for a district serving seven hundred to twelve hundred Mennonite refugees, and within each district were ten to fifteen *Gruppenmaenner*, or
small group leaders, who could relay messages to refugees directly.
Neufeld cites the significance of the group leaders in contacting the scattered refugees and escapees from the Russian zone, intervening with
repatriation officers, and addressing refugees' varied questions and concerns. He further observes that 'These men and women cared for the
church services and spiritual welfare within their group and in many
cases presided themselves.'[26] Neufeld's statement, though inconclusive,
leaves open the possibility that women continued to exercise spiritual
leadership in the context of small groups of refugees located away from
the camps themselves.

In the Berlin camp, which was accessible to only a few MCC relief
workers and not to North American Mennonite Church personnel, and
in which there were so few adult men, women may have had more
opportunities to assert their leadership skills. According to Elfrieda
Klassen Dyck, herself someone who undertook many daunting tasks
during her eight-year work term in Europe, it was women who took
most of the leadership in organizing special events at the Berlin camp.[27]
Her husband, Peter, recalled that one minister in the camp, who thought
he possessed authority because of his status, 'was never looked upon
for ... initiative, for something new.' He further observed that 'new ideas
and initiative usually didn't come from the elected leaders ... but [they]
came spontaneously from the grass roots where the real leadership people were.'[28] Nevertheless, in keeping with tradition, the elected leaders
were only men. At the Berlin camp, a church council (*Kirchenrat*) consisting only of men was elected in July 1946. As Peter Dyck recalled, 'it
never occurred to anyone to officially elect a woman to the *Kirchenrat*.
That just was not done.'[29] As well, housefathers were appointed for each
house, although there was also one housemother.[30] In Mennonite
camps, the unofficial and creative leadership of women was acknowledged and encouraged, but at an official level the norms of North American and Russian Mennonite culture were assumed to hold. In these
contexts, the separation between the public male realm of institutional
leadership and the private female domestic world was considered a natural part of God's universal order. The loss of men and the realities of
war had broken down some stereotypical gendered behaviour, but traditional thinking on sexual roles was unaltered, a fact that became
increasingly evident in the ordered setting of the camps.

A variety of indicators suggests that within refugee camps, gender roles began to reassume a traditional, more stratified order in which women were expected to defer to male authority. For instance, in the Fallingbostel camp, men and women were divided into two separate groups to discuss the Sunday school lesson, because 'if all together, the women in true Mennonite fashion, did not speak at all (and were not expected to).'[31] Official decision-making bodies, especially those that were concerned with spiritual matters, were generally all-male, such as the brotherhood meeting that met to discuss moral problems among the refugees.

Religious life among the refugees was perhaps the most significant manifestation of a return to traditional hierarchical norms. Unlike in Ukraine prior to German occupation or along the trek, during which informal religious practice led by women had predominated, public ritual and formalized structure and doctrine took hold in the camps. Male ministers from North America, sometimes accompanied by their wives, were commissioned to undertake church work among the Mennonite refugees. The North American male hegemony over formal religious life contrasted not only with the precedents of female leadership established among the refugees, but also with the more liberal traditions of Dutch and German Mennonites. A Canadian minister reported astonishment over the fact that in the Netherlands, he had met at least three female preachers in the Mennonite Church.[32]

A priority for the ministers from overseas was religious rehabilitation, given the widespread perception that many of the refugees lacked spiritual and moral foundations. Church services and Bible and Sunday school classes were scheduled, choirs were formed, and, most importantly, catechism classes were held for those who desired baptism. A central tenet of the Mennonites was a belief in a voluntary church of believers symbolized by baptism at an age of consent, rather than as an infant. Preparatory baptismal classes that provided instruction in Mennonite doctrine were considered especially important in order to preclude the 'search for pleasure and enjoyment' that had set in among the youth as a release from the terrors of war.[33] After reading letters from European relief workers, a Canadian described her concern for the 'appalling spiritual mist that has enveloped ... the young people.'[34]

Particularly for the young adults among the refugees, who had grown up during the 1930s without formal religious instruction, the spiritual life that permeated the camps represented something very new. Some refugees were hardened against religion because of their wartime experiences and personal losses. More common was the sentiment of one young woman who recalled that 'a whole new world' had opened up for her when she was exposed to Mennonite religious practice.[35] The 'new-found concern for religion' common among DPs was, according to Mark Wyman, an antidote to the despair felt by many refugees and also an expression of gratitude for having survived the war.[36] The forms of religion zealously offered by North American workers and eagerly embraced by Mennonite refugees gave the latter a restored sense of belonging to a community.

The new concern for religion may have also had more pragmatic roots. Given the heavy program of religious rehabilitation in the camps, as well as the links between a Mennonite identity and immigration eligibility, many refugees saw baptism as a way to establish personal authenticity. In the Mennonite tradition, an individual was not officially a member of the Mennonite Church prior to that religious rite of passage. Baptisms in refugee camps became extensive, partly due to the zeal of North American ministers who wanted to win souls for their particular branch of the Mennonite church. At the Gronau camp, one hundred individuals were baptized in the course of the first year.[37] Peter Dyck became concerned about the widely held view among refugees that 'it is better for immigration if one is baptized' and cautioned ministers against performing 'hasty' baptisms. He found it depressing that many people, when asked why they had become baptized, simply shrugged their shoulders and said it was 'better all around.'[38]

The competition for members on the part of two Mennonite denominations – the General Conference Mennonites (referred to as *Kirchliche* in their Russian setting) and the Mennonite Brethren (or *Bruedergemeinde*) – was one factor accounting for the zeal with which ministers undertook baptismal instruction. The Mennonite Brethren Church was founded in Russia in 1860 after a crisis in moral and spiritual deportment and outside pietistic influences had prompted a split from the main church body. Many refugees had little appreciation for this division, which in North America was rigid to the extent that marriage between individuals from the two groups was considered exogamy by the Mennonite Brethren and proscribed as a result. As churches in the Soviet Union were closed during the 1930s, the denominational differences had receded behind the common will to maintain any religious practice at all. Certain MCC relief workers became frustrated by the rift imposed from the outside on religious life in the Mennonite camps. In a confidential letter to a Mennonite leader in Canada, one worker complained about the denominational separation that certain ministers were promoting. The worker noted that once the churches were closed in the Soviet Union, nobody spoke about different kinds of church, and that individuals were happy simply to have access to the word of God. Such unity continued through the German occupation and the trek from Ukraine. But in the refugee camps, the emphasis on division had reached the point that the Mennonite Brethren choir had to avoid singing certain chorales because they were from the General Conference hymnal. The denial of 'wonderful' music to the young people and to part of the church was a disgrace, as far as this worker, himself from Mennonite Brethren background, was concerned.[39] A General Conference minister from Canada also complained about the 'aggressive' approach taken by Mennonite Brethren clergy among the refugees in Europe: whenever one of their own 'good-natured' General Conference men was in charge, then the other side would go 'fishing' for recruits, he said.[40] The competition between the two sides extended into efforts to promote their separate denominational newspapers in different locales where refugees were living.[41]

The relief effort concentrated, at one level, on meeting the immediate physical needs of the refugees and re-establishing religious practice in their lives. Yet political questions were also among the first priorities. Most pressing was the need to define the national identity of Mennonites from the Soviet Union. Mennonite refugees came under scrutiny first with respect to their eligibility as recipients of United Nations relief and secondly, regarding their eligibility for emigration to North America.

In order that Mennonites might receive assistance from the International Refugee Organization as legitimate refugees, MCC set out to prove that Mennonites were neither Soviet – which would have subjected them to repatriation – nor German by nationality. The officials of MCC considered it a major victory when they were able to make the case to the IRO, through an elaborate study process and lobby, that Mennonite refugees from the Soviet Union were really Dutch in ancestry.[42] This was true, although Soviet Mennonites were separated from their Dutch ancestors by four centuries. The fact that almost all Mennonite family names could be traced back to the Netherlands, as well as the similarity between the Dutch language and the Low German dialect spoken by Mennonites, helped to establish the claim. MCC further argued that Mennonite refugees who became German citizens during the war or men who joined various German military units had done so only under duress and, for the most part, involuntarily. Neither of these arguments were, however, applicable to Mennonites displaced from their homes in Prussia or Danzig; they had already been citizens of the Reich before 1939. As a result, the latter were never eligible for IRO assistance.

The positive outcome, for MCC and the refugees, of a lengthy negotiation, belies the complexity of the eligibility issue. As T.D. Regehr has demonstrated, IRO officials were never really convinced of the Mennonites' Dutch ancestry, but continued to process them for relief and immigration assistance mainly to expedite the refugee problem in postwar Europe. Suggesting that the competing claims of MCC and IRO both contained validity, Regehr concludes that 'even these cherished values [of truth and honesty] may appear differently to people in complex, difficult and morally ambiguous situations.'[43] MCC officials such as C.F. Klassen were critical of the refugees for adopting a situational morality that compromised truth and other Christian norms when they presented themselves as German, rather than Soviet, by nationality. In Klassen's words: 'We lament the fact that they have resorted to an untruth in order to save their lives. But this is already a matter concerning the inner territory of church discipline.'[44] But, in effect, Klassen and his colleagues were doing the same thing by constructing a questionable, if not entirely 'untrue,' argument about the national identity of the refugees.

The complexity of the issue and the ambiguity of truth were especially evident from the vantage point of the refugees themselves. The question of German citizenship, of Germanness generally, is altered somewhat when the memories of individual refugees are probed. Although MCC officials insisted that citizenship had been obtained involuntarily, this argument to a certain extent invalidates the ability of refugees to make choices for themselves. While few of them actually sought out German citizenship, certainly a large number of Mennonite refugees were quite happy to go through the naturalization process once in German territory, since they considered themselves to be more German, at least culturally, than Soviet. One woman expressed the sentiments of others when she said that she felt regret when MCC had instructed her to deny her German citizenship in order to emigrate. 'It was a lie,' she said, and so she deliberately kept German citizenship for her infant son, who had been born in Germany.[45]

The affinity that Mennonites felt for German culture, if not so much for the state, is evident in the way they welcomed the German occupation forces in their homeland in 1941 and the way they readily evacuated their homes with the German retreat two years later. Many in fact hoped that Germany would win the war, although such sentiments were based as much on antipathy for the Soviets as on nationalistic identification with Germany. Particularly for young people who grew up in the years after the closure of churches, their self-identification and differentiation from Soviet society was as Germans, not as Mennonites. As several memory sources indicate, language and culture, rather than religion, differentiated people during the Soviet era.[46] The idea of being Mennonite was in fact quite new for the generation of children and youth.

The relationships that Mennonite women developed with German soldiers during the occupation and also later in Germany further demonstrated the ethnic compatibility they felt. Some may have even used these relationships to define their own national identity. Mary and her older sister both had German soldier boyfriends who were unable to return to their families in the Eastern zone after the war ended. The young women felt that if they were threatened with repatriation, they would immediately marry their boyfriends and thus avoid being sent back to the Soviet Union.[47] A significant number of marriages did take place between Mennonite refugees and *Reichsdeutsche* (German nationals) in the immediate postwar years.

Some refugees perceived the criteria for eligibility in a gendered way, even if perceptions had little grounding in official procedure. One young man concluded that his family was rejected for immigration to Canada because they lacked a male provider. While he, together with his mother, grandmother, and six siblings, was encouraged by MCC to go to Paraguay, his unmarried aunt waited in Germany to emigrate to Canada with her fiancé, and his uncle was able to go to Canada after his release from a Soviet POW camp.[48] His own family's experience, as well as his memory of the many widows with children who had gone to Paraguay, created the impression that MCC had in fact deliberately directed fatherless families toward South America.

At least one relief worker felt that women were less able than men to argue their cases before immigration officials. Referring to the process of determining whether Mennonites had become German citizens involuntarily, C.F. Klassen argued to IRO officials, 'How can a helpless woman, for instance, prove this? ... She is confused, she does not know any more what to say. She is afraid of any official, because she became so very suspicious.' Klassen went on to apologize for cases in which women had lied about their identity in order to avoid 'Soviet agents,' saying, 'We understand the circumstances they were in, but we can't justify the means.'[49]

Despite Klassen's statement about helpless women, which may have been made for mainly tactical reasons, many women refugees went before screening officials and capably argued their case. Part of the guidelines of eligibility included establishing oneself to be a bona fide Mennonite – as opposed to a German national – which usually was confirmed by a typical Mennonite surname or the ability to speak Low German. Katharina, a widow with seven children, did not have a Mennonite name because her second husband was of German Lutheran background. She arrived at Gronau, having lost her first husband during the deportations of the 1930s and her second husband on the warfront in Poland. The seven children included some from her first marriage, some her second husband's first marriage, and three who came from the second union. When questioned about her identity, she demonstrated her ability to speak the Low German dialect and, with the help of her friends, proved her Mennonite upbringing.[50] In order to ease her own eligibility hearing, another woman resumed the use of her Mennonite maiden name for herself and her son after she separated from her husband, who was German. As a result, she was thought to be a single mother with an illegitimate son.[51] Rather than being helpless, refugee women adopted a variety of strategies to establish identities and make a case for themselves.

For some refugees a greater hurdle than establishing national identity was the process of medical screening. In contrast to the previous world war, aggressive efforts to combat typhus and other epidemic diseases following the Second World War meant that, excepting those released from Nazi concentration camps, the health of displaced persons was 'remarkably good.'[52] Yet most refugees were in a generally weakened state due to years of inadequate food, insufficient shelter, and the stress of an insecure future. One refugee widow wrote to an MCC relief worker describing the health of her son: 'My ten-year old, whose father has been in exile since 1937, is suffering from undernourishment and one of his lungs is not well. He was once a blooming, healthy child, but six years of privation with the irregular life of wandering have destroyed the strongest constitutions.'[53] In a similar vein, Marga Siemens wrote from Bad Harzburg, Germany, to her uncle in Saskatchewan in 1947. She thanked him for the care package he had sent, but said, 'Unfortunately I can not eat the lovely things. I am ... always sick. I have endured great pain and have prayed to God to let me die even though I don't want to leave my son with other people. My whole body cramps up until a fainting spell releases me from the pain. Now I am only skin and bones.'[54] Such characterizations were common.

For those individuals who did have major or minor health problems, their medical examination by immigration officials could close or open the door to a new home. While health or disability was not an impediment to acceptance by Paraguay, Canadian immigration regulations had strict physical fitness criteria for eligibility. The rigid enforcement of health regulations by Canadian immigration officials was in fact one reason why so many refugees were compelled to go to Paraguay. In a report dated November 1948, Gronau camp director Siegfried Janzen noted that 'comparatively many cases' had failed examination by Canadian officials and had sought admission at Gronau to wait out their six-month deferment. Most common conditions were eye disease (mainly trachoma), tuberculosis, and 'a general run-down condition.'[55]

Bribery was not uncommon as a strategy to ensure a family's success during medical screening. One family made it through their medical examination when the mother, described in a memoir as 'an intelligent woman,' slipped the physician a package of American cigarettes, prompting him to overlook the fact that two of the daughters had spots on their lungs, which indicated exposure to tuberculosis.[56] Conversely, knowing how important an 'okay' was to hopeful emigrants, examining physicians could also use their power of approval to obtain favours from refugees. In one case, a Canadian doctor had become quite attached to his assistant and interpreter, a young refugee girl whom he called 'his little "slave driver."' When it came time for her family's medical exam, the doctor 'let her Grandfather slip by without paying too much attention,' despite contrary evidence that the old man's lungs were damaged. In return, the doctor demanded a kiss, placing the girl in a confusing and embarrassing situation. According to the report on this incident, the kiss never transpired. The writer of the report excused the doctor by saying, 'He was just trying her out and amusing himself'; however, the facts point to a clear case of sexual harassment.[57] The situation also reveals the ongoing vulnerability that women experienced as women when confronted by systems, in this case government immigration screening, that were dominated by men.

Families who had already experienced much fragmentation in some cases found themselves separated again over the process of medical screening. One family – two daughters with both parents – that, remarkably, had remained intact through the war found that the father had tuberculosis and had to spend two years in a sanitarium in Germany. Since they all wanted to emigrate together, the two daughters with their mother lived at the immigration transit camp at Fallingbostel from February 1947 through May 1949. In the end, the father was still not permitted to enter Canada, so while the daughters immigrated to Canada, their parents followed some months later to the United States, where they had relatives. The family was reunited a year later when the parents attended the wedding of one daughter in Manitoba.[58] In many similar cases, parts of a family unit were left behind in Europe to wait out a medical deferment while other members went ahead to Canada. Sometimes, healthy individuals refused opportunities for earlier emigration in order to avoid separation from family who had to remain behind.

With respect to certain medical conditions, families might have to make difficult decisions that invariably involved separation. For instance, one widow with five daughters was faced with the undesirable option of remaining in Germany in an ongoing situation of deprivation to keep her family together, or leaving behind the eldest girl (age nineteen), who had active tuberculosis and could not emigrate until cured. The MCC worker dealing with the case advised the woman to go to Canada. She did so, although the move caused enormous pain after the woman had struggled so hard to keep her family together.[59]

A diagnosis of mental illness was one condition that stood as a permanent obstacle to emigration. In a case requiring MCC's intercession, a forty-six-year-old woman with four children faced a family breakup due to the 'feeble-minded' condition of her fifteen-year-old son, although she insisted he was only 'hard of hearing.' Initially, the IRO said the rest of the family could emigrate to Canada, but the boy could never go, despite MCC's guarantee for his care. Other officials said that the mother had to stay in Germany with the boy and his younger brother (age twelve), but the two older daughters could go on to Canada. As an alternative to leaving the boy in Europe, MCC decided to find a Paraguay-bound family to adopt him, a plan that his mother agreed to. Apparently this plan was acceptable to IRO authorities.[60] For a family already shaken by the loss of its father and the trauma of war, the suggestion by MCC that they give up the ill son seems acutely insensitive. Rather than lobby to bend the policy for this family, the agency's representatives sought alternatives that didn't challenge a rigid bureaucracy. Although the final outcome for this family is not immediately evident from the sources, the comments regarding their processing provide evidence of the painful decisions and situations facing some refugee mothers.

The efforts to identify oneself as a bona fide refugee, according to IRO criteria, and to pass security and medical screening were all necessary if an individual wanted to emigrate. Canada was the preferred destination, particularly since it had accepted approximately twenty-one thousand Mennonites from the Soviet Union only two decades earlier. Many of the refugees had relatives among the immigrants of the 1920s. However, Canada's immediate postwar priority was the transport and rehabilitation of Canadian service personnel and their families. Thus prospects for the large-scale movement of displaced persons and refugees from Europe seemed dim. Due to fears of renewed economic depression and high unemployment, public opinion in Canada was initially set against postwar immigration. As these worries proved unfounded and it appeared that economic boom and industrial expansion were on the horizon, attitudes and policies toward the immigration of DPs and refugees gradually changed. Canada's immigration policy in the first decade following the war focused on a gradually expanding program of sponsorship by close relatives, as well as a bulk labour program that placed workers under contract with specific industries as well as in domestic service.[61]

But in the two years immediately after the war, Canada's doors remained firmly closed. Anxious to find a new home for the thousands of Mennonite refugees in Europe, who in varying degrees were acutely frightened of being sent back to the Soviet Union, the Mennonite Central Committee investigated prospects in South America. Paraguay was an immediate option, given that several thousand Mennonites already lived there and that eligibility requirements were almost non-existent. The first major transport of Mennonite refugees left Germany on 1 February 1947, bound for Paraguay, followed in 1948 by three more shiploads of individuals whose chances of getting to Canada were remote.

In Canada, an organization called the Canadian Mennonite Board of Colonization (CMBC) was actively lobbying the Canadian government to broaden its immigration policy and to widen the admissible categories under the close relative scheme.[62] Initially quite narrow in scope, the close relative provisions were gradually broadened and, significant for the Mennonite migrants, came to include a category for 'the widowed daughter or sister (including any unmarried children under eighteen years of age) of any Canadian capable of receiving and caring for such persons.'[63] Because of their connections with earlier Russian Mennonite migrants, about three-quarters of the refugees were eligible for immigration as close relatives.

Those refugees who had no close relatives to sponsor them sought admission to Canada under one of the Special Projects schemes implemented by the Department of Labour. Initially, these projects were aimed mainly at potential labourers for the mining, forestry, and agriculture industries, but were later extended to include female domestic labour. Many Mennonite families thus immigrated as farm labourers, sponsored by cousins or other relatives who were not considered close according to the prescribed categories. A community appeal on the part of the CMBC also prompted applications from Canadian Mennonites who wished to sponsor non-related Mennonite refugees for farm employment. In early 1949 the Canadian government approved the Farm Labour Movement scheme, which created an additional immigration opportunity for displaced persons without close relatives in Canada. Over one thousand Mennonite refugees became eligible under this category, most of them matched with Canadian Mennonite sponsors through the CMBC.

After the peak years of immigration in 1948 and 1949, MCC in Europe and CMBC in Canada became mainly concerned with what were known as 'hard-core cases.' These were individuals who did not meet Canadian eligibility requirements for medical reasons; because they were considered German nationals, having resided in Prussia or Poland; or, in the case of young men, because they had served in certain 'reprehensible' units of the German military, such as the Waffen SS, or because they were considered security risks in a general sense. In a few cases, moral reasons were cited as the cause for delays in processing. One such case was that of a couple, both of whom were born in Russia, and their four-year-old son. In 1954, an MCC refugee worker in Germany remarked that the 'case apparently hinges on fact that he had a wife in Russia; and that [the child] is illegitimate.'[64] In a similar case, MCC advised a woman with two illegitimate children and no relatives in Canada to try for the United States.[65] Other cases were simply described as hopeless or pathetic, although specific reasons for their ineligibility are unclear. The lack of sponsorship in Canada or the United States may have been the main obstacle to immigration for a sixty-two-year old woman mentioned by MCC worker G.R. Gaeddert in a 1951 report. Although she was skilled as a cobbler and apparently did 'good work,' Gaeddert remarked that it was 'too bad that she has some peculiarities that might count against her.' Her peculiarities, whatever they were, may in fact have been emotional difficulties stemming from rape by Russians and Poles, obliquely referred to by Gaeddert who says, 'she has suffered greatly at their pleasure.'[66]

Further reasons for delayed emigration lay with refugees themselves. As one MCC worker reported in 1952, some families were divided on the question of emigration: 'Most often men or fathers want to emigrate but women or mothers hold back because of fear what the new land will hold for their families.'[67] As time went on and refugees began to put down roots in Germany through employment and personal relationships, and as the fear of being sent back to the Soviet Union dissipated, the anxiety to leave European soil diminished. Other causes for hesitancy included reports coming from North America about the difficult labour that new immigrants had to do, and also fear of some of the theological tendencies in Canadian churches.[68]

By the end of 1949, the majority of postwar Mennonite immigrants, about six thousand, had arrived in Canada. In 1950 the Canadian government decided to admit German nationals to Canada, given that those immigrants arriving to date had been absorbed successfully and that serious labour shortages remained in key areas of industry.[69] This change in immigration regulations opened the door for Prussian and Polish Mennonite refugees still waiting in Danish and north German refugee camps. Through 1953, several hundred continued to arrive each year, although the numbers coming from Europe steadily declined after that.

Published accounts, while generally acknowledging the striking number of widows among the postwar immigrants to Canada, rarely give statistical breakdowns that demonstrate the sexual and familial demographics of this group. An analysis of the family registers (*Familienverzeichnisse*) compiled by the Canadian Mennonite Board of Colonization provides a portrait, by age, sex, and position within the family and/or marital status, of postwar Mennonite immigrants during the three years of highest immigration. The years 1947–9 were those during which most eligible Soviet Mennonites immigrated to Canada. For these years of highest migration, 58 per cent of the total were female, 42 per cent male (see the Appendix, Table 2). These percentages include immigrants of all ages.

A breakdown of these statistics by age reveals that the greatest ratio of females to males occurs above the age of thirty. That is, while a general equilibrium exists between children and young adults (who would have been children during the war), a striking predominance of women over men is apparent among adults arriving in Canada (see the Appendix, Table 3). In 1948, a female–male ratio of slightly greater than 2 to 1 existed among the adult immigrants. Within this sample, the smallest gap in the ratio is for individuals up to the age of thirty, where women are 62 per cent of the total. At the other end of the age scale, one finds the largest differential, where women sixty years and older are 77 per cent of the total in that age group. In the age range thirty to fifty-nine, the percentage of women is slightly higher than the average 68 per cent of the total. These statistics make sense given that many individuals in their twenties, arriving in Canada in the late 1940s, were less than sixteen years during the war. The depletion of males in this age group was due mainly to losses of young men conscripted into the German forces in 1944.

While the sex imbalance in the adult population is noteworthy, what is especially striking is the number of widows – 896, or 15 per cent of the total – of which 451 had dependants under the age of sixteen (see Appendix, Table 4). This compares dramatically with the 150 widowers (only 8 with dependants), who represented 3 per cent of the total.

Comparable statistics that illuminate the demography of Paraguayan immigrants are not available. Their unique situation, in which the predominance of women and children was particularly striking at the outset, is examined in the next chapter. In Canada, the sex imbalance among the postwar Mennonite immigrants became less pronounced as they were scattered across the country and integrated into Mennonite communities from Ontario to British Columbia. As boys and young men grew up and as women married (either within or outside the immigrant community), the striking dominance in numbers of female-headed families diminished. Even though the demography changed, the community's identity as fatherless and leaderless remained, and the stigma that women without men possessed stayed with them.

For those Mennonites who had survived the war, had made it to the Allied occupied zones in the West as refugees, had applied for immigration eligibility, and had successfully passed the various levels of screening, a new life was about to begin. The encounter with North American Mennonites in Europe had begun a process whereby the experience and norms of the refugee community were juxtaposed to those of the society that received them and to those of their co-religionists in the new land. Whether migrating to Paraguay or to Canada, the Mennonite newcomers maintained their identity as *Fluechtlinge* (refugees) for years to come, a label ascribed to them by earlier residents but also one they held onto themselves. The perception that they were neither settled nor rooted in their new homes had much to do with the psychological and emotional attachments they maintained with family members left behind and with their physical homes in the Soviet Union and eastern Europe that had been vacated with such haste. For the most part, however, the psychological effects of the refugee experience were submerged beneath the more immediate challenge, which was to settle themselves into new homes. In both Paraguay and Canada, the scars of war were either quickly healed or covered over as Mennonite immigrant families built and bought homes, found or created livelihoods, and sought to find a place in their new national environments.

4

'Weak' Women in Paraguay

On 1 February 1947, the ship *Volendam* left the port of Bremerhaven, Germany, bound for Argentina. On board were 2,303 refugees, most of them Mennonite. Donna Yoder, an American relief worker in Europe, described the make-up of passengers on the ship: 'The first person to go on board on Monday was a little old lady and her daughter. The lady is not well and we wonder if she will stand the journey, but she has determination. There were little babies too ... There were twins, little kiddies with wooden shoes, old grandmothers, young folks and all. Not many men though, but some young boys and a few young men.'[1] There were in fact 444 men sixteen years and older aboard the ship, but this was less than half the 950 adult women. Twenty-one days later, the *Volendam* arrived in Buenos Aires. It was the first of four large transports that moved a total of 5,616 refugees to South America in 1947 and 1948.[2] Approximately 4,500 of these refugees were Mennonites destined for Paraguay, where land had been purchased specifically for settling the newcomers, and where they would add to an already existing Mennonite population of about 5,000.

This chapter, set in Paraguay, examines the experiences of those Mennonite refugees who migrated to South America. Focusing on the early years of settlement, I describe the conditions under which immigrant families established new homes in the wilderness and the particular problems facing predominantly female communities. Relations with North American workers assisting the settlers as well as earlier Mennonite colonists in Paraguay are central to the discourse surrounding the initial experience of the refugees. The sex imbalance and the dilemmas it engendered were especially obvious in Paraguay, where the newcomers were settled apart from the resident Mennonite population. The harsh realities confronting them caused many immigrants to question and resent the decision to send them to Paraguay, and before long an exodus to Canada began.

The refugee families who immigrated to Paraguay are frequently described in the correspondence, minutes, and published reports of relief workers as *schwache*, or weak, families. Their weakness, or feebleness, was directly attributed to the absence of fathers or adult males. This described weakness was in sharp contrast to the harshness of the environment – sometimes called the 'green hell' – that they would now call home. As women and their families cleared land, built homes, grew food, and attempted to sustain themselves with minimal resources and minimal outside aid, the characterization of frailty was really an abstraction that did not reflect reality. The process of pioneering was for the new immigrants in many ways a continuation of the previous two decades, in which strategies of physical and emotional survival were developed in situations of inescapable hardship. As a result of the past and present demands placed on refugee families, they were in many respects 'stronger' than the average whole family. Yet Mennonite refugees were lacking certain elements that may have been deemed essential to the creation of a strong person or family unit, that is, the father figure as head of the family and the formal structures and practices of institutionalized religion. As a result, families were perceived to be weak at both the physical and spiritual levels. The main agenda of North and South American workers entrusted with supervising the resettlement was thus a combination of material assistance and religious rehabilitation.

The early years of settlement in the Paraguayan wilderness represented, on the one hand, further despair for the refugees, who for the most part had little idea of the hardships that awaited them when they began their transatlantic journey. On the other hand, the relatively isolated setting and bare bones existence in South America afforded a certain freedom from the rigid codes of behaviour that characterized North American Mennonitism in the 1950s. One manifestation of this relative freedom was the formation of common-law marriages between women and men whose first spouses had been left in the Soviet Union. As well, the shared past tragedy and present difficulties created a commonality of experience among the refugees that led to supportive communities and, in one Paraguayan village, a culture of women.

When Mennonite refugees from Europe arrived in South America, there was already a sizeable population of Mennonites in three colonies in Paraguay.[3] The first of these, called Menno Colony, was established in 1928 by several groups of conservative Mennonites emigrating from the Canadian Prairies. These first settlers, descendants of Mennonites who had emigrated from Russia in the 1870s, left Canada due to the pressures of assimilation, manifest most strongly in policies that took away Mennonite autonomy in education. Menno Colony was located in an isolated area known as the Chaco in the western half of Paraguay. The descriptive label 'green hell' came to be applied to the Chaco because of the prevalent 'heat, drought, sandstorms, ants, and grasshoppers' that made early settlement extremely difficult.[4] Fernheim Colony was founded nearby in 1930, and populated by Mennonite refugees who had fled the Soviet Union in the late 1920s hoping to emigrate to North America but directed to South America after the doors to Canada were closed. In 1937, about one-third of Fernheim's population moved to east Paraguay where they founded the colony Friesland. The climate here was more tropical, though the thick jungle-like forest required greater efforts in clearing the land. Despite having already lived in the Chaco for two decades, residents of Menno colony were just beginning to rise above the bare-bones self-sufficiency of early settlement.

The adversity that would plague the postwar refugee immigrants over the next few years in their new home began as soon as the *Volendam* docked in Buenos Aires, Argentina. Two separate groups of about three hundred people each were immediately transferred by riverboat to Paraguay. After revolution broke out in Paraguay, preventing further travel, the remaining refugees were forced to live in a makeshift 'tent city' in Buenos Aires for over three months. In the meantime, as news of the hot, dry climate and agricultural difficulties in the Chaco spread among the newcomers, the decision was made to investigate land prospects in east Paraguay. The result was the purchase, by the Mennonite Central Committee (MCC), of a 25,000-hectare tract of land near the Friesland colony; the new immigrant community was named Volendam after the ship that brought them to South America. In July 1947 the first group of fifty-six immigrants set out to commence the 'gigantic task of carving a home out of the primeval forest.'[5]

The majority of the first refugee transport opted to settle in the new colony of Volendam, but approximately 870 chose to continue, as originally planned, to the Chaco in western Paraguay. Here MCC purchased 74,000 hectares of land to form a new colony called Neuland, located just south of Fernheim. Of the second sailing of 860 refugee immigrants who arrived in South America in February 1948, 803 persons went to Neuland, while the rest went to Volendam. The passengers on the remaining two ships, which arrived in March and October of that year, were distributed more or less evenly between the two colonies.[6]

The two new colonies, although very different environmentally, represented equal, if distinct, challenges and hardships in settlement. In Volendam colony, dense forest had to be cleared with machete, saw, and axe before roads and villages could be laid out. The digging of wells, one or more for each of the twelve villages, was also strenuous; the deep subsoil of heavy red clay or rock had to be penetrated with pick and crowbar and sometimes even hammer and chisel. Each well required an average of ninety days' labour. The bush was so dense that, in some cases, settlers had to crawl on hands and knees from the street path to their building site. To make this endeavour worse, much of the bush was thorn-covered. Trees measuring a full metre in diameter and climbing vines as thick as a human arm had to be cut with a limited number of hand tools. The hardships of pioneering were exacerbated by new and strange dangers in the form of wild antelope and ostriches, rattlesnakes 'noted for their size,' jaguars, and 'vicious zebu bulls.'[7]

In Neuland, the terrain was divided between campo – grassland plain – and bush. Clearing the land was somewhat easier because there were fewer trees, but the wood was so hard that often axes would bounce right off and it became necessary to burn the trees out. The soil was sandy and relatively easy to plough but was not suitable for the kinds of tropical fruits and vegetables that could be grown in Volendam. Beans, cassava, and sweet potatoes were the main crops in the early years. Kaffir, a form of sorghum, was also grown as feed for horses and cattle, to roast for coffee, and, when mixed with white flour, for baking bread. The climate in the Chaco was hot and dry, and the settlers were plagued with all manner of insects and pests.

It was thus into a strange and mostly untouched environment that the refugees, with minimal equipment and provisions, set about creating new homes for themselves. Even with some outside assistance, the task was daunting and dispiriting. One young refugee woman recalled that she and her younger sister broke down and cried when they saw what lay ahead of them in Paraguay: 'We didn't know what we should do. But crying didn't help anything. We had to do what we could do.'[8] MCC worker J.W. Warkentin described the experience of one female-led family – Margareta Enns with two daughters and three sons – pioneering in Volendam colony. The two daughters and the eldest son were part of the first group of fifty-six persons to arrive at the scene of what was to become the colony. Lots were drawn to determine the location of their building site, and then the 'brave trio' set about clearing a spot for their house with a 'few hand tools.' The house itself was constructed from tree trunks as wall supports, bamboo sticks as sheeting laths, and tall grass saturated with mud as shingles for the roof. Margareta and the two smaller boys joined the three others to make mud bricks to complete the walls.

On a return visit to the Enns home four months later, Warkentin was gratified to find that the walls were finished and whitewashed on the inside, and that the family was eating watermelon, beans, and other vegetables from their own garden. He observed that 'the family was very happy and contented.' A neighbouring woman was reported to have said, 'never before have we been as poor as we are now, but we have never been happier.'⁹ To what extent Warkentin was accurately assessing the state of mind of these two women is open to question. His statements may have in part been aimed at defusing the concern, on the part of both immigrants and North American Mennonites, that perhaps MCC had made a big mistake in settling the refugees in Paraguay. In that respect his description was a public relations tactic. On the other hand, the women may have indeed been displaying the kind of happiness that arises from pride in accomplishment. This pride is evident in the photograph of an 'old mother of eighty years' standing beside one of two cookstoves and one baking oven that she constructed entirely on her own out of mud and sod, and about whom it was remarked, 'it must be admitted that she did her work very well.'¹⁰ Another noteworthy photograph depicts two women, wearing dresses, atop a scaffolding surrounding a house under construction. The caption says: 'Their husbands and brothers in Siberia, these women are building their own homes with adobe brick in the Chaco.'¹¹

Relief workers were struck by the daunting obstacles facing female-led families in Paraguay and also by their ability to meet the challenge. In her report on a visit to the new colony of Neuland, MCC worker Ella Berg made several comments about the sex imbalance there. Her assignment was to distribute Christmas bundles prepared by North Americans and to hold children's worship services in certain villages. In all six villages, only once was she hosted in a home where the husband and wife were together – 'a rare thing.' Her first billet was with a widow who had two young children; the furniture in the two-room house (still without proper ceiling and whitewash) consisted of 'a very plain cross-legged table, two stools, a camp cot, and a broken-down carriage.' In one home, the mother of four children had become a semi-invalid after breaking her leg while loading a tree soon after her arrival. In the village of Halbstadt, Berg 'saw again how bravely a mother and two daughters carry on. One of them had charge of the land work and did some top-notch plowing with Fred and Charlie, the oxen.' Berg noted that 'each of the few men in a village is assigned to help several women by giving counsel and assistance in the heavier work.'[12]

Even after the first year or so of constructing basic shelter and planting a few crops for food, household maintenance continued to be intensive and difficult. After visiting the Paraguayan colonies in the early 1950s, American sociologist Winfield Fretz wrote, 'People who have not experienced the life of the Mennonite housewife in Paraguay have little idea of the burdens under which she lives and labors.'[13] Several years later his views had only intensified and he commented that the women looked old at forty years and completely worn out at sixty. Somewhat ahead of his time, Fretz made a public plea for kerosene-burning refrigerators to ease the workload of women in Paraguay. Although he was perhaps erroneously setting up a strictly gendered division of labour that was not as applicable to Neuland and Volendam as it was to the older colonies, Fretz nevertheless questioned whether it was not time to give 'at least one big push to help the women.' After all, 'we have helped the men in the colonies with loans for tractors, land, cattle, seeds, and industrial equipment.'[14]

Some women were able to use their skills in occupations other than subsistence farming. Single women and young widows were drawn into work as office help for relief workers or as cooks and aids in hospitals as these were established. As was common for many immigrant farming families, daughters were sometimes sent to the cities of Asuncion and Filadelfia to work as domestics. With minimal health care at the outset, any woman with nursing or midwifery skills was a significant asset and was stretched to the limit pulling teeth, delivering babies, and tending injuries. At the beginning, one nurse served the entire colony of Volendam. 'She was brave, she did everything,' recalled one Volendam resident.[15]

One immigrant nurse recalled that there were 'all kinds of sicknesses' among the refugees; another colonist agreed that 'health was bad.'[16] Among the postwar immigrants from Europe were many individuals who would not have passed the stringent medical screening for Canadian immigration, but who were able to emigrate to Paraguay, where regulations were less strict. As a result, many refugees were 'blind, lame, crippled physically and mentally sick.'[17] A Volendam nurse recalled a widow with three children who had 'especially bad arthritis' and who, after all the running as a refugee, could hardly walk anymore. With little flesh left on her bones, the tropical climate of Paraguay was 'poison' to her and others like her.[18] Given the 'war-weakened' state of the immigrants, as well as the 'unaccustomed climate,' one MCC worker expressed surprise that no serious epidemic had occurred.[19] Importing physicians for temporary service as well as building hospitals and training nurses was a priority in the new colonies.

Many families received small and larger amounts of money from relatives in Canada and also from Mennonite women's organizations and churches in North America; however, this kind of direct financial assistance did not begin immediately. For the first months up to several years, refugees in the initial stages of settlement received material assistance from the Mennonite Central Committee and the older Mennonite colonists in Paraguay. At the outset, residents from the Menno, Fernheim, and Friesland colonies provided accommodation for the 'weaker' families for several months while land was cleared and houses built. Fernheim reportedly carried out its part by maintaining five hundred persons free of charge for three months.[20] Construction units were formed in Fernheim, with every six farmers responsible for erecting a house for 'the poor women [who] were justly concerned who would help them build their houses.'[21] Vernon Neuschwander reported that in Neuland forty-one houses for widows were thus built 'in record time' by Fernheim colonists.[22] As well, Fernheim colonists lent each family a tame cow for five years and a pair of tame oxen for each complete farm; each family also received six chickens and thirty kilograms of peanuts for seed. Kitchenwares and a variety of farm implements were also lent to the new settlers.[23]

The encounter between new immigrants and older colonists represented a mixture of both positive and negative relations. On the one hand, there was a common language, ancestry, and religious culture between newcomers and residents in the Fernheim and Menno colonies. The connections with Fernheim were especially close given that residents had fled the Soviet Union as refugees only two decades earlier. Fernheimer Peter P. Klassen writes in his history of Mennonites in Paraguay: 'Particularly between Fernheimers and the new immigrants there was so much common ground and family relationships that initially it was decided that Fernheim would simply enlarge newly laid out villages in the south.'[24] Immigrants from Fernheim could share the new-comers' feelings of displacement, given that they too had fled the Soviet Union in a crisis and been accepted into Paraguay as refugees.

On the other hand, a common history and similar culture did not pre-vent the development of tensions. Sociologist Raymond Breton has observed that migration can cause a clash of cultures not only between the host society and a newly arrived ethnic entity, but also within ethnic communities that have been separated by different times of migration.[25] While an outright 'clash' may be too strong a characterization of the relationship between the two groups, it was clear that diverging experi-ence had wrought some distance. At a meeting of new immigrants in June 1948 it was expressed that a common colony between Neuland and Fernheim would probably not happen, 'since Fernheim had made no effort to work cooperatively.'[26] After the initial assistance with clearing land and building houses, it seems that Fernheim was reluctant to inte-grate the newcomers into pre-existing colony life. The two colonies were a good day's drive apart, so that once the immigrants were established in their newly built houses, there was minimal contact. One immigrant suggested that after delivering Neuland settlers to their new colony, the attitude of Fernheimers was basically one of 'hands off.'[27] In at least one case, an immigrant woman with her child and brother-in-law were to return to east Paraguay because the Fernheim household where they were being accommodated wanted them removed as soon as possible. Although it isn't explicitly stated, it could be that sexual relations had developed between the woman and man, given the comment 'How much further is this issue regulated?' that accompanied the expression of concern over the case.[28] Diverging lifestyle practices and morality may have strained the relationship to the greatest extent, as will be seen.

Between Menno colonists and the immigrants there was even greater distance, both physical and cultural. Menno colony was established by emigrants from Canada who were several generations removed from their Russian heritage. Not only had they come from different Russian Mennonite settlements, Menno residents, who were descendants of fam-ilies that arrived in Canada in the 1870s, had not experienced the tumul-tuous events that shaped the lives of Fernheimers or the immigrants. At the outset, it seemed that substantial persuasion was required before the older colonists were ready to offer their wholehearted assistance. 'Numerous discussions' occurred with Menno colony residents; and although they at first 'never gave a negative answer neither did they come to any definite arrangements or agreement' when encouraged to help the immigrants with clearing land, digging wells, and building houses.[29] Part of the hesitancy was likely due to the fact that the earlier settlers were barely getting on their own feet after several decades of pioneering in the wilderness, and there was also some resentment that they had done so without the same kinds of material assistance that the postwar refugees were receiving.

The Mennonite Central Committee, with administrative offices in the United States, was a key provider of material support for the refugee immigrants. It was initially expected that settlers in Volendam would be self-supporting after 1 December 1948, less than two years after their arrival. MCC worker J.W. Warkentin reported in August of that year that the plan was to keep the immigrants on full maintenance until 1 October, to gradually reduce their allowance in the following six months, and to discontinue it entirely by 31 March 1949. Fernheim resident Jakob Isaak made a public plea that support for Volendam settlers be extended at least until after the harvest of 1949, stating: 'Keep in mind the women and mothers who must feed as well as train their children without a husband and father ... If, in addition to the hard labor, these poor souls must bear the worry of what they shall eat or wherewithal they shall clothe themselves in the immediate future, the burden will be unduly heavy.'[30] Full maintenance was the equivalent, in U.S. dollars, of twenty cents per person per day in both Volendam and Neuland.[31] MCC also supplied a minimal number of household and farm implements and some basic garden tools.

The financial support received from MCC was not without its return obligations. Although Mennonites in Canada had contributed a substantial amount to fund the transport of the refugees, thousands more would be spent in the settlement process itself. Already in the summer of 1947, MCC expressed the wish that the first arrivals would soon be able to repay their transportation debt in order to fund further shiploads.[32] Thus, not only was material support of relatively short duration, but immigrants were expected to repay a portion of the maintenance provided in the early years. This incensed one Canadian minister, who questioned how MCC could spend money on the Paraguayan immigrants 'In the Name of Christ' – MCC's motto – and then record it all as debt, expecting repayment from impoverished individuals.[33]

As accounts of the hardships faced by South American immigrants reached Canada, financial and material aid began to flow south from churches and relatives. In 1950, refugee youth in Leamington, Ontario, presented a play entitled 'The Thorny Crown of a Mother' at the local Mennonite church, after which an offering was taken for Paraguayan immigrants.[34] The need of the widows in Paraguay aroused sympathies especially among Mennonite women in Canada, and thus a network of women helping women was created. For instance, the first project of the Alberta Women's Missions Conference was to assist widows in the village of Einlage, Paraguay, with $835, an undertaking that required 'ingenuity' on the part of Albertan Mrs H.L. Sawatzky, who needed to establish 'favourable rapport' with the local bank before the money could be sent.[35] The budgets of Canadian Mennonite churches and their women's organizations frequently included ongoing donations for widows in Paraguay during these years. That such need was occasionally quite acute is suggested by the fact that churches in Canada sometimes received specific support requests for individual women. In what was obviously not an isolated incident, in 1954 Sargent Avenue Mennonite Church in Winnipeg received an urgent request for sixty dollars for a certain Mrs Wiebe in Paraguay. The church council decided to send her only ten dollars, stating that it was impossible for the church to keep up with such requests.[36]

Settlers in Neuland and Volendam recall with gratitude the donations, both large and small, received from relatives and also total strangers in North America. A Volendam resident said that the occasional ten dollars sent by a relative in Saskatchewan allowed her family to hire Paraguayan labour to assist with tree cutting. Later, they received regular gifts from a Mennonite family in Ohio, linked with them at random by MCC.[37] Jealousies were triggered, however, when some families began receiving money from relatives in Canada, and differences in income started to show up in the kinds of houses people built and the furnishings they acquired.[38]

Despite the jealousies, financial support from individuals in North America may well have been more welcome than aid from MCC and settled colonists, partly because it was removed from the kind of paternalism that may have made local aid more awkward to receive. For instance, as in some parts of Canadian Mennonite communities, in Paraguay there was a financial institution called the *Waisenamt* (orphan's office) that managed the estates of widows and orphans. Under this system of estate devolution, which had its origins in nineteenth-century Russia, two or three 'goodmen' were appointed to oversee a widow's property. In Neuland and Volendam, each woman who was head of a family had to name a goodman, whose duty it was to help and look after her. The assistance received in clearing land, building a house, and planting crops was undoubtedly welcome, yet, to the extent that such aid was accompanied by managerial control over a widow's affairs, her own capacity for decision making on behalf of her family was undermined. That women were not entirely pleased with this intrusion in their lives is reflected in a saying attributed to widows in Paraguay: 'One bad husband is better than two goodmen.'[39]

There is also evidence that North American financial gifts prompted similar intervention by male leaders within a colony. In Volendam, a *Hilfskomitee* (relief committee) was organized to distribute gifts arriving direct from a *Hilfskomitee* in western Canada. The committee consisted of nine men – four ministers, four church deacons, and the *Oberschulz* (colony administrator) – and allocated funds according to a list of the needy submitted by a deacon from each village. Winfield Fretz, the American sociologist studying the Mennonite colonies, applauded this system for 'insuring some element of equality in the distribution of gifts.'[40] This may have been true, but it also reinforced the discretionary power that was carried by male leaders within village and colony.

The establishment of villages resulted in one of the most fascinating aspects of the Paraguayan refugee experience, namely the creation of a village of women. For the most part, villages were organized according to the wishes of the refugees themselves, frequently following patterns from their former homes in Russia. In some cases, relief workers intervened to ensure that 'strong' individuals – namely men – were well distributed among the 'weak' families. Following the arrival of the second Volendam transport in October 1948, there was concern in MCC circles over the 'pettiness' of a group of eight strong men who resisted efforts to separate them, thereby rendering one village very weak by their absence.[41] That some men may have been reluctant to settle near widows and their families is corroborated by the experience of one Volendam family. This widow with four children under the age of twelve was upset to learn that her male neighbour was annoyed because she was located next to him. His greatest concern was that she would not keep up with him in clearing the surrounding forest, thus inviting in wild animals.[42] The extra responsibilities placed on the limited number of men was undoubtedly another deterrent to being a lone man among widows.

The village of Friedensheim in the colony Neuland was more commonly called the *Frauendorf* (women's village) because, in its earliest form, all of the 147 adult inhabitants were women. The eldest male at the outset was a thirteen-year old boy. The women of Friedensheim had come together as a group while fleeing the Soviet Union. Initially, earlier colonists and MCC workers reportedly 'balked' at the idea of a village of women, saying, 'you can't do that, you won't survive.' The women countered with the question, 'Weren't we told that we were free to group ourselves into villages as we pleased?' When asked how they would manage such heavy tasks as cutting trees, digging wells, and building houses, the women responded that they would help each other.[43]

In helping each other undertake the hard tasks of settlement, a community of women was created, joined by common experience and common suffering. A village of women without men was also, to a certain extent, free from the suspicions, sexual tension, and traditional patterns of authority that exerted themselves in villages with even a limited number of adult men. It is possible that mutual support and undertaking the difficult tasks in a cooperative manner came more easily in the *Frauendorf*, where all the households were woman-headed, than in other villages. Joan Chandler suggests that lone women are often compelled to become self-sufficient rather than seek help for certain tasks from other people's husbands, since women without husbands 'are viewed with reserve, if not suspicion, or are targeted by men with sexual ambitions.'[44] In a context where there were no men to 'borrow,' women in the *Frauendorf* were more free than in other villages to assist one another, where the problems associated with husband-borrowing may have led to greater self-sufficiency on the part of female-headed households.

Beyond the physical labour that was shared in the *Frauendorf*, women supported one another emotionally and psychologically in a way that may not have been possible had some of them lived with husbands. Peter Dyck, an MCC worker who helped facilitate the migration to Paraguay, recalled meeting a woman who had lived in the *Frauendorf* and who later immigrated to Winnipeg. His remarks on her personal prosperity and the flourishing church life of which she was a part in Canada were met with the following response:

She talked about how they used to sit in the Frauendorf after a hard day's work, outside their mudhouses, all the women in a circle around a smoky fire to keep away the mosquitos [sic]. Somebody would have a guitar and they'd sing. They would sing and share, they would cry but they would also laugh a lot. They were all the same. Nobody was rich, nobody had advantages over the other, they were all going through the same experiences, everyday the struggles of pioneering would knit them closer together, and they would all be waiting for news from their missing husbands. These experiences welded them together, they understood each other.[45]

The woman went on to describe to Dyck the loneliness she felt in Canada, having lost this community of women. For her, the informal spirituality that was nurtured by singing by the fire, the shared pride of accomplishment in building mudhouses for themselves and their children, and the removal of status barriers based either on material goods or the presence of a husband, all filled a void that a more prosperous and stable environment could not.

Despite declarations of independence on the part of the residents of the *Frauendorf*, there were ongoing concerns on the part of MCC for the development of the village. In September 1948, C.A. DeFehr, a prominent Canadian Mennonite businessman who spent several years assisting the refugee settlement, wrote to a Mennonite leader in Brazil, thanking him for a substantial donation that would be distributed among the most needy women. In the same letter, he noted that the village of Friedensheim, where forty women without men had settled, had recently celebrated the opening of its school. DeFehr said that missions donations were most welcome in the village to assist with clearing the land – a task especially difficult for women – digging wells, and building the school.[46] Echoing this perspective, MCC worker Vernon Neuschwander wrote in November 1948 that the 'plowing is not going too good with the widows.'[47]

To what extent the problems experienced by the widows in Friedensheim were unique is difficult to ascertain, given that the same attention is not focused on some of the villages with more men. It is evident, however, that MCC workers were quite unprepared to deal with the tremendous needs in this village and in others where 'man'-power was limited. Although much was expected of the Fernheim colonists in terms of assistance to the newcomers, it was noted that 'every one wants to do his own plowing at home first.'[48]

Beyond assisting the new immigrants economically, North American Mennonite organizations saw as their mandate the 'religious rehabilitation' of the refugees, who had been without formal religious institutions for almost two decades. Although the material needs of the refugees were the most immediate, relief and church workers shared the sentiment that 'the ravages of war and nomadic refugee life has [sic] left its scar on the spirits of many of the immigrants.'[49] North American workers marvelled at the 'simple way' in which some immigrants expressed their faith but also lamented over those who 'believe in nothing, and have fallen into low moral practices.'[50]

Given the various degrees and manifestations of perceived religious disintegration among the refugees, the restoration of religious beliefs and structures was considered a priority. This rehabilitation operated at a number of levels. First of all, it meant dealing with questions of life-style that were understood as problems of morality. For Mennonite denominations, it also meant opportunities to plant churches and save souls. In the case of two of these denominations – the General Conference Mennonites (GC) and the Mennonite Brethren (MB) – the campaign to win members in the new immigrant colonies resulted in a certain amount of 'competition and strife.'[51] The battle for Mennonite souls had already made itself felt in Europe but was intensified after the refugees migrated. In 1950 an observer of church life in Paraguay noted that due to 'influences from North American individuals ... tensions [between GCs and MBs] are developing at certain points.'[52] A resident of Volendam reflected that the denominational walls imposed on the immigrants by Canadian ministers 'really hurt.'[53] One specific manifestation of this tension lay in the area of marriage. Even though marriage between individuals from different conferences had been unproblematic among postwar refugees, the Mennonite Brethren in North America prohibited such marriages unless the General Conference half of the couple were willing to be rebaptized in a manner acceptable to the MBs. An important difference between the two groups was the Mennonite Brethren insistence on baptism by full bodily immersion in water, as a more definitive symbol of spiritual rebirth, in contrast to the General Conference practice of sprinkling or pouring water on a baptismal candidate's head. Gradually, the taboo on 'mixed marriages,' as they were called, exerted itself in Paraguay as local ministers complied with North American pressures in order to maintain 'good relations' with their benefactors. In one case, 'considerable ill feeling' arose when a young woman was forbidden to pray in public and to take communion within her own church because she had a boyfriend from the other conference.[54] Undoubtedly, the differences seemed petty and the interconference hostility mean-spirited to refugees who were trying to make sense of their huge losses and were asking larger questions about the presence of God, or lack thereof, in their lives.

For many of the refugees, the establishment of formal church life, whether GC or MB, was not necessarily the first priority. Most refugees had established an informal religion based on private ritual, one that had sustained their spiritual needs over the past two decades. With the building of churches, the appointment of ministers, and the reinstitution of such formal rituals as baptism, religion took on the forms and norms of North American and other Paraguayan Mennonite churches. Given the sex imbalance among the refugees, this process of formalization, which also followed the prevailing male-ordered hierarchy, made for some incongruous results and accentuated the absence of men. For instance, the General Conference Mennonite Church in Volendam in 1952 had 147 members: 42 men and 105 women.[55] At the time, a common practice in Mennonite churches in Paraguay, and some in Canada, was that women and children sat on one side of the church and men on the other. Thus churches in the new colonies were visually unbalanced because the left side – where the women and children sat – was always full, while the right side had only a few men and older boys.[56] As had been the case during the German occupation of Ukraine and in the refugee camps of Germany, members of church choirs and their directors were mainly women. At the outset, when there were insufficient male ministers to service all the immigrant settlements, women continued in their practice of undertaking worship services on their own. In one instance, this caused some consternation for Ella Berg, an MCC relief worker from North America, accustomed to male leadership in this realm. While distributing Christmas bundles in Neuland colony, she was surprised and reluctant when she was asked to lead worship services in one village. 'At Saturday night prayer meeting and Sunday morning service, I was asked to take charge. At first I protested, but they assured me they were mostly among themselves (women) and someone had to do it.'[57] In this case, female spiritual leadership was unproblematic for female refugees, but presented a challenge to the North American woman who was used to the conventions of male authority in religious matters.

   Aside from creating systems to perform baptisms, build churches, and institute formal religious practice, rehabilitation turned to issues of morality. Part of the concern for the morality of the new immigrants lay in minor aspects of external conduct and deportment. The fashion of immigrant women was one of these. Although the refugees were welcomed by and received material assistance from the earlier settlers, different historic paths had created significant gaps in the experience and outlook of the first pioneers and the newcomers. As would happen to a degree in Canada as well, the refugees were viewed as worldly, particularly by the conservative Menno colonists. In one instance, a delegation of men from the Menno colony complained to C.A. DeFehr about the short dresses and cut and curled hair of the refugee women. DeFehr pointed out that the women had not chosen or made the clothes that they wore; rather, they had received them in refugee camps and quite simply owned nothing else. The men apparently replied that if that was the case, perhaps their criticism should be redirected at the North American women who gave the dresses for relief in the first place. Seemingly, this was a 'woman's' problem. As for the 'kinky' hair, DeFehr offered that women in refugee camps curled their hair 'to pass the time,' but fortunately, 'here in Paraguay they will be so busy they won't have time to curl it again.'[58] The practice of styling their hair was not just a means for refugee women to alleviate the boredom; many had cut their hair to reduce the problem of lice but also in order to look less German in countries where that might be a hindrance.[59]

If fashions did not vex relief workers as they did the residents of the older colonies, other issues were more problematic. There was little screening of the first group of immigrants to South America aboard the *Volendam*, beyond establishing that they were Mennonite. But because of problems that emerged with this first group, MCC in Europe henceforth subjected potential Paraguayan settlers to a process of moral screening. Points to be considered in determining the eligibility of a refugee included the problem of mixed marriages, that is, where a Mennonite married a non-Mennonite; evidence of Nazi or Communist ideological sympathies; attitudes that were 'anti-Church, anti-Bible and anti-Mennonite'; and moral problems such as common-law relationships and illegitimacy.[60] In the case of Mennonite women who had married non-Mennonite men and had subsequently left the Mennonite Church, and where both she and her husband were living, they were considered ineligible for emigration. But if the husband was missing, and the woman desirous of returning to the Mennonite fold, it was deemed 'probable' that she would be eligible. One might conclude from these stipulations that the process indirectly encouraged the emigration of women without husbands. Rather than promote the inclusion of able-bodied adult men as prospective settlers, the screening process, in its goal of maintaining a purely Mennonite migrant group, actually may have reinforced the sex imbalance among the new settlers.

The most problematic issue was the existence of common-law marriages among the refugees. These relationships, gently termed 'companionate marriages' by the head of MCC in the United States, William

Snyder, caused ongoing headaches for relief workers and denominational leaders and ministers in both Europe and South America.[61] Perhaps unintentionally, Snyder was offering the perfect definition for those relationships that developed between men and women who had lost their first spouse through death or disappearance but who had no confirmation of death. Such relationships grew out of the need for companionship, physical intimacy, material practicality, and greater economic security. A typical beginning of the companionate marriage was one in which 'William' helped 'Helen,' who was struggling to get the centre beam of her house in place, and she in turn replaced some missing buttons on his shirt; he might help her break in the wild ox and she would return the favour with some freshly baked zwieback; soon William and Helen were sitting on each other's porches and before long they were sharing a house.[62]

Most of the literature that discusses the postwar colonies treats the existence of companionate marriages in Paraguay only obliquely. In their 1991 personal account, Peter Dyck and Elfrieda Dyck deal with the issue in a more direct and honest way. They describe the experiences of a young woman named Elizabeth whose husband had been arrested by the Soviet secret police eight months after their marriage and who immigrated to Paraguay with a seven-year-old son. In a conversation years later she had told the Dycks that the Chaco was the 'green hell' in a double sense for widowed refugees. What she meant was that the women had to cope not only with the harsh natural environment, but also with their own natures as women. She went on to point out that church ministers, stuck in 'their traditional thinking about morality,' assumed that common-law marriages were based primarily on sex, when in fact Elizabeth argued that loneliness and economic necessity were more fundamental reasons for men and women to join households.[63]

In describing as 'traditional' the morality of the ministers, Elizabeth was indirectly referring to the situational morality that of necessity was adopted by many refugees under wartime conditions. In oral interviews with immigrants to Paraguay, the existence of companionate marriage is freely acknowledged as an almost logical outcome of the circumstances. As one woman reflected, 'now it is very hard for us to understand. But during the war so many things happened that otherwise never would.'[64] She clearly acknowledged the creation of a situational morality that was at odds with the normative standards of the Mennonite Church, in which sexual relations outside of marriage were considered sinful and thus were prohibited. Companionate marriages grew out of emotional and material needs that were unfamiliar to Mennonites who did not share the experiences of the refugees.

A refugee who had been a young man growing up in the Neuland colony also acknowledged that 'retroactively, it's natural that [common-law relationships] would have developed.' He recalled one serious incident early in the life of the colony when an immigrant minister who had lost his wife began to spend a great deal of time at the home of a widow and her family, initially to obtain various household services such as cooking, sewing, and laundry from her. Seemingly, the relationship progressed further, and because of his status, the man was 'kicked out of the church pretty fast' and returned to Germany. The woman, who did not know the fate of her own husband, had to publicly apologize in church.[65] In the young man's memory, this incident was a deterrent to much more 'hanky-panky' in the colony, yet sources indicate that the problem did not go away as a result.

That companionate marriage was a reality, but nevertheless a problem to be dealt with, was keenly felt by religious workers and other Mennonites in Paraguay. Even though couples who had entered into common-law marriages prior to emigration apparently made and signed pledges to cease such relationships, this did not solve the problem, according to an MCC worker.[66] One Fernheim resident, reporting to the Mennonite World Conference at Akron, Pennsylvania, in 1948, described the desire for a 'helpmeet' on the part of widows and widowers as 'one of the most embarrassing and difficult problems to the new settlement in Paraguay.'[67] In the minutes of a South American Mennonite ministers' conference held in July 1949, it was noted that the question was already 'acute' when the first refugees arrived from the east.[68]

At this particular conference, convened in Fernheim, Paraguay, and attended by ministers from all the Mennonite colonies as well as some from North America, it was felt that decisive action must be taken since no satisfactory solution to this 'disastrous' problem had been found, despite positions taken by North American conferences (see chapter 6) and despite being dealt with at a previous conference in Friesland. That the problem was becoming worse had been presented in 'shattering' ways by ministers from Volendam and Neuland, who urgently requested that the assembled group reach a decision on the matter. Sixteen persons from Paraguay, Uruguay, Brazil, and North America were appointed to draft a recommendation that was unanimously accepted.[69] The essence of their ruling allowed for remarriage if a spouse had not been heard from for seven years. If a spouse was known to be living in the Soviet Union or Europe but had married again, then remarriage was also permitted. But if a spouse was known to be alive and unmarried, then any relationship begun by the Paraguayan resident had to be terminated.

The outcome of this decision was mixed. The ruling seemed to cover all situations in which one-half of the couple had been missing prior to 1942, which would have represented the majority. In cases where a couple was separated within the seven-year period or where a husband/wife was found to be living unmarried in the Soviet Union, then existing common-law relationships would have been subject to discipline. For some couples it meant terminating a relationship in order to maintain their standing in the church. Others chose excommunication from the church rather than endure yet another separation from a loved one. That there were a sufficient number of cases not clearly covered by the guidelines to cause extensive heartbreak is suggested by some memory sources.[70]

The formal resolutions taken against common-law marriages and regarding remarriage caused a degree of discomfort not only for those subject to such rules but also for those in the position of enforcing them. The chairperson of the Mennonite Central Committee in the United States wrote to one of his colleagues in Paraguay, saying that he 'trembled when the conference acted and decided on the basis of theory, without a grasp of what the situation really is.' He suggested that the rules be interpreted and applied in a practical way and that, 'rather than hold an absolute standard which cannot be inforced [sic], it might be better that each case should be decided on its own merits.'[71]

The adult women and men among the new colonists were not the only ones subject to moral scrutiny. The behaviour of young people and children was occasionally called into question and their misbehaviour attributed to the lack of discipline that resulted from a father's absence as well as a lack of proper religious instruction. Sometimes the questionable behaviour was sexual in nature. This is suggested by one MCC worker who warned of three young people 'it would be wise to have examined for V.D.' on arrival in Paraguay. Although nothing further is said about the two boys, about the girl it was said, 'Anita F. caused us considerable trouble during the voyage because of her friendships with crew and officers.'[72] About the same transport – the *Charleton Monarch* – C.A. DeFehr wrote that in this particular group there were quite a few depraved girls and also women who made themselves conspicuous already at the port in Casado, Paraguay. He further said that 'the brethren' (presumably he is referring to the male leadership) from Fernheim colony were very anxious and indignant, fearing that their own youth would be led astray by the newcomers, an outcome that had already occurred in one case.[73]

Anxiety also existed over the lack of school and religious training that the children of the immigrants were receiving. Although instruction of any kind was a relatively low priority for all families struggling to establish themselves at a subsistence level, it seemed there was concern particularly for villages where there were fewer men. In June 1948, C.A. DeFehr wrote to an MCC colleague about the village of Friedensheim (the *Frauendorf*), which at its inception had no adult men; after almost a year, only five of forty-five families had a man. He was concerned particularly by the fact that the village had neither a schoolteacher nor a minister. DeFehr was trying to find a solution that would address the problem of fifty-two school-aged children who were 'to this day still running around' without any instruction.[74] Several months later he used Friedensheim as an example of how loose the young people could become if they were not given religious instruction. He was gratified that after the arrival of a teacher/preacher, all the youth in the village were participating in a choir.[75]

The gender role disruption that occurred within female-headed refugee families did not relate only to the assumption, by the widowed mother, of roles hitherto held by the father/husband. In many families that were without a father, the eldest son would frequently take on leadership roles, often well beyond his actual years. In one family the eldest son at 13 1/2 years became the 'symbolic head.'[76] This meant attending town meetings and voting on behalf of his family. In a semi-fictional account of a widowed family settling in Neuland in 1947, the author makes a similar observation: 'boys not yet twelve stepped into the places left empty by their fallen or exiled or executed fathers, and took the burdens of sustenance upon their young, suntanned shoulders, smiled with slow confidence, and did what had to be done.'[77] As boys grew older and some men were released from European prisoner-of-war camps in the early 1950s, the number of able-bodied men in the colonies increased, but competition for the scarce resource of male labour likewise increased. Widows happily saw their daughters get married because 'when you have a man in the family it was so much easier.'[78]

The need for male leadership, even if only symbolic, may have been more acute for refugees in South America than for those who went to Canada. This greater need would relate to the highly patriarchal nature of family life among Paraguayan Mennonites, in which, according to sociologist Fretz, 'The father is the unquestioned head of the family, and in case of death is normally succeeded by the oldest son.' Fretz further noted how women in Paraguay deferred to their husbands and played 'the role of servant.'[79] The sociologist was likely taking his cues for analysis from the more conservative gender roles within Menno colony families. Yet as the most established of the Paraguayan colonies, Menno may well have been the model for success promoted among the newcomers. An immigrant woman who settled in Volendam with her widowed mother and three siblings recalled that, 'it was a man's world, still is, but at that time it was much more.'[80]

Placed into a setting where patriarchal family values were prominent, the fatherless nature of many refugee families was that much more pronounced. In this context, strength became synonymous not only with physical ability, but with the presence of a male head. The identification of those that were dead or exiled in the Soviet Union as 'the strong and able-bodied and those possessing qualities of leadership' set up a sharp contrast with the refugees, frequently characterized in general terms as 'the old, the weak, the crippled, some women and children.'[81] The dichotomy between male/strength and female/weakness was especially pronounced in Paraguay, where there were more physically weak refugees than had emigrated to Canada. In observing that the 'manhood' of the Mennonite fellowship had been severely weakened, one MCC overseer was speaking not only of numbers of men, but of qualities of maleness that included strength, virility, and dominance. The family itself was also emasculated. This was evident in the comment of one MCC worker who described a village in which only three of forty-two families had a father: 'Because of this unfortunate circumstance, it will take a number of years before the group will grow strong again through the children who will eventually fill the present gaps.'[82]

Despite the efforts of MCC to gain assurances from refugees that Paraguay would be their permanent home, for numerous families South America was not the end of their travels. Some backtracked to Germany, perhaps in hope of family reunification but also to return to the familiarity and civility of German culture. By September 1962, a total of 583 Mennonites had returned to Germany from South America, the vast majority from Paraguay.[83] The main migration that the MCC workers were attempting to forestall, however, was what would become an ongoing wave from Paraguay to Canada, beginning shortly after the new colonies were established. Already in January 1948 MCC was concerned that some immigrants were leaving Paraguay before their debts were paid, prompting the committee to 'officially discourage emigration from Paraguay, particularly while the immigrants are indebted.'[84] In 1949, Cornelius Dyck remarked on the growing problem of 'Canadian fever' among Neuland colonists.[85] One immigrant said that, aside from the immediate hardships, the new settlers were justifiably frustrated by the limited futures that Paraguay offered to their children, and that this caused 'a fair amount of discontent.' He interpreted the attitude on the part of MCC toward this frustration as, 'We shipped you there, we bought the land and so forth and now you're abandoning us.'[86]

In an effort to improve the quality of life in Paraguay and thereby deter further emigration out of the country, MCC officials also bent their own screening policy with gender in mind. In the case of about six young men in Germany who candidly admitted that they wanted to emigrate to Paraguay only as a stepping stone to Canada, one MCC worker suggested that an exception be made to their policy of disallowing anyone who was not prepared to settle permanently in South America. The worker felt that, until they were able to go to Canada, the men would be an asset to the new colonies and could be assigned to work such as 'building homes for women who have lost their husbands.' But because they were not eligible for assistance from the International Refugee Organization, the men would be indebted to MCC for their transatlantic travel costs as well as the trip from Paraguay to Canada.[87]

Despite the efforts of MCC to curb the spread of 'Canadian fever,' according to one source more than 60 per cent of the refugees that went to Paraguay after the war eventually immigrated to Canada, mainly during the years 1955 to 1960.[88] The high point of outmigration from Neuland occurred in 1957, when 283 persons left the colony.[89] Motives for leaving South America were varied, but economic opportunity and family reunification were predominant among the reasons for emigration. Katie stated that she and her family moved to Canada in 1957, motivated primarily by a desire to keep together a family that was already cut in half. Her two older brothers and father had been left behind in the Soviet Union. She had one sister who had already moved to Canada, so in order to keep the remaining family members together, Katie with her mother, husband, and their three young children, decided to follow.[90]

With most migrants settling in such cities as Winnipeg and Vancouver, one observer concluded that 'the fast rhythm of city life was more satisfying than the silence of the Paraguayan jungle.'[91] A more likely attraction than the fast rhythm was the employment and educational opportunity that the city offered. Unlike the earlier colonists in Paraguay, a large proportion of the postwar refugees were not agriculturalists, and this fact contributed to the difficulty that many had with the subsistence farming they were expected to undertake. As one immigrant, who was a teenager at the time, reflected: 'To my mom and her generation who had grown up to some extent in Europe and also in Germany and knew what modern activities and modern appliances and modern support was like ... Going back to plough with oxen, using an axe to clear the land, this was unbelievable!'[92] The mayor of Neuland colony further attributed departures to the fact that the many single women with children were hardly in a position to run a farm and so sought an easier lifestyle elsewere.[93]

For many immigrants, the disbelief over the living conditions that met them translated into resentment, especially toward the Mennonite Central Committee for sending them to Paraguay. There was disapproval, particularly in retrospect, that MCC had sent so many widows with young children to South America.[94] Given the striking demographic imbalance in this migrant group, a few individuals were left with the impression that MCC deliberately sent more widows to Paraguay than to Canada because the former was viewed as the preferred destination for the weak, unfit, and crippled. One young unmarried woman who had lost her entire family in the war felt she had to go to Paraguay because her overwhelming sadness seemed to preclude emigration to Canada: 'Only glad people go to Canada,' she said. Even though she had relatives in Canada, she felt that MCC encouraged her to go to Paraguay because she was trained as a nurse and her skills would be in much demand given 'all the sick people' who were going to South America.[95] It is not surprising, given that many refugees believed themselves to have little choice in deciding where to emigrate, that so many were quick to opt for Canada when that became an option. One man recalled that on arrival in Paraguay, news came that the doors to Canada were now open, and 'how the women cried.'[96] Although the actions of MCC seem short-sighted and somewhat ill-advised in retrospect, in the immediate postwar environment the intense pressure from a number of sides to move the Mennonite refugees out of Europe prompted MCC to take quick action in the context of limited options. However, the attention given to overcoming the hurdles of global policies toward the emigration of refugees and displaced persons meant that little thought was given to exactly how these predominantly female pioneers would manage in the green hell of Paraguay.

The perception that female-headed refugee families were weak was not entirely inaccurate. With more than a decade of loss, starvation, violence, and displacement behind them, many widows and their families undoubtedly felt an overwhelming sense of defeat at seeing their new home in the Paraguayan wilderness. Although they had left the instability of war-torn Europe behind them, the prospect of starting from scratch had the effect of weakening both body and spirit for many new immigrants, women and men alike. However, the weakness ascribed to them meant more than just the physical and emotional realities of their immediate lives. The discourse surrounding the reception and settlement of the postwar refugees suggests that they were viewed as weak, first of all, because many families lacked that which made for 'strong' families, namely a husband/father. The language of rehabilitation further suggests that the refugees were considered to be weak at the moral and spiritual level as well. The combined factors of the absence of formal religious structures and the creation of a wartime morality that was at odds with the norms of Mennonite tradition all created an immense gap in experience between the new colonists and the other Mennonites.

5

Becoming Settled in Canada

In the early summer of 1949, Katie Wiebe, with her mother and sister, stepped off the transatlantic steamship *Samaria* and onto Canadian soil at Halifax. Although they still had a week-long train trip to their final destination in southern Alberta, they had, for all intents and purposes, arrived. For Katie, the ocean voyage had been an indication of better times to come, despite the fact that wartime losses and suffering were always present in obvious, visual ways, most particularly in the numerous missing family members. The food on board the ship was more ample than anything Katie had experienced; she tasted oranges for the first time. The many children and young adults on the ship meant a level of gaiety that included dancing, singing, and games to pass the hours. Katie expected her new home in Canada to fit the 'imaginary fairyland' she had constructed in her mind.

For Katie, as for many other refugee immigrants, the fairyland 'soon turned out to be a reality.' The land was full of opportunities but they were realized only through hard work. In the case of the Wiebe family, that meant work as farm help for their relatives in Alberta – in particular, Katie recalled with distaste, 'thinning beets, bean hoeing and picking, corn picking and the hardest of all, beet topping by hand in the fall.'[1] While all the immigrants anticipated hard work to pay their travel debts and to begin to make a living, first impressions of Canada were often disappointing as expectations of wealth and progress were unmet. The Isaak family, among the first Mennonite refugees to arrive in July 1947, were dismayed to encounter 'large unpopulated areas of tree and prairie' and a country that was 'less civilized' than the richness they had been expecting. Furthermore, their relatives' home was smaller than the Isaak's home in Russia and did not even have running water.[2] One sixteen-year-old newcomer, enthralled with the plentiful food available during the train trip from Halifax to Alberta – 'we had never tasted such white soft bread or drank such cold rich milk before' – also found her enthusiasm dampened when they reached the prairies, which reminded her of the Siberian steppes. 'At this point we were ready to go back to Germany,' she said.[3]

The disappointment over the Canadian terrain and climate, the hard work, and other difficulties in adapting to Canadian society did prompt some immigrants to return to Germany, although not in the same numbers as occurred from South America. Yet not all immigrants had negative first impressions. Particularly for those who were met and hosted by immediate family members in Canada, the reunions were profoundly joyful. Maria Reimer, destined for Waterloo, Ontario, had an unexpected surprise when she was met at the Toronto train station by her sister and brother-in-law, whom she immediately embraced after a twenty-four-year separation. The couple had migrated to Canada from the Soviet Union in the 1920s. About the drive to Waterloo, Maria remarked: 'Ontario [was] far lovelier than I expected.'[4]

This chapter will deal with the experience of single women immigrants, widows, and their children as they became settled in Canada. Finding jobs, repaying transportation debts, purchasing homes, and becoming economically stable were top priorities. Attaining stability in terms of health, both physical and mental, was also part of becoming established, as many immigrants carried with them the effects of deprivation and personal tragedy. Regardless of their initial opinion, most immigrants set their sights on the future, resolutely undertaking the challenge of settling into Canadian life.

The immigrant community was aided in the settlement process by individuals and institutions within the Canadian Mennonite community. This chapter also introduces aspects of the relationship that developed between the refugees and Mennonites already resident in Canada, an encounter that caused both comfort and unease for the newcomers. In the late 1940s, there were already about 120,000 Mennonites in Canada, the majority with roots in migrations from Russia in the 1870s and 1920s. Most Mennonites were rural and agricultural in their economic orientation, but this would change drastically in the next two decades as they urbanized and professionalized. The refugees entered an environment in which their Canadian co-religionists were struggling with the pressures of modernity at many levels.

Studies of various postwar immigrant groups have demonstrated that, above all else, the persons who made Canada their home after the war were 'a hardworking people.'[5] Especially noteworthy is the fact that in most immigrant families, all members old enough and physically able to work contributed in some way to the family economy. Furthermore, immigrant women, married or single, with children or without, were more likely than not to join the labour force.[6] The wage-earning immigrant mother in particular was at odds with the family ideal of the 1950s, in which, as Franca Iacovetta has suggested, the 'dominant rhetoric assumed a gendered arrangement in which husbands supported a wage-dependent wife and children, and women took on the task of running an efficient household and cultivating a moral environment for their children.'[7] This popular idealization of the stay-at-home married woman did not reflect the experience of displaced persons arriving in Canada after the war.

By far the majority of Mennonite immigrants to Canada, men and women alike, worked for wages in some capacity. In fact, Canada's labour-oriented postwar immigration policies demanded it. Certainly no one in the Canadian Mennonite community questioned whether the newcomers would work, nor was any suggestion raised that it was problematic for women with dependent children to be doing so. If the rhetoric surrounding the question 'Should women work?' was prevalent in society generally, it could also be found in microcosm within the discourse of the Mennonite community, as a brief survey of Mennonite media suggests.

Although Mennonite women were enrolled in higher education and were entering the workforce to an unprecedented extent beginning in the early 1950s, domesticity continued to be idealized as the proper and most rewarding role for women. For instance, in 1956 an occasional column entitled 'Conversation with Wives' or 'Conversation with Mothers' appeared in the biweekly newspaper *The Canadian Mennonite*. In her first article, columnist Anne Bargen set the tone for the series: 'To be a capable housewife is a wondrous feat, which taxes the whole personality of a woman.'[8] In 1957, in response to a debate by the Association of Mennonite University Students on the greater involvement of women in society, Bargen contended that woman's greatest purpose remained that of making a house into a home.[9] *The Canadian Mennonite* column 'Kitchen Kathedral' appeared in 1957, its title quite indicative of its emphasis. Radio CFAM in Altona, Manitoba, a station with substantial Mennonite content, featured distinctively women's programming from its inception in 1957. Among the programs aired were 'Homemaker's Chat,' 'Afternoon at Home,' and 'Hints for the Homemaker.'

Alongside the opinion pieces that celebrated domesticity ran the debate over the pros and cons of Mennonite women's increased participation in the workforce. Through the 1950s and on, Mennonite periodicals in Canada and the United States carried articles with such titles as 'Why Christian Married Women Work' and 'Woman's Place in the World.' Reflecting the middle-class character of most Canadian Mennonites, cautious affirmation of women in the workforce was based on arguments about utilizing women's God-given talents, about self-fulfilment, and about making a contribution to society.[10] Negative reactions to the wage-earning woman, on the other hand, often pointed to the acquisitive and materialistic motivation behind the married woman's desire for a salary.[11] Neither side of the debate acknowledged the economic necessity that drew most Canadian women of the time into the workforce. And although the discourse included the experience of single women, it did not generally mention widows, and certainly not unmarried women with children.

Ironically, many Mennonite refugee women might have welcomed the opportunity to 'stay at home' and not 'work out'; most of them had worked extremely hard already for much of their lives, many since childhood. Unfortunately, they did not have the luxury of debating the issue, as did some of their Canadian sisters, but were bound by immigration policy, and the responsibility of providing for themselves and their families, to find jobs that paid. The absence of adult males in many families meant that widows and single women became the primary providers for their dependants. Certainly, the 'gender-stratified household' containing the 'production-oriented husband and the domestic-centered wife' that, according to Royden Loewen, characterized one Mennonite community in the postwar era, did not apply to many immigrant households.[12] Mennonite refugee women arriving in Canada did try to run efficient households and did attempt to provide a moral example to their children, but they also 'worked out,' many until they reached retirement age. Unlike Canadian-born women, many of whom were moving into the growing sector of clerical work, immigrant women were generally relegated to the lower rungs of the 'female job "ghetto,"' which included domestic service, low-skilled factory jobs, work in hospitals and laundries, and seasonal labour in the agricultural sector.[13]

Working as household help, be it on the farm or in the city, was the most common paid job that Mennonite women performed. Although a relatively small number of Mennonite women arrived under the Canadian government's Domestic Service Contract Scheme – only twenty-nine by the end of 1948 – many more who arrived as close relatives or farm labourers undertook essentially the same work. Domestic labourers arriving on contract were expected to be paid thirty-five dollars per month (this rose by five dollars in 1951), in contrast to male workers immigrating on contract to the lumber and mining industries who received at least forty-five dollars per month.[14] The Domestic Service Contract Scheme was initially oriented primarily toward single women, but as the need for domestics intensified, and as the number of widowed refugees with dependants became apparent, officials became more lenient about accepting women with children. Nevertheless, Mennonite Central Committee (MCC) and Canadian Mennonite Board of Colonization (CMBC) workers frequently had to make special petitions to allow female-headed families and other exceptions fit the criteria for sponsorship as domestics. As late as September 1952, an MCC worker in Europe, Anne Giesbrecht, wrote to the CMBC in Saskatoon, requesting that an employer be found for a certain Frieda Suckau, aged thirty-four with two children, and that a letter guaranteeing employment and housing for all three be provided, since Labour Department officials had apparently rejected earlier cases of domestics with dependants.[15]

Domestic service held both advantages and disadvantages for Mennonite refugee women. Some women received their first informal English lessons in the household where they worked, often from the children in their care.[16] Learning about Canadian and Mennonite household customs and cooking was another positive aspect of being 'househelp.' Because of the scarcity and narrow variety of foods that most of the younger immigrants had experienced in the Soviet Union, many women had limited culinary skills. Agatha recalled that she knew little about baking or cooking when she arrived in Canada in her early twenties, but that after several household situations, her meatballs and bread became 'very popular.'[17] The process of learning new traditions was not without woe. Although emotions of consternation and humiliation were likely present at the time, frequently these learning experiences are remembered with humour. For instance, Katie Dirks Friesen, while employed by a Swedish family, mistakenly used coffee grounds in baking a coffee cake, instead of the leftover liquid coffee. She felt unsure about the instructions given to her, but discovered that 'actually the batter looked real good with the dark flecks in it.' Her employers were sensitive to her language difficulties and corrected her gently, but Katie was mortified at the time and 'did not tell anyone at all about the incident.'[18]

Although the feeling of being part of a household was comforting for some women who had been homeless for many years already, the privacy of the live-in domestic situation also presented one of the greatest hazards of the profession. Sexual harassment by an employer was one aspect of the darker side of domestic service, and Mennonite women were certainly not free from the risks, even if working in a Mennonite home. Susan arrived in Canada with her sister in 1948 and worked as househelp in a variety of temporary situations. At one placement, where she helped out before and after the arrival of a new baby, Susan was repeatedly molested by her male employer: 'with my milk pails full of milk he pressed me to the wall and squeezed me and even gave me a kiss. I was so very ashamed. He always did that. [His wife] was so good to me. I felt so guilty. I couldn't look her in the eyes. I didn't like it when his body came to mine always in such a corner. I was very uncomfortable. But I had to stay there. They gave me $45 a month.'[19] Like many immigrant domestics, Susan was caught between a distasteful situation – more so because her employers were distant relatives – and her need to earn money to repay her debts and send money to family members left behind for health reasons in a refugee camp in Germany.

One pre-existing Mennonite institution that received a boost with the arrival of the postwar refugees was the Girls' Homes, or *Mädchenheime*. These homes in the major urban centres in western Canada were operated separately by the General Conference Mennonites and Mennonite Brethren and functioned as boarding houses, employment bureaux, and city churches for Mennonite girls and women working as domestics.[20] The first two homes were established in Winnipeg in the 1920s, following the arrival of approximately 21,000 Mennonites from the Soviet Union. The majority of these immigrants settled on farms, but many families sent daughters to the city, where positions in domestic service were plentiful. During the war years, the attendance at the homes declined as daughters were needed on the family farm to replace their absent brothers, or as other jobs, such as factory labour, became more lucrative. With the arrival of Mennonite refugee women after the war, the need for the homes increased. The Vancouver Girls' Home, for instance, became a 'beehive of activity' in 1948 as 'people were eager to hire these lively, energetic, and dependable Mennonites.'[21] In Calgary, the Girls' Home was re-established, after closing several years earlier, specifically to meet the 'pressing needs' of the many 'young women and widows' who had arrived after the Second World War.[22]

In their early years, the Girls' Homes had functioned as temporary residences for young women who were seeking live-in situations, as well as providing help in securing employment, monitoring the women, and interceding in cases where difficulties with employers arose. The homes and their administrators also served as moral regulators, ensuring that the young women not fall victim to the immoral temptations that abounded in the urban setting.[23] By the late 1940s and early 1950s, the main function of the homes was social, offering the women a place to meet and socialize on their days off and to attend Bible studies and prayer meetings led by a Mennonite minister. For instance, in 1953 the Girls' Home in Calgary had a bed capacity of only twelve, but was visited weekly by at least fifty young women who received counselling and spiritual guidance there.[24] For single young women living and working an urban environment, the Girls' Homes were significant focal points in their transition from refugee to citizen.

Canadian Mennonite leaders attempted to ensure that the guiding influence of the church did not miss those Mennonite domestics sent on government contract to remote districts where no Girls' Home existed. The head of CMBC, Jacob J. (J.J.) Thiessen, seemed to make a great effort to establish contact with immigrants who were fulfilling one-year government labour contracts as domestics, farmworkers, and lumberworkers. Thiessen corresponded on more than one occasion with young women placed in such centres as Trois Rivières and Quebec City in Quebec, and Kingston, Guelph, and Perth in Ontario, all locales with no Mennonite population. His letters typically contained a request that they complete a CMBC immigrant registration form, inquiries as to how they fared in their placement, and words of encouragement to uphold their contract obligations and take comfort in the fact that at the end of a year they might relocate and be closer to their co-religionists.

For their part, the young women who replied to Thiessen were effusive in thanking the CMBC for facilitating their immigration and to Thiessen for taking an interest in their situation. They expressed resigned acceptance of their labour obligation but spoke of their loneliness so far from any relatives or friends, and often provided a chronology of the disappearance or death of their own closest family members. As well, women frequently apologized to Thiessen for their poor handwriting and many spelling and grammatical errors. Two women in the province of Quebec were particularly discouraged by the foreign language and Catholic religion that surrounded them. Anne Luise Regier,

Work crews along the Dnieper River between Zaporozhe and Dnepropetrovsk, 1943.

German occupation forces and ethnic German civilians in the Molotschna settlement, 1942.

On the westward trek from Ukraine, 1943.

Taking cows to drink on the trek from Ukraine, 1943.

Sleeping child during a stop on the trek from Ukraine, 1943.

Refugee children loaded on a boxcar.

German officers survey massacred German civilians in the aftermath of the
Soviet advance into East Prussia, 1944.

Women preparing vegetables for noonday meal, Gronau refugee camp, 1947.

Refugee women gathering fuel, Germany.

Elfrieda Klassen Dyck, Mennonite Central Committee escort on the *General Stuart Heintzelman* bound for Paraguay, 1948.

A Mennonite family in front of their newly built home in Volendam, Paraguay.

A Mennonite woman in Volendam, Paraguay, prepares a meal on the mud stove she built herself.

Refugee women working at the home for the aged in Yarrow, British Columbia, c. 1948.

First baptismal group at Sargent Avenue Mennonite Church, Winnipeg,
Manitoba, with ministers J.J. Thiessen and Jacob Toews in the rear, 1949.

working at Trois Rivières, wrote in August 1948: 'It is usually going well in my position. The people are very clean, only with the language is it sometimes difficult. Then comes beloved Sunday, when we would so much like to go to church. It is difficult, but the hope that we are only required to be a year in this area eases the pain a great deal.' Her loneliness was exacerbated by the fact that she had lost her parents and siblings in various ways and to date did not know whether they were dead or alive.[25] Along with his own offers of ongoing advice and support, Thiessen solicited the help of a woman of Mennonite background living in Montreal, asking if she could make contact with the two immigrant women working in the province of Quebec.[26]

Reporting on the work of the CMBC later that year, Thiessen said: '[The domestics] appreciate our interest in their well-being very much, since many feel lost and lonesome among strange people whose language they do not understand.'[27] As members of a close-knit, ethno-religious group, Mennonite women immigrants had the immediate advantage of having a connection with organizations and individuals that were concerned for their well-being and adaptation. This interest was nevertheless accompanied by expectations that newcomers conform to Canadian Mennonite standards of behaviour and thought, the consequences of which are discussed further in chapters 6 and 7.

For some immigrant women, domestic service was only one of several positions held during their first few years in Canada. Indeed, the labour histories of many newcomers were characterized by mobility in terms of both type and locale of employment. Changes of employment were sometimes necessitated by circumstance, but mobility was also a positive strategy for new immigrants to find better work and higher wages. Low levels of unemployment in postwar Canada and the ongoing demand in the sector of domestic service made such mobility possible.

The abundance of employment opportunities meant that women could easily take leave of domestic service, after completing whatever contract obligations they had, and seek alternative ways to make a living. In this way they might increase their wages, have greater freedom, especially when leaving live-in situations, and possibly develop a higher skill level. As Donald Avery has observed, high job turnover 'typified' the DP domestic.[28] When Elizabeth, age twenty-six, first arrived in Canada in the fall of 1948, she obtained work as a cook at a lumber camp in northern Ontario. Homesick for her widowed mother and six siblings, who had moved on to British Columbia, she left the camp after a year, 'fed up' with the hard physical work and poor pay. From November 1949 through to the spring of 1950, she cooked for a household in Vancouver, then spent the summer season cooking for employees at a canning factory in the interior of the province, taking along her younger sister as a helper. In the fall, Elizabeth returned to the Fraser Valley, where her family had settled, bought a sewing machine, and took sewing lessons in the hope of earning a living with her hands.[29]

Justina's career path was characterized by a single-minded upward mobility, as she was always seeking a new position that would increase her wages. During her first year in Canada, Justina held various positions as domestic help, first in rural Saskatchewan and then in Manitoba. After a bad experience in her last situation, she spurned further domestic work and moved to Winnipeg, where she had heard that better-paying factory jobs were plentiful. Initially she worked with several other refugee women at a chocolate store, earning fifteen dollars per week. After three months there, Justina obtained a position at a glove factory, earning money by piecework. Here she increased her earnings to $17.50 per week and sometimes to $20 dollars 'if you were very fast.' Justina, like other new immigrants, was anxious to earn as much as possible to repay her travel debt and to send money to relatives still in refugee camps in Germany.[30]

The seasonal nature of the agricultural industry also dictated a certain amount of mobility, especially for new immigrants who were frequently the main pool of labour during the busy periods of the farming cycle. In the Fraser Valley of British Columbia, where strawberries, raspberries, blueberries, and hops were primary agricultural crops, work in the harvest or the processing industry was one of the main sources of income for immigrants and others. The Fraser Valley also attracted immigrant families because of its already significant Mennonite population in such towns as Yarrow, Abbotsford, and Chilliwack. Women would frequently quit househelp jobs when the berry season began in order to earn better wages either picking berries or working at the fruit-processing factories. Upon her arrival in Canada in October 1948, Katie Dirks Friesen, then twenty-one, spent the first winter attending Bible school in Abbotsford. When spring arrived, she did domestic work for several months, then spent the summer picking berries and hops. She and her mother also got jobs working the night shift at a fruit-processing cooperative, jobs they sometimes combined with daytime picking. When the hop season ended, Katie returned to Bible school, and followed the same work cycle the next year, this time replacing domestic service with restaurant work.[31]

The need to maximize earning power prompted some women to be more mobile than they would have wished. Sisters Maria and Katja with their two young sons arrived in the Fraser Valley in the fall of 1948, too late in the season to pick berries. The two women drew lots to decide who would seek employment in Vancouver and who would stay at home with the children. Maria earned forty dollars per month working at a delicatessen in Vancouver while Katja supplemented those wages through seasonal work on the berry fields. Before long, however, Katja was offered household work in Vancouver and reluctantly left the two boys living with relatives until they finished the school year and could join their mothers in the city.[32]

While Mennonite farms and households frequently offered an immigrant her first opportunity to earn wages, some Mennonite institutions also took in a substantial number of Mennonite refugees as workers. The Mennonite-operated Concordia Hospital in north Winnipeg, for instance, sponsored young and old women to work as aids and in the kitchen and laundry. For immigrants who made their homes in urban areas, factory labour was a common source of employment. In many cases, individuals were able to secure a job in a particular factory through relatives who already worked there. Maria found her first job at the Goodrich Tire factory in Kitchener, Ontario, although immigration officials had assumed she would enter domestic labour. Because of union opposition to DP labour at the plant, Maria, along with other new immigrants, had to leave. She quickly found work at the non-unionized Kaufman Rubber factory down the street, and remained there until she had her first baby.[33]

Finding employment was not difficult, but managing relations with employers could be more of a challenge. Some new immigrants felt taken advantage of, with respect to both work demands and wages, by employers who viewed their offer of work as a gesture of charity. The fact that many employers were near or distant relatives of the immigrants created an environment of familiarity and eased the process of integration. However, in cases where relationships were not amiable, the blood ties that existed between employer and employee made tensions that much worse. Anna was disconcerted by the amount of work assigned to her and her sister when they arrived at their cousin's prairie farm in 1949, saying 'we worked just about night and day.' She unequivocally recalled that the sponsoring relative was 'mean' and 'took advantage' of them. The female employer's begrudging attitude extended, on one occasion, to a refusal to purchase sanitary napkins for Anna during a shopping trip to town, forcing the young woman to use rags as she had done in Russia.[34] In another case, a young immigrant woman left her position in Alberta after only half a year because her uncle's wife was physically abusive toward her young son.[35] For immigrants, the Canadian workplace included the hardship of learning new work skills along with a new language, occasional difficulties with employers, and loneliness for those who were separated from family members.

The long-term work histories of Mennonite immigrant women were varied. Those women who were young and single when they arrived in Canada tended to follow the dominant gendered order of 'working out' until they married and had children, after which they were occupied with their own housework and childcare. Those women who were widows, or remained single, continued to work for wages as health permitted. Rita was a single mother who, after working for several years at a dry cleaners, found a position as a filing clerk with a large insurance company. She remained in the insurance business until retirement in the 1980s, having worked her way as high as a woman could.[36] Agnes Klassen-Harder, who immigrated to Ontario with three daughters at the age of forty-seven, had the following work history: first she had temporary employment at the Boese food canning factory in St Catharines, followed by a permanent job at the John Forsyth shirt factory in Kitchener, where she worked for many years; later she took a position with the Mutual Life insurance company, and finally, as a live-in housekeeper for a wealthy widow. Following Agnes's death, it was said, 'She always earned her own living with ingenuity and the labour of her hands until her retirement in 1971.'[37]

Older widows who arrived in Canada with children who were teenagers and young adults sometimes did not work outside the home at all. As one man recalled of his mother, she had 'worked like a slave' on the collective farm in the Soviet Union and simply did not have the health and strength to work anymore.[38] Whether young or in early adulthood, children were frequently significant contributors to the family economy, thus sharing much in common with the experience of other immigrant families. Among immigrant families engaged in agricultural labour as the main source of income, children would work alongside their parents during the fruit-picking or vegetable-hoeing season. In one female-headed family, three children – age fourteen, thirteen, and ten – helped with the beet harvest in southern Alberta, while their two-year-old sister came along because she grew lonely when left with a babysitter.[39]

In urban families, children found other strategies of contributing to the family income. After first migrating to Paraguay, Jacob was thirteen in 1955 when he arrived in Canada with his widowed mother and three siblings. His older brother worked as a butcher's assistant, while Jacob worked an hour after school each day for a manufacturer of shovels and chains. At the age of fourteen he went to work weekends at a garage where his uncle was employed. Meanwhile, Jacob's two younger sisters earned money babysitting, sometimes over an entire weekend. The earnings of all four children went into the family coffer, administered by their mother. In Jacob's recollection, any expenditures would be a communal decision, and not even his mother would remove money from the family savings without consulting her children.[40] Generally speaking, young widows with school-age dependants were the hardest off, since their children were a 'liability' in that they could not contribute much to the family in terms of earnings, except in summer. By contrast, one widow with six children was described by another refugee as 'rich' because four of her children were single adults who could contribute substantially to the family income.[41]

The financial priority for all immigrant individuals and families was to pay down travel debts to sponsors, in most cases relatives who had made application for specific refugee immigrants and had advanced their travel costs, or to the Canadian Mennonite Board of Colonization. Canadian citizens who applied to sponsor refugees under the Close Relative Scheme were obliged to make advance payment for the transatlantic travel of the immigrant, in addition to guaranteeing employment and accommodation for a year. By December 1948, $822,000 had been raised from Canadian Mennonites for this purpose. The cost per immigrant ranged between $200 and $300, depending on the sailing and the final destination in Canada.[42] Many families paid their debts within a year of arrival in Canada, sometimes less. One young widow with three children who arrived in May 1948, sponsored as a farmworker by a distant relative, was able to pay her debt of about $800 by the end of that summer.[43] Although the Russian Mennonite immigrants of the 1920s had taken two decades to pay off similar travel debts, the majority of postwar immigrants were debt-free within five years. Given that the earlier immigrants were faced with economic depression soon after their arrival, while the postwar immigrants benefited from an economic boom, the quicker repayment of debts by the latter is not surprising. At a 1951 celebration of refugee resettlement, the president of the CMBC announced, 'It gives me great pleasure to share with you that the majority of the immigrants have kept their promises and paid their [debt]. Good intentions, favourable economic circumstances, and employment opportunities have contributed to this.'[44]

In the rare cases where immigrants were unable to repay their debts, the CMBC sometimes interceded to have the amount owing waived. For instance, in July 1950, J.J. Thiessen appealed to officials of the International Refugee Organization (IRO) to drop transportation charges of $233 for fourteen-year-old Rudolph Wazura. The boy's mother was 'a widow and not very strong physically [and] had a hard time to repay her own fare and to make a home for herself and her son.' Their sponsor had passed away in the meantime. The IRO promptly agreed to cooperate and cancelled the account.[45] In at least one case, immigrant families themselves made an appeal directly to the IRO. In February 1950, a family of three sisters (two widowed with one child each and the third single) and their sixty-eight-year-old mother wrote to Hector Allard, head of the IRO in Canada, requesting that part of their ocean fare, which had been prepaid by their sponsor, be refunded. The family was having trouble repaying their debt to their sponsor, who was a cousin, and generally having trouble 'making ends meet.' Together, the three sisters averaged thirty-four hours per week at factory labour in Winnipeg, but reported that their earnings were low. They had to struggle to provide their children with adequate food and their ill mother with the expensive medicine she required. In closing their letter, they said: 'If you could refund to us ocean fare, we would be ever so thankful to you, and perhaps mother would feel better, too. She is so weak now she cannot even go to Church.'[46] Unfortunately for this family, the IRO considered transportation refunds only if the sponsor was a displaced person him/herself, and so their request was denied.[47] Presumably the sisters either continued to struggle and economize or they received assistance from their local Mennonite church or the CMBC. In several other instances, immigrants were either unable or unwilling to repay debts owing, despite persistent efforts of Mennonite leaders to make them accountable. In the case of one family – a widow with six children aged five to twenty-six years – that arrived in 1949, CMBC officials spent the next decade attempting to recoup the relatively small sum of about $50 remaining in their debt for rail fare. In 1961, after all efforts to locate the family failed, the debt was cancelled as 'hopeless.'[48]

The above cases represented a small minority: most immigrants repaid their debts through their own labour and thrift. For individuals who had made do with the barest of material resources for most of their lives, being thrifty was not difficult. Part of the success in paying off debts and accruing savings lay in frugal management of earnings. Lena arrived in Winnipeg at the age of sixteen with her two younger brothers, who boarded with relatives while she lived at the hospital where she worked in the laundry. Lena earned fifty dollars per month, of which she kept two dollars for spending money, the remainder being punctually sent to her grandmother's cousin in British Columbia, who had financed the travel costs of the three orphans. Most of her spending money was used to purchase street car tickets so that she could attend night school two evenings a week and learn English.[49] In one female-headed family, repayment of the travel debt was such a priority that the eldest daughter had to defer her wedding plans until their financial obligations had been fulfilled.[50] Similarly, Katie Dirks Friesen had only five dollars to her name when her wedding day arrived in 1950, since all her earnings from the day of arrival in 1947 had been given over to her mother to cover their debts and pay for their house.[51]

Along with obtaining work, securing a roof over their heads was an immediate necessity for refugee families. Upon arrival, accommodation was usually found with sponsors or other relatives resident in Canada. After repaying their travel debts, the main priority for most immigrants was the purchase of a house. Home ownership was part of being Canadian, particularly in the postwar era when construction and sales of housing boomed in the context of government reconstruction policies and an urbanizing population.[52] Furthermore, home ownership provided immigrants with a sense of rootedness and belonging, and freed them from indebtedness to or feelings of intrusion upon relatives. As well, rental accommodation could be problematic for some refugees due to discrimination against DPs on the part of landlords. As was the case for many other postwar immigrants, the purchase of a house provided Mennonite families with a psychological and material sense of stability.

Many immigrants were able to purchase houses in a relatively short period of time. One female-headed family that immigrated to Canada from Paraguay in 1955 was able to purchase a house within a year from the combined earnings of the mother and all four children, age nineteen and under.[53] Katie Friesen, together with her mother and aunt, also purchased a 'crude shell' of a house within the first year, since the house they had occupied in the first summer was meant for seasonal agricultural workers and was not adequate as a winter dwelling.[54] The pattern of home-buying after debts were paid was so prevalent among the refugees that in the Mennonite-populated community of Virgil in the Niagara Peninsula, it was noted that 'new streets emerged ... inhabited primarily by immigrants.'[55] The fact that female-headed families repaid their travel debts and also became homeowners so soon after immigration was described in one church history as 'all the more noteworthy' given the absence of a 'family man.'[56]

Although the sources offer no specific comparison of the rate at which female-headed versus male-headed families were purchasing homes, women may have been faced with obstacles to home-buying that were directly related to their gender. Suspicion on the part of Canadian Mennonites as well as lending institutions that widows were less likely to be financially solvent over the long term may have affected situations in which a woman did not have sufficient cash to purchase a house up front. Gertrude, a young widow with two school-aged children and her own mother to care for, was able to purchase a half-finished house for three hundred dollars after several months of picking berries in the Fraser Valley. She was able to pay for the digging of a basement and the pouring of the foundation, but didn't have the seventy-five dollars needed to move the tiny house onto its foundation. Gertrude's uncle insisted that she would be unable to obtain a loan from the bank, but Gertrude's employer, a doctor for whom she did housework, intervened with the bank manager and signed for the loan on her behalf. She paid the loan off within a month and a half, although it meant eating little more than 'potatoes, bread, sometimes noodles, just meat for Sunday.' The house purchase included two acres of land and, following two good crops of berries, Gertrude was able to build onto her house.[57]

The intervention of several men occurred in the purchase of a home by Margareta Ruppel, the sister of J.J. Thiessen, the head of the CMBC. In the spring of 1949, N. Isaak, a colleague of Thiessen's, wrote from St Catharines, Ontario, informing the Saskatoon-based church leader that a seven-room house, considered a bargain, had been found for his sister and her daughters. Ruppel, accompanied by two community men, had visited the house and decided to purchase it at a price of $4,300 with a down payment of $1,500. The remaining mortgage of $2,800 was arranged at the bank by the two businessmen. Ruppel had been encouraged to share the purchase with her sister-in-law, but she preferred to do it on her own, intending to help pay the mortgage by renting out several rooms. Several days later, Thiessen responded with gratitude to Isaak for assisting his sister, noting that he had already been informed about the purchase because Thiessen's signature had been required by the bank.[58]

The hesitancy of banks to make loans to widows may have been behind the decision by the British Columbia Mennonite Relief Committee to establish a fund of $12,000 to assist immigrant women with children whose husbands were dead or missing. The concern that many women with small children and no 'masculine help' were renting accommodation, was another justification for the fund,[59] out of which were granted interest-free loans of up to $500, repayable over five years, for the purpose of building or buying a house.[60] I have not determined exactly how many women took advantage of this assistance, but memoirs and conference records indicate that women did take out loans from the British Columbia committee. For instance, Anny Penner Klassen, a forty-two-year-old widow with two children, borrowed $500 in 1950 and bought three-quarters of an acre of land in Yarrow and moved a one-room house onto it. She said: 'We were thankful to have our own home, even though it was small.'[61] At the annual meeting of the committee in November 1950, it was reported that in the year prior to 1 October, $13,830 had been paid out in loans for houses, while $1,320 had been taken in as repayment.[62] Thus, the $12,000 set aside had already been exhausted, although repayments were beginning to replenish the fund. The following year, the chair of the committee reported that ten 'women without men' ('Frauen ohne Maenner' was frequently the designation given to these women) were on the waiting list for loans, as there were insufficient funds in the treasury. He further commented that the situation was aggravated by the fact that British Columbia was the only province with this type of assistance for widows, and that women from other provinces were consequently moving west to apply for house loans.[63] By 1954 it was reported that $17,000 had been lent for house purchase or construction, sixty families had been assisted thus far, and seventeen women had already repaid their loans.[64]

While the arrangement was generous in its repayment schedule and in the fact that no interest was charged, there is evidence that loans were accompanied by a certain amount of church intervention into the type and locale of housing chosen by a widow, as well as an assessment of her suitability. In one case brought to the attention of the British Columbia Provincial Relief Committee, concern was raised about a widow with children who had taken a loan and built a house a considerable distance (thirteen miles) away from the nearest Mennonite church in Kelowna. Members of the committee decided that her present house should be sold and another purchased closer to Kelowna. Although the minutes of the meeting suggest that this action was taken following a request for advice from the woman, one wonders why she would have chosen the original site for building a house had that not been her intention in the first place. Unfortunately, there are no clues to her own motivation in the matter. In the case of another woman who had applied for a loan, it was reported that 'she made a good impression,' but the committee decided that she must first complete repayment of her travel debt.[65] In yet another instance, a woman's application for a house loan had already been approved when it was learned that she was 'living in sin' with her brother-in-law (presumably both had lost their spouses). Since she was not willing to separate from him, the committee revoked its approval of her request.[66] These incidents suggest that widows who took advantage of the loan option with the committee were subject to monitoring by that same body, which needless to say, was all male.

Other forms of independence for women were necessitated by the absence of a man in some households. For instance, the purchase of an automobile was another step toward upward mobility and was an especially noteworthy purchase by widows in an era when many women were just beginning to get their drivers' licences. In the town of Leamington, Ontario, where many Mennonites lived, a woman sitting behind the steering wheel of a car was practically unheard of before 1940; according to N.N. Driedger, a local minister, 'driving a car was clearly a masculine function.'[67] Postwar immigrant Anny Klassen bought a new Volkswagen in 1956, and 'in time I learned to drive it.' This brought an end to her routine of riding her bicycle to work.[68] Even when an adult male was part of the immigrant household, women were sometimes the pathbreakers in getting behind the wheel of a car. Susan, who was the eldest child in a family that remained together throughout the war, and who had assumed many responsibilities beyond her years and was often treated by her father 'like a son,' obtained her driver's licence in 1955, soon after her marriage. She commented on the surprise that some men exhibited when they saw a woman driver: 'Sometimes when I met a man on the road he would sort of go on the grass when he was coming the other way. My goodness I thought, if that man in Abbotsford [the licensing agent] says that I can drive on this road just as you can, then it's too bad for you if you want to drive there because I'm driving there too.'[69] The kind of responsibilities shouldered by this young woman during the war made it obvious to her that practical things such as 'getting around town' had nothing to do with gender.

The majority of immigrants obtained economic security through earnings accrued by the work of their own hands. Memory sources refer to few organized efforts of material assistance for the refugees; informal gestures of charitable giving were more likely forms of mutual aid. Certainly, the tradition of looking to extended family members for social assistance when other institutions were lacking has been characteristic of immigrants and refugees historically. In making application for immigrant families, sponsoring relatives and prospective employers obligated themselves to ensure that new immigrants would be supported for one year. Thus, until the time that they could become self-supporting, refugee families were provided with shelter, clothing, and food. Household goods collected by local churches and given as gifts to refugees also helped many families make a start. Common was the experience of one widow with four children, who, stopping in Ontario to meet relatives before continuing on to her sponsor and employer in Alberta, was given a 'shower' at which she received gifts of clothing, quilts, and towels to help her get started.[70]

Although most of the assistance offered to the newcomers was of a personal and informal nature, the principle of mutual aid operated at the institutional level, too. Some churches and conferences established funds, such as the housing fund for widows, but assistance was not always only for basic material needs. In her autobiography, Katie Dirks Friesen noted that she was able to attend the Mennonite Bible school in Abbotsford because the Conference of Mennonites in British Columbia had decided that no fees would be charged for recent immigrants from the Soviet Union.[71] Similarly, the Mennonite Brethren church in the southern Alberta town of Coaldale offered free tuition to the twenty immigrant youth who enrolled at the Bible school there in 1949.[72]

In October 1947 First Mennonite Church in Winnipeg established a fund intended for three purposes: for transportation of European refugees, for assistance to alleviate need in Europe, and for assistance for refugees once they arrived in Canada. The desire of the church council was that each family would donate twenty-five dollars to the fund and each single person give half that.[73] In 1950 the United Mennonite Conference of Ontario recommended that Ontario churches contribute $2.50 per member toward the conference refugee treasury in order to pay the health bills of new immigrants.[74] Similarly, the British Columbia Provincial Relief Committee resolved to pay doctors' bills of newly arrived immigrants for a period of three to six months, or more if there was good reason to do so.[75] Unfortunately, the records of these churches and organizations do not reveal with any precision whether members actually followed through and contributed to the funds or the extent to which immigrants drew from them. While some immigrants attested to little help from the church, others had more positive experiences. Lina Wohlgemut, a widow with three children, received ten dollars 'periodically' from the 'deacon's assistance fund' at her church.[76]

Situations of financial need were usually dealt with by assessing the merit of each case and by special collections in individual congregations rather than through set up funds from which immigrants could draw according to the discretion of church deacons or other fund administrators. For instance, at the Virgil Mennonite Brethren Church at Niagara-on-the-Lake, Ontario, a special offering amounting to $138 was collected to purchase artificial feet for a refugee boy whose feet had been frozen during the trek from the Soviet Union.[77] An indirect way to assist immigrants economically was to exempt widows in particular from certain financial obligations toward the church. At the 1952 annual church meeting at Scott Street Mennonite Brethren in St Catharines, it was noted that widows were exempt from local church and conference dues.[78] Although there was no distinction made between postwar immigrant widows and other widows, the timing of this particular guideline coincided with the impact that refugee widows were having on Canadian Mennonite congregations.

The advent of certain government social programs had the potential to assist some immigrants who required financial aid. In the published history of the Blumenort (Manitoba) Mennonite Church, it was observed that the role of the deacons, who had been active in addressing the needs of impoverished widows, changed with the onset of universal old age pensions in Canada in 1951. Even so, the ten refugee widows in the congregation did not qualify for Canadian pensions because of the twenty-year residency requirement.[79] The universal family allowance program, instituted in 1944, also had the potential of increasing, albeit in small measure, the spending money in immigrant families. At its inception, the program had a residency requirement of three years, but this was reduced to one in 1949, thus making the allowance available to immigrant families following an initial year of sponsorship and self-support.[80] Some Mennonite conferences and congregations warned their members against accepting this form of government assistance, viewing it as unwanted state intervention in the family. Mennonites had long been ambivalent about government programs, fearing that favours from the state would compromise religious beliefs such as non-resistance, especially during war, when such beliefs were publicly called into question. However the British Columbia Provincial Relief Committee considered it a 'great help' when the residency requirement for family allowances was reduced to one year, especially in light of flooding and poor harvests in the Fraser Valley in recent years.[81] The responses of women also varied. Some mothers, widowed or not, did accept family allowance cheques. In one instance, a 1949 immigrant from East Prussia – a widow with three preschool children – chose not to apply for mothers' allowance even though she was eligible as a single parent. She was motivated partly by pride in supporting her children independently, but also by 'not liking the idea of the government checking up on how she would spend the allowance.' She later did accept a family allowance cheque of $5 per month, since it did not carry the same stigma of need.[82] Another young widow, although she received no financial aid from the church, refused government assistance, saying, 'I didn't want any welfare. We managed.' Later she also accepted family allowance stipends.[83] Clearly the lack of a means test, which marked the significance of the 1944 legislation, had a direct impact on the willingness of proud and self-sufficient women to apply for the grant.

The various forms of material assistance received by refugee widows and their families from churches, relatives, Mennonite relief organizations, and public sources were nearly always welcome aids that enabled women to get established sooner than if there had been no help. Mennonite women, like other immigrants who were part of distinct ethnic groups, were thus advantaged by their immediate inclusion in a community that considered itself responsible for the welfare of the newcomers. Yet, as Franca Iacovetta has suggested, relationships between postwar immigrants and networks of volunteers and welfare professionals were inevitably inegalitarian, especially given that assistance and sympathy for refugees and immigrants were accompanied by pressures to conform to 'Canadian ways.'[84] Although Mennonite refugees were not necessarily pressured by their co-religionists to become 'Canadian,' there were subtle and not-so-subtle measures that influenced the newcomers toward accepting the norms and standards of behaviour of Canadian Mennonites. The complex and often uncomfortable relationship between the old-timers and the newcomers will be dealt with at greater length in chapter 7, but at the level of economics, the encounter was ambiguous, characterized simultaneously by the care and concern that motivated gestures of mutual aid and by the unequal power relations that resulted. That the pre-existing Canadian Mennonite community may have preferred the inequality that situated them on top is suggested by their discomfort when the immigrants began to succeed economically.

The speed with which many of the postwar immigrants attained economic stability prompted Canadian Mennonites to perceive the newcomers as materialistic and acquisitive. Elfrieda Klassen Dyck, who had grown up in Canada and served as a relief worker in Europe among the refugees, explained the acquired reputation thus: 'They worked terribly hard and they did well. It didn't take them long to own a house and a car, which was very different from those of us that came in the 20s, who also worked hard but had to survive the Depression of the 30s.'[85] Along with the label that they were materialistic went the criticism that the immigrants did not give enough to the church.

Certainly there were large differences in the degree to which and the rate at which immigrants became well-off economically. Even within the refugee community, the concern was expressed that some immigrants were excessively oriented toward 'making a buck.'[86] Undoubtedly upward mobility and aspirations of material success were a means of validating the refugee identity in a context where these people normally felt ashamed of who they were. As Mary K. Roberson has observed about Palestinian families of the Occupied Territories, financial success helped transform the psychology of a refugee from 'stigma to pride.'[87] Much of the indignation over the relatively quick financial success achieved by some families arose from the markedly different economic contexts into which the Russian Mennonite immigrants of the twentieth century entered. The perception that the later immigrants were doing a bit too well too soon exacerbated the tensions that arose from different historical experience. For instance, one female-headed family was taken aback when asked by a sponsoring relative to pay interest on their travel debt after one year. When the family promptly paid what was asked, the sponsor published a letter to the editor in the local paper that criticized DPs for being so well off. He was compelled to retract his statements, however, when he learned that another church member had loaned the family money to pay the interest.[88] This incident, along with others like it, demonstrates how large the gap in understanding could be between members of what society viewed as a 'closed community.'

Even while most immigrants were becoming financially stable, if not all wealthy, their years as war refugees continued to have repercussions in terms of physical and mental health. Because of years of malnutrition and near starvation, combined with overexposure to the elements during the flight from the Soviet Union, some refugees had ongoing health problems, necessitating treatment years later in Canada. One young widow concluded that poor diet, stress, and overwork had led to her stomach being 'loose in the body,' a condition requiring two surgical procedures in British Columbia.[89] Another woman, who had given birth to five children between 1935 and 1946, underwent a series of operations in Canada to 'correct problems caused by over-exertion during her child-bearing years.'[90] Other refugees had unnamed illnesses vaguely described as 'problems with nerves' or 'general weakness.'

Unspecified physical complaints could also have been somatic manifestations of repressed psychological trauma. In an oral history project with Cambodian refugee women in North America, researchers found that 'conscious avoidance of remembering the trauma [of dead children and disappeared husbands] and any concurrent feelings of pain' was common, but was frequently accompanied by ailments such as 'headaches, stomach aches, dizziness, [and] heart trouble.'[91] This occurred for some Mennonite women as well. One young woman, Gerta, who saw her mother raped and lost both parents in the war, commented that Canadian Mennonites were either unwilling or unable to understand the experiences of the refugee immigrants. As a result, the 'horrible experiences' were not talked about but instead manifested themselves, in Gerta's case, in a fragility of emotional health. She said: 'I would probably not have wanted to talk about it much because I cried a lot more than I ate. My hands are not steady. The doctor saw it and asked, what is the matter with you. I said that's a long story. I can't help this. I have very bad handwriting.'[92]

Even less concrete in diagnosis were illnesses expressed in mental and emotional disturbances. It is difficult to document or assess how widespread or serious were cases of mental illness among postwar Mennonite immigrants. Peter Dyck, MCC worker among the refugees in Europe, recalled at least one Mennonite woman in Holland who was admitted to a psychiatric hospital there: 'She just blew a fuse, blocked out the past, and became a child again.'[93] That postwar immigrants may have had a higher than normal occurrence of physical illness and/or psychological disturbance is suggested by a number of sources. For instance, at Sargent Avenue Mennonite Church in Winnipeg, a congregation with a high percentage of postwar immigrants, the church historian reported in 1971 on the noticeable number of members of the church who, though not elderly, had illnesses requiring hospitalization. He attributed this in part to the fact that many of Sargent's members had been born and raised during the years of famine in the Soviet Union and that many had later experienced a decline in health in prison camps. As well, quite a few individuals had difficulties with nerves, a condition that could be traced back to shattering wartime experiences.[94] More substantive or quantitative evidence, however, has not been found to determine whether the postwar immigrants had a higher rate of mental illness or suicide than the general or Canadian Mennonite population.

That a number of files in the records of the Canadian Mennonite Board of Colonization deal specifically with individuals who were patients in mental hospitals suggests that this was an issue of not insignificant magnitude. The questions raised in these files deal not so much with the particular symptoms or illness of an individual patient, nor the causes thereof, but with the issue of financial responsibility for the costs of institutionalization, as well as the threat of deportation from Canada. The following case is illustrative of these questions. Margaret Bartel (not her real name), a young, unmarried woman, immigrated to Canada with her parents in 1951. Their home had been in Danzig, and the family became eligible for emigration as sugar beet workers in southern Alberta. Shortly after arriving, Margaret became ill and was sent to the Bethesda Home for the Mentally Ill in Vineland, Ontario, an institution operated by the Mennonite Brethren Church. As treatment, her physician there recommended a lobotomy, which Margaret underwent at a provincial hospital in Hamilton. While in hospital in Hamilton, an order for Margaret's deportation was issued by the Department of Citizenship and Immigration on 17 March 1955. The order was deferred for a year. On Margaret's return to Bethesda in early 1956, the administrators of the home learned that the department had reopened the case, which was surprising given that the home had never been informed of the initial investigation. A flurry of correspondence followed between the business manager at Bethesda; the head of the CMBC, J.J. Thiessen; officials with the provincial relief committee in Alberta; and the director of the Department of Citizenship and Immigration, C.E.S. Smith. The government's representative was assured by Thiessen that all of Margaret's hospital expenses had been covered by Mennonite church organizations and would continue to be covered in the future, thus addressing the government's main concern that she not become a public charge. In March 1956 the deportation order was stayed for yet another year.[95]

Whether the threat of deportation was really serious in cases like Margaret's, or whether the government was simply following procedure, is difficult to assess. Certainly Mennonite officials took the threat very seriously. In 1961, following a lengthy period when no further action on Margaret's case was taken, J.J. Thiessen took the initiative to discern the exact policy of the government with respect to such individuals. He wrote, 'Among the immigrants who came to Canada after the second world war under the auspices of our organization, we have a number of cases which required treatment in mental institutions and where deportation proceedings were started. We are wondering how long these patients will be under the danger of being deported.'[96] Government officials assured Thiessen that deportation orders were unlikely to be carried out if an immigrant continued to receive treatment at no cost to the Canadian public.[97] Thiessen's interest in establishing the general policy surrounding these cases suggests that there were more than a few isolated situations like Margaret's.

Even where mental illness or emotional fragility was not in evidence to any extreme, there were behaviours and characteristics attributed to postwar immigrants arising from their refugee experience. Certainly the loss of husbands and fathers, particularly when death was never confirmed, created ongoing and unresolved grief. In studying the psychosocial trauma experienced by women refugees who survived a 'disappeared' husband, Michael D. Roe has observed that 'the uncertainty does not permit a complete grieving process to occur,' even when there is little likelihood that the missing person will be found alive.[98] Many other wartime experiences similarly were unresolved. One woman recalled that the need not to reveal her Soviet birthright while a refugee in Germany induced a silence born out of the fear of committing a blunder should she open her mouth. As a result, she and her siblings were 'shy and introverted' and also suffered from 'chronic inferiority complexes.'[99] Similarly, one young woman recalled that her mother taught a survival strategy that meant in essence, 'don't talk back, don't say anything, don't fight, just be quiet.'[100] Other psychological traits attributed to the immigrants included uncertainty and guilt.[101] For a large portion of individuals, traumatic wartime experiences were buried, and any emotional or physical manifestations of those memories were denied.

When Mennonite refugees from Europe stepped onto Canadian soil, the initial tasks before them were practical and material. Some had government labour contracts to fulfil, others had housing and jobs readied for them by close relatives, and still others had employment obligations with sponsors who were distant relatives or not related at all. Almost all of the immigrants had travel debts to repay, which most did within a minimum amount of time. Beyond fulfilling the obligations that resulted from their admittance to Canada, the refugee immigrants set about establishing themselves in the new land. This meant buying homes, learning English, possibly going to school, and changing employment as often as necessary to increase wages and job satisfaction. In all of this they were assisted by institutions, as well as by individuals within the Canadian Mennonite community – individuals who, as the postwar immigrants were frequently reminded, did not have the same kind of supports when they arrived earlier in the century. For the immigrant community, establishing themselves economically and materially was, for the most part, easier than settling in psychologically. Their prewar and wartime experiences stayed with them, resulting in mental illness for some, and, for many others, ongoing pain over the loss of loved ones. In attempting to fit into Canadian Mennonite churches and communities, the disparate experiences of the newcomers frequently became apparent, most keenly in standards of behaviour and in the presence of so many fragmented families.

6

Re-creating Families

When Mary Rempel immigrated to Canada in 1948, her first job was in the laundry of a small hospital in north Winnipeg. It is not surprising that Mary described the matron and other employees at the hospital as 'a family' since, over the course of the past decade, she had repeatedly been forced to redefine the form and function of family in her own life. In 1937, at the age of five, Mary and her younger brother lost their father when he was arrested and disappeared in the Soviet Union. In 1943 her mother secretly married a soldier with the German occupation, and from this union Mary gained a second younger brother. Mary's stepfather was killed in action toward the end of the war, and her mother died following surgery for varicose veins in Germany in 1947. The three orphans immigrated together, and, when other family members followed, Mary's Canadian household included her grandmother and two aunts. Her family changed once again when she married at the age of nineteen. The newlyweds' household also included Mary's two brothers.

In this chapter I will discuss cases of family fragmentation among postwar immigrants and how they were dealt with by Canadian Mennonites. The presence, among the refugees, of unmarried mothers posed problems at the level of immigration regulations but also in terms of the immoral sexual behaviour that their situation implied to a community that reserved sexual relations strictly for marriage. The main focus of the discussion is the problem that remarriage presented for widows with no confirmation of a prior spouse's death. Efforts, both compassionate and disciplinary, to deal with this issue caused considerable turmoil in some Mennonite churches during the 1950s and 1960s. The struggle reveals that both immigrant Mennonites and Canadian Mennonites were attempting to overcome the deviation from the ideal that fragmented families seemed to represent.

As Mary's family went through its various transformations in form and function, there were few points at which it could be considered a 'normal' nuclear family. Mary's background as a refugee immigrant was foreign to most Canadians, and so was her experience of family. Yet her marriage at a relatively young age suggests that Mary was trying to recreate the type of family form that had eluded her for most of her life, one which would make her feel like she had successfully adapted. The notion of 'the happy, united family' became, as Annalee Gölz has suggested, a 'potent ideological force' in the postwar era.[1] Historians and others have described the glorification of the gender-stratified nuclear family that characterized postwar ideology, and the accompanying emphasis on 'familism.'[2] Many Canadian families had endured wartime separation and were, as Joy Parr has suggested, 'yearning for a settled domesticity after the disruption of depression and war.'[3] As Elizabeth Heineman points out with respect to the Federal Republic of Germany in the immediate postwar years, the significance of the 'complete family' seemed to escalate at exactly the historical moment when the nation was confronted with an unusually high number of female-headed families due to wartime losses of men. German government legislation, such as the Law to Aid Victims of War (1950), provided some measure of assistance to unwed mothers and to war widows, yet did so within an ideological context of reconstructing these 'non-families' or 'half-families' into complete ones – that is, with a husband as head.[4] In Canada, various groups of professionals, such as social workers and psychologists, were imposing idealized and homogeneous notions of 'every family' based on Anglo-Saxon, middle-class values that served to discount and discourage the real diversity that existed in Canadian families.[5]

There has been little historical analysis of family ideology specifically within Mennonite communities. While sociologists have generally agreed that the family has been a 'near-sacred institution' for Mennonites,[6] most studies have not offered a structural definition for the family but have assumed a normative ideal based on the nuclear model. Certainly, in a time of rapid change for society generally, and for Mennonites in particular, a stable family was considered crucial to the maintenance of Mennonite-Christian religious values and conduct. With the arrival of refugees and displaced persons from Europe, all Canadians, Mennonites included, were confronted with family configurations that did not fit the nuclear ideal. Aside from the many female-headed families, there were orphans accompanied by grandparents or aunts, single adults alone or with siblings, a few widowers with children, and groupings of several generations. The very existence of refugee families, in all their fragmentation, dispels the myth of monolithic postwar familism. They also presented Canadian Mennonites, in this case, with the challenge of incorporating remnants of families into their communities and, if possible, creating new families that were stable and independent.

Amid all the familial configurations represented among the postwar Mennonite immigrants, several provoked greater concern and raised more perplexing issues than others. One configuration that exhibited both the feature of an unnatural family form and blatant evidence of moral error was the family headed by an unmarried mother. Margaret Little has noted that during the war and postwar era there was escalating anxiety in Ontario concerning unwed mothers: 'It was generally believed that both desertion and illegitimacy were escalating at an alarming rate, shattering the very foundations of the heterosexual nuclear family.' Although, according to Little, there was little evidence in support of this, workers from charitable and public organizations promoted the notion that the 'moral fibre of the nation and of the nuclear family unit was at risk.'[7]

The presence of unwed mothers among Mennonite refugees was also a challenge to the Canadian Mennonite community, first of all at the level of immigration policy. One family type that was not initially admissible under Canadian immigration regulations was that of an unmarried woman with a child, who was termed 'illegitimate.' Although some of these women were able to immigrate as part of extended family groupings under the Close Relative Scheme, those who had no close relatives in Canada and wished to be sponsored as farm labourers faced initial refusal from the Canadian government. Even in the case of unmarried mothers sponsored as close relatives, the government requested special affidavits from sponsoring applicants, presumably to guarantee their assumption of responsibility for the illegitimate children.

The main official of the Canadian Mennonite Board of Colonization, J.J. Thiessen, wrote to the director of the Department of Immigration, A.L. Jolliffe, on several occasions in the summer and fall of 1949, requesting the admission of 'unmarried women with children.' In response to Jolliffe's initial refusal, Thiessen asked for consideration on 'compassionate grounds' since many of the young women were 'war casualties' (presumably he meant rape victims). He assured Jolliffe that there were Canadian sponsors willing to take such women as domestic workers and that the CMBC would assume responsibility for the 'unfortunates.' He also noted that no difficulties had thus far arisen with those single mothers who had immigrated under the Close Relative Scheme. Subsequently, Thiessen stressed that the CMBC would assume responsibility for providing for the children and 'not allowing the immigrants to become public charges in Canada.'[8] In a 28 September letter to Jolliffe, Thiessen cited eight specific cases of women aged twenty-one to thirty-eight, each with one child ranging in age from one to twelve (most were under five). He said: 'We regret that these are irregular cases but we look on them as unfortunate war casualties in need of the rehabilitation the Mennonite church can provide.'[9]

Despite the paternalistic language of rehabilitation in Thiessen's petitions, which suggests moral failing on the part of the young women, there is also a lack of outright condemnation for the women, as well as seemingly genuine sympathy for their situation. Interestingly, certain Mennonite leaders seemed to have had less trouble than government officials in integrating unwed mothers and their children into the notions of family. For instance, in July 1949, Cornelius F. Klassen, the Mennonite Central Committee's relief and immigration ambassador in Europe, wrote to J.J. Thiessen, expressing his distress over the government's stance:

That Ottawa applies such a narrow interpretation to the term 'dependents' and that illegitimate children are only permitted to come if the father is present, shuts out quite a lot. This is very, very unfortunate! The fathers of these children are, in the case of rape, first of all unknown. We are only glad that the mothers were not infected by the monsters. Ottawa must be yielding in this case. These unwed mothers with their guiltless charges must be given the opportunity to make a new beginning. They are not bad people and when sponsors on the other side are ready to receive them, Ottawa should let them in. It is cruel to do otherwise![10]

Klassen's comments were among the very few that made a direct link between wartime rapes and the pregnancies that resulted among refugee women. Thiessen responded to Klassen with understated agreement, expressing regret that the 'boundaries of family unity were so severely drawn and that girls with illegitimate children were thus not allowed through.'[11] It seemed that the Immigration Department was willing to admit the women as labourers, but not together with their children, suggesting that without fathers present, unwed mothers with dependants did not constitute a family unit. One high-level official with the Department of Labour in fact suggested that 'a good many' of the women with children who had entered Canada already may have 'manufactured stories that their husbands were behind the iron curtain, thus concealing illegitimacies.'[12]

Like many other persistent lobbying efforts of the CMBC, in this case the government reversed its stance, as Thiessen telegraphed to Klassen in October 1949.[13] The fact that Thiessen made a personal visit to Jolliffe in Ottawa to make his case undoubtedly helped to sway the official's position. However, while Jolliffe granted admission to the eight specific cases 'on purely humanitarian grounds,' he emphasized that this 'favourable action' did not represent an overall change in immigration policy with respect to such cases.[14] In the months following, Thiessen made additional pleas for small groups of unmarried mothers, repeating promises that his organization would not allow the women or their children to become public charges.[15] As far as can be established, all the unmarried mothers for whom special petitions were made, were subsequently admitted to Canada, usually as farm labourers or domestic workers.

Establishing the exact number of unwed mothers or 'illegitimate' children among the Mennonite refugees is virtually impossible, but various document sources, supplemented by memory sources, can provide some clues regarding the prevalence of this particular family form. On arrival in Canada, the CMBC recorded information about each immigrant household on a *Familienverzeichnis* (family register).[16] In its most detailed version, the family register offered the following data: full name; birthdate; birthplace; marital status; last place of residence in the USSR; place names and dates regarding the refugee trek and migration to Canada; information about sponsors; and lists of missing family members, including where and why they were left behind. Each form included all the members of a family unit, however defined at that moment by the CMBC or by the family itself.

Tabulations drawn from the 1948 CMBC family registers reveal twenty-six cases specifically defined as unmarried mothers, but in many other situations there is ambiguity surrounding the parentage of a child. The existence of an unmarried mother with a child is not immediately apparent from the way in which individuals were grouped together on a form. There are at least twenty-five additional cases in which a woman in her forties or fifties (widowed or not) is listed together with one or more single daughters, possibly with several other teenagers or children, and then a very young child (less than five years). In these cases, uncertainty arises as to who is the mother of the young child – the middle-aged family matriarch, or her daughter. For instance, one record lists a widow and seven children or dependants, ranging from twenty-five to one year of age. There is no information on the record to indicate that all seven are other than the widow's own children; they all bear the same surname. However, the 1946 birthdate of the youngest child – ten years after the family's father was arrested and exiled – raises questions, and in searching for other information about this family through oral interviews, it was learned that the eldest daughter was the mother of the one-year-old. Thus, this family group contained within it two single-parent groupings. The manner in which the identity of the child's mother is not obvious on the form parallels the way in which the child's very existence is masked in oral narratives of the family's story. Both circumstances suggest that illegitimacy was indeed problematic, to the point of denial, both for the Canadian Mennonite community and for the family itself.

A further clue to the prevalence of children born out of wedlock among the postwar immigrants can be found in the family and membership registers of Canadian churches. In one Mennonite church, the detailed membership register reveals seven cases in which children were born during or shortly after the war and in which the mother did not marry until sometime later.[17] For the most part, one cannot know the circumstances surrounding the child's conception and birth, although in one case, for a child born in January 1946, the register states, 'Father unknown,' suggesting that this was a situation of rape. In cases where a marriage occurred months and possibly years after the birth of a child, the identity of the father is open to question, at least where the only evidence derives from the church records. Examples such as one where a couple married in Canada in 1957, both having immigrated in 1948, with one child born in Germany in 1945, can be found sporadically throughout the genealogical records of Canadian Mennonite churches.[18]

A careful reading of immigration documents can offer other clues to the existence of young women who gave birth prior to marriage. One case file deals with the proposed immigration of a young couple with two children. Since the father was from Danzig, immigration authorities were concerned to know his activities between the years 1939 and 1945, presumably to determine the nature of any participation in the German military. In explaining their background, an MCC worker in Europe noted that the woman was a Soviet Mennonite who left her home in 1943 and that the two were married in Germany in 1947. These facts are unremarkable until one checks the birthdate of their first child – November 1945 – thus leading one to speculate that the mother was a victim of the mass rapes that occurred in the winter of 1945, when Soviet forces overtook the territories of eastern Germany.[19]

The point here is not to determine with certainty which births were cases of illegitimacy, but to illustrate the way in which families could be defined on paper so as to create ambiguity. Certain memory sources more vividly illustrate the way in which illegitimacy cast a cloud of deviancy over the immigrant family. Even if the existence of children conceived outside of marriage could be obscured on paper, Canadian Mennonites quickly became aware of such family configurations in their midst. One woman living in the Russian zone of occupied Germany at the end of the war gave birth to a daughter after trading sex with a Soviet officer for food and protection for herself and her three other children. After immigrating to Canada, the woman knew that people talked about her past, although nothing was said directly to her. When the 'illegitimate' daughter grew up in Canada, negative rumours surrounded her own morality – she was thought to be 'loose' and 'easy' – simply because she was born out of wedlock.[20] The perceived immorality of one immigrant also had implications for how other family members were regarded. In the fall of 1950, the executive committee of the British Columbia Provincial Relief Committee heard the case of Susanna, who reportedly had led a 'loose life' in Germany, the result of which was a baby born after her arrival in Canada. The child was adopted. The concern lay with Susanna's application for her sister Mary, who was detained in Gronau due to health concerns. After determining, based on a report from an immigration official, that the two sisters were not similar in character, and that the Girls' Home in Vancouver would take Mary in, the executive committee agreed to act as a guarantor for Mary's sponsorship. It was further noted that Susanna had her own accommodations and worked in the city; more importantly, she had been converted and baptized into the Mennonite Brethren Church.[21]

In another case, a young immigrant woman named Hertha, following the Mennonite practice of adult baptism, asked to be baptized but was refused by two Mennonite churches in Alberta and Ontario. As an unmarried mother with a young son, it was expected that she repent of her sins before being baptized. Hertha had in fact married the child's German father during the war but had sought an annulment when she discovered that he already had a wife from whom he was separated but not divorced. The complicated circumstances of her marriage and her own stubborn personality prompted Hertha to withhold this information from the church, allowing church members instead to think of her as an unwed mother.[22] After twelve years in Canada, she finally was baptized after a visiting Lutheran evangelist interceded on her behalf with her Mennonite pastor. The evangelist compared her situation to the biblical story of the adulterous woman who received forgiveness from Jesus. This comparison maintained the image of Hertha – for herself, the evangelist, and the Mennonite Church – as a sinner who required forgiveness.[23]

The community response to unmarried mothers suggests that their status as women with 'illegitimate' children was an issue of greater concern than the circumstances that surrounded the conception of the child. There may have been little differentiation between women who bore children as the result of rape or women who voluntarily engaged in sexual liaisons, even if the particular circumstances were known, which was frequently not the case. The silences that women and their families imposed on their personal stories, combined with community gossip, meant that there was limited understanding of the wartime experiences of women. Because the new immigrants were already under a cloud of questionable morality, it may have been that those single women who came with small children were assumed to have had extramarital sex. The evidence suggests that an element of genuine sympathy lay behind the efforts of CMBC officials to bring unmarried mothers with children to Canada. As well, there were instances of community acceptance to offset the negative anecdotes related above. Yet, the general attitude toward these women was that they added a dimension of immorality to the immigrants who, in their very fragmentation, represented a discomfiting aberration to the ideal family of the postwar era.

Although their status did not, for the most part, raise any moral red flags, the large number of widows among the postwar immigrants created yet another deviation from the 'normal' family. During the peak years of migration, 1947 to 1949, widows represented 15 per cent of the total number of immigrants registered with the Canadian Mennonite Board of Colonization. This number is not insignificant, given that the number of married immigrants (20 per cent) and the number of single adults (23 per cent) were only slightly higher and included both men and women. The distinguishing feature of the family structure of the postwar immigrants, attested to also in numerous memoirs, was the high proportion of widows, both young and old.

The overall treatment accorded immigrant widows by their Canadian Mennonite churches varied. Most of the discourse surrounding them viewed refugee widows as 'unfortunate,' 'weak,' and 'tragic.' A similar attitude prevailed in postwar Germany, where, according to Annemarie Tröger, the numerous 'women's families' created during the war 'were increasingly tagged as communities of the "needy," the last resort for economic and social losers.'[24] Some memory sources suggest that Mennonite immigrant widows felt maligned because of their status. One woman said: 'They started to criticize us in church [but] it wasn't our fault that the men were taken away during the war and the women came by themselves. For years and years we didn't know whether they were alive or where they were. Nobody seemed to understand that.'[25]

Since many of the women who arrived as widows were relatively young – in their thirties and forties – they may have been viewed with some suspicion by Canadian women, who perceived them as sexual competition. Women without men were, as Joan Chandler notes, a 'moral threat' whose reputations came under considerable scrutiny, particularly by other women.[26] According to one memory source, women from the postwar immigration were informally told by members of the church that they would be better off marrying 'English' men than Mennonite men.[27] Furthermore, women who were without men but with children were viewed as a burden that a potential second husband should avoid. A single man who had immigrated to Alberta after the war was counselled against marrying a widow with four children: 'What do you want with her and all her children. You should find someone younger who could bear your children,' he was told.[28] Ironically, and a vivid illustration of the double standard that existed, a young immigrant widow with no children was encouraged to marry a Canadian Mennonite widower because she would be 'doing missionary work,' given that he had two children.[29]

Immigrant widows were in the demanding position of being heads of their families, and of having control and decision-making power over family finances, for instance; yet they were cast in the powerless and stereotypical role of the burdensome widow in Canadian Mennonite communities. While women experienced the ambiguity of their own experiences of strength, independence, and resourcefulness and the weakness that was attributed to them in community attitudes, spoken and unspoken, they also shouldered dual roles within their own house-holds. In particular, widows with dependent children had to assume the gender roles of both mother and father. One widow, whose husband was evacuated to the eastern Soviet Union in 1941, immigrated to Canada with two preschool children. She recalled that it was 'very hard' being a single parent, especially in trying to fulfil the roles of both father and mother.[30] Reflecting on the significance of her mother's influence, the daughter of a widow similarly remarked, 'she was really a mother and a father. She was the only one that we could turn to.'[31]

As women without men in Canadian Mennonite communities, the immigrant widows were an anomaly. Particularly for those who had lost their husbands in the Soviet purges of the 1930s or during the war, marital status was ambiguous. Most of these women never received any official confirmation of their husbands' fate, although it was common to obtain second-hand accounts of starvation in a Siberian labour camp or violent death on the war front. The women functioned for all intents and purposes like widows and generally were treated as such, but their official marital status remained a grey area. In fact, in some reports and correspondence, women who had confirmation of a spouse's death were referred to as 'true' widows. The uncertainty of the identity of those without such confirmation became most obvious when the option of remarrying presented itself.

Many 'widows' took the position that if the slightest possibility existed that their husbands were alive, then remarriage was out of the question. Indeed, the emotional attachment that women continued to feel for men who had been absent from their lives for several decades and with whom some had lived for a relatively short time – sometimes only a matter of months – was striking. Annemarie Tröger, who has analysed the stories of German women in the Second World War, observes that the 'myth of marriage as the warm and secure refuge in difficult and unsafe times' was ironically sustained most strongly by war widows and single women, who idealized the missing men in their lives. These women in particular tried to justify their marriageless state by placing marriage on such an ideal plane that finding an adequate partner was out of the question.[32] Certainly, the idealization of lost spouses is evident in the memories of Mennonite widows, who without exception recalled their first husbands in glowing terms.

The grief that many widows continued to feel over the uncertainty of their husbands' fate was very real. When Anny Penner Klassen received news in 1956 that her husband had died in early 1942 in Siberia, she held a memorial service at her home in order to formally acknowledge his death, and perhaps subconsciously confirm her identity as a widow. She remarried four years later.[33] Some women were able to come to terms with the death of their spouses through dreams or premonitions. For instance, shortly after receiving her newlywed husband Aaron's last letter in August 1944, Agatha Janzen had a dream about him, in which she saw him lying on the battlefield with blood gushing from a wound in his head. Agatha considered this a premonition and believed that her dream occurred as Aaron was actually dying.[34] The strong attachment that women felt for their missing husbands prevented many from contemplating remarriage – even after several decades had passed – unless some indication, either tangible or intuitive, allowed them to bring closure to their first marriage.

For other women who had survived successfully without a spouse and were quite happy with their emotional and economic independence, remarriage was not a desirable option. One immigrant woman recalled that her mother had declined opportunities to remarry, 'largely because she did not want her children to have a step-father.'[35] Maria, a widowed mother of six children, expressed her ambivalence about men in a humorous way. According to her daughter, Maria received regular visits from a single man (possibly a widower) who lived across the street from her new home in British Columbia. When the visits became a little too frequent, Maria had said: 'If I married him, I would have to sleep with him. Oh No!'[36] The son of another widow observed that his mother was focused on 'making it' economically, rather than finding a husband, and that she often spoke of men with disdain, saying 'they don't know what life is all about.'[37] One immigrant remarked that 'very few' of the young widows that she knew remarried, especially after 'they settled in their life.'[38]

For yet another group of women, loneliness, the yearning for physical intimacy, and the quest for greater economic stability made remarriage a desirable option. However, the ambiguity of her marital status quickly became apparent when a widow indicated her intentions to marry again. The problem that this presented came to the attention of Mennonite churches in North America when it was learned that a significant number of common-law marriages existed among the scattered Mennonite refugees in Europe and also in the two newly established Mennonite colonies in Paraguay.

In 1947 Franz Janzen, a Canadian minister working among Mennonite refugees in Germany, wrote to the Board of Spiritual and Social Concerns (known as the *Fuersorgekomitee*) of the Canadian Mennonite Brethren Conference, asking for guidance on how to deal with the cases of remarriage that he had encountered. He pointed out that, although German law allowed for remarriage after five years of hearing no word from one's previous spouse, he was searching for a biblical answer to a very difficult question. Janzen felt it important that the Mennonite Brethren Church state its position on the matter, not only in Europe but also from Canada, and further, that perhaps a specific amount of time – five, ten, or fifteen years – might be determined after which an individual would be free to remarry.[39] The *Fuersorgekomitee* responded, after 'mature reflection and serious thought,' with the following statement addressed to the refugee community: 'Weighing most heavily on you is the long separation from precious family members, especially the separation from husbands without word over their fate. With deep emotion we saw in Paraguay the love and faithfulness to missing husbands. So it must remain until certain news of their death. For the children of God, the Holy Scriptures offer no way for remarriage. Death alone can separate husband and wife.'[40] Janzen learned of the refugees' experiences first-hand, saw with his own eyes their need to form intimate relationships, and, as a result, hoped that some liberal position might be adopted. North American leaders, however, were more rigid.

The problem of 'family disorganization,' as one Mennonite sociologist put it, was dealt with in 1947 by the two largest Mennonite conferences in North America.[41] Both the General Conference (GC) Mennonites and the Mennonite Brethren (MB) Conference took the position that it was impossible to permit a church member to remarry as long as there was uncertainty whether the first partner had died or not.[42] A remarriage that took place contrary to this ruling meant that a church member would be automatically excommunicated. The General Conference position was modified somewhat two years later when the Conference of Mennonites in Canada (the GC body in Canada) decided that those who chose to remarry could not be received as members into the church, though they also could not be refused communion, if they chose to partake of it.[43] Although the Canadian and Paraguayan governments, as well as Mennonite leaders in Paraguay, allowed for remarriage following a seven-year separation in which no word from the missing partner had been received, Canadian Mennonites held that no marriage could take place in the church where any doubt remained of the survival of the missing spouse.

More rigid positions tended to come from the top of the denominational hierarchy, but those in leadership positions, such as Franz Janzen, were not necessarily in agreement with absolute opposition to remarriage. For instance, in late 1949, the South-Saskatchewan representative on the Board of Spiritual and Social Concerns of the Canadian Mennonite Brethren Conference requested that the committee reassess its position against remarriage adopted the year before. C.C. Penner reported that the participants at the ministers' and deacons' meeting of the South-Saskatchewan MB Conference had found the committee's position 'too harsh,' given that the Canadian government allowed for remarriage after a seven-year waiting period.[44] In the minutes of its 1950 annual meeting, the Board of Spiritual and Social Concerns noted the request, but stated that as a satisfactory solution had already been found, the question had been withdrawn.[45]

At the level of congregations the issue was even less clear-cut. The official conference policy notwithstanding, some congregations chose to weigh each individual situation on its own merit. In many congregations, an initial attitude of rigidity and condemnation with respect to standards of morality that seemed to be compromised by problematic remarriages, gave way to greater tolerance and situational decision-making as the complexity of the issues and emotions involved became apparent. However the issue was dealt with at the local level, remarriage presented congregations with a totally new and highly perplexing problem. Of issues dealt with at the Waterloo-Kitchener United Mennonite Church in the postwar era, that of remarriage was considered 'more weighty' than the reform of the church's constitution. This congregation adopted the General Conference resolution that disallowed remarriage unless definite information was obtained regarding the demise of an individual's first partner.[46]

That Canadian Mennonites were initially at quite a loss as to how to deal with the issue is suggested by one early case that came up in Vineland, Ontario. The minister of the United Mennonite Church there, Nicolai Fransen, wrote to J.J. Thiessen in March 1948, regarding the situation of a young immigrant man who had arrived in Canada four months earlier. Apparently the young man, Jacob, had married a Catholic woman from the Soviet Union at a registry office in the Warthegau region of Poland. Three weeks later Jacob was taken into the German army, and, after one visit with his new bride, she disappeared with no trace, despite search efforts by the Red Cross after the war. Now he wished to marry a woman from Manitoba, whose uncle, a Mennonite minister, had indicated he was not against the marriage. Fransen sought

Thiessen's advice, since this was the first case of its kind in Ontario as far as he knew. He added that he feared Jacob would go his own way even if they did refuse. Thiessen responded in a straightforward manner, stating that the position adopted by the General Conference Mennonites and Mennonite Brethren was that no marriage could be carried out unless certain proof were obtained that the missing party was dead.[47] Unfortunately, the correspondence does not offer information regarding the outcome of this case; one might speculate that Jacob went ahead and married outside of the Mennonite Church, as other individuals would choose to do.

The story of one woman from Sargent Avenue Mennonite Church in Winnipeg was repeated many times elsewhere in Canada. That circumstances relating to her situation appear in brief references in church records over a ten-year period suggests that there were neither simple nor quick solutions to the issue of remarriage. Anna was born in the Ukraine in 1918, married there, and gave birth to a daughter in 1939.[48] The specific circumstances of her husband's fate are not mentioned, except for the fact that he was left in the Soviet Union when Anna and her daughter emigrated to Paraguay following the war. Anna probably immigrated to Canada around 1950. In 1955, church council minutes note Anna's remarriage to Gerhard, also a postwar immigrant, even though it had been learned that her first husband was still living in the Soviet Union. To complicate the situation, Gerhard too had a wife living in the Soviet Union. Given the circumstances, the church officials maintained that it would be impossible to tolerate her membership in the church. The bishop of the church indicated that he would report this to Anna in a 'gentle' manner. It appears that Gerhard was not a member of that congregation and therefore no action against him was called for. A note in church minutes from October of that year notes that Anna (she is still referred to by the surname of her first husband), despite her removal from the church's membership role, continued to attend Sunday services regularly. It would seem that she was still attending ten years later, since her case came up again in 1966. This time the concern is over her suitability, given her situation, as a Sunday school teacher. In a later church register (specific year unknown), Anna and Gerhard are listed together as a family under his surname. Additional information indicates that together they had a daughter in 1960 who was baptized at Sargent Avenue Church in 1976. It would seem that as the years passed and Anna continued to associate with the congregation, her membership was eventually restored.

Another case at Sargent revealed how complex family fragmentation and reconfiguration could become. Born in the Soviet Union in 1909, Heinrich had married a Russian woman in 1930. Two children were born in 1933 and 1940. Heinrich immigrated to Paraguay in 1946, his family left behind in the Soviet Union. Elizabeth, also a Soviet Mennonite, was born in 1911 and married in 1933. Her husband was arrested and exiled in 1937, the year that their only child was born. Elizabeth also immigrated to Paraguay after the war. In Paraguay Elizabeth and Heinrich met and were married in 1952, then immigrated to Canada. At the time of their marriage, neither Elizabeth nor Heinrich had received any word of their respective spouses, although shortly thereafter Heinrich learned that his first wife and children were still living in the Soviet Union.

In the early fall of 1960 their case first came to the attention of the Sargent church council, from whom they were seeking acceptance as church members. Although the congregation had dealt with individuals who were intending to remarry without confirmation of a previous spouse's death, this was the first instance in which the second marriage had already taken place. Now the church was faced, not with the decision of excluding a member, but with the question of whether to accept as church members a married couple, one of whom had a spouse still living. Heinrich and Elizabeth's petition came before a meeting of the congregation, where a vote was taken, resulting in 147 for and 3 against the acceptance of the couple as members at Sargent.

At one level, the vote was a highly definitive affirmation for Heinrich and Elizabeth and for the reality of their new family formation. It also demonstrated the dilemma facing the church, given that the marriage was already eight years old. If Sargent did not accept them, another congregation probably would; thus, church growth was also a factor. In fact, some couples who were refused remarriage, or were excluded by Mennonite churches, left for other denominations altogether, such as the Lutheran Church.

At another level, the decision was an affirmation of the 'happy united family' that was normative for that community. Remarriages offered the approximation, if not the complete restoration, of the ideal family configuration. In Canadian churches with a significant number of female-headed households from the postwar migration, the presence of so many widows was frequently cited as a problem, and their very existence was a painful reminder of the dislocation and tragedy experienced by the Mennonite settlements in the Soviet Union. By tacitly allowing remarriages to take place, churches were diminishing the number of potentially burdensome widows in their midst, and were also putting behind them a history of community disintegration that was almost too painful to acknowledge.

In a number of cases, the church's acceptance of remarriage may have been justified on the grounds that the supplicant was viewed as the 'innocent' party, given the prior remarriage of his or her spouse in the Soviet Union. Several cases dealt with at the Niagara United Mennonite Church in Ontario suggest that the weighing of guilt or innocence was an influential factor in the congregation's final decision. For instance, Isaac was married in 1941 in the Soviet Union, only to be separated from his new wife when he was drafted into the German military. After the war he had been held in a prisoner-of-war camp. His wife in the meantime had been sent back to the Soviet Union, where she remarried in 1951. In 1962 Isaac was married for the second time (by a Lutheran minister in St Catharines), and was accepted as a member, seemingly with little debate, into the Niagara United Mennonite Church in 1966.[49] Isaac's young age and the apparent lack of children from his first marriage may have been additional factors that made the congregation willing to recognize his second chance at family life. Similar leniency is evident in other cases involving individuals in young adulthood whose first experience of marriage had been very brief.

Greater tolerance for remarriage also existed when an individual exhibited earnest effort to obtain confirmation of a previous spouse's death or when it seemed 'likely' that a missing spouse was no longer alive. In the case of a young woman married only a few months, many letter-writing efforts had resulted only in a 'missing-in-action' report regarding her husband. Nevertheless her congregation agreed that the available evidence pointed to the fact that he had fallen during a particularly hard battle in France in 1944 and so recognized her remarriage.[50] The unlikelihood of a woman's husband still being alive, despite a lack of certain evidence, was the stated reason given at First Mennonite Church in Winnipeg, where the congregation voiced no objections to a remarriage in their midst. In this 1959 case, it seemed 'reasonable' that a man, exiled in 1938, was no longer living after twenty years.[51] In this case, the passage of time was a softening ingredient to the official stance. In both of the above situations, permission was qualified by the reminder that all such cases were still subject to the resolution against remarriage by the denominational body and each must be considered on its own merit.

The struggle that congregations experienced over cases of remarriage revealed above all a tension between strict conference-directed positions based on tradition and biblical interpretation, and the complex reality of the lives of most postwar immigrants, who were eager to become part of the church. While Canadian Mennonites became more situational and somewhat less rigid in their management of the remarriage dilemma over time, the softening may have resulted as much from immigrant pressure and their proven contribution to church life as from an internal shift in position. For instance, in 1959 an immigrant widow wrote a letter to J.J. Thiessen (in his position as chair of the Conference of Mennonites in Canada) in which she pushed the conference to re-examine its position on remarriage. Her letter, which was at times poignant, at times sarcastic, and definitely challenging, raised a number of issues that were central to the handling and outcome of remarriage cases.

The woman, Ingrid (not her real name), was particularly concerned with those cases like her own, in which one-half of a separated couple had already married a second time. Ingrid had been married for twenty years; she had lived with her husband for only four years when they were split apart during the war. After immigrating to Canada, she learned that her husband had remarried in the Soviet Union and had two children with his second wife. After corresponding with her husband, Ingrid received word from her brother-in-law that her letters were damaging and that her husband had shut himself off and was neglecting his children. She wrote to Thiessen that she wished her husband well and knew it would be better for him if she either died or remarried. Ingrid went on to point out, with some sarcasm, the response of the conference and church elders to her hopes of remarriage: 'The Conference says however – No! From the *Aeltester* [elders] one gets the answer: Naturally you are free, when your husband has already been married for 8 years and has children. And you should also remarry, however you must leave the church and resign from all church work. And we cannot marry you, you must go to a Lutheran pastor.' 'Do you call that free?' she asked Thiessen. Ingrid rhetorically asked whether it was right that a woman be put out of the Mennonite Church for remarrying, so that she ended up losing all spiritual feelings, or (perhaps worse?) teaching Sunday school in the Lutheran denomination. At the same time, she urged that, despite the church's position on marital breakup, a situational approach be adopted that took into account the circumstances of the times.

Perhaps even more shocking to Thiessen and his colleagues was

Ingrid's comparison of the remarriage issue with the biblical parable of the Good Samaritan. In her allegory, Ingrid identified herself and others like her as the wounded man lying on the road, having been robbed by murderers of his – or, in this case, their – loved ones. The conference was the priest who saw the wounded, heard their moans, but responded, 'Why should we dirty ourselves?' Similarly, the local congregation was the Levite, who also passed by, exhorting the wounded to carry their cross with honour, as Jesus had done. The Good Samaritan was the 'man on the street' who, without thinking long, lifted the 'bloody heart,' applied ointment, and hastened the healing process. 'Who do you think,' she challenged Thiessen, 'of these three would receive the greatest reward?'

After scolding the conference for its hypocrisy, Ingrid proposed that the conference establish a policy whereby, once a certain number of years had passed after one-half of the couple had remarried and had children, the 'innocent' half be free to also remarry without being excluded from the church. She implored Thiessen to take her letter to the conference delegates. Thiessen passed Ingrid's letter on to six of his colleagues, one of whom replied that a deviation from the conference's earlier position on the question could hardly be expected, nor did he feel that recognition of an innocent party would truly ease anyone's conscience.[52]

Ingrid's appeal summarized a number of issues that were central to the remarriage debate: the question of whether one-half of a separated couple could be considered innocent; the apparent hypocrisy in a church position that sympathized with the need for couples to remarry yet rejected them as church members, even losing devout members to other denominations; the highly doctrinaire and principled attitude of much of the church's leadership versus the situational approach that immigrants had taken throughout much of their lives. Yet in reality, even while the conference made no official alteration in its stance, many congregations did, as we have seen, deal with remarriage on a case-by-case basis. That the church was really dealing with each situation on its own merit is revealed in a 1968 statement in Sargent church minutes, which notes that in the earlier years a rigid stance of exclusion had been taken toward remarriages, but at the present 'we have become more tolerant and try to find practical ways to address the issue.'[53]

For women who did remarry, with or without opposition from their churches, the outcome also varied. Some cases of remarriage were undoubtedly happy and no more problematic than any other marriage;

yet there is substantial evidence, particularly in the memory sources of postwar immigrants, that for some the choice to remarry had not been a good one. Katie, who immigrated to Canada in 1948 with four daughters, decided to remarry in 1955. Confirmation that her first husband died in 1942 arrived just prior to her wedding, though she had decided to go ahead even without official word. Initially her daughters, all but one of whom had left home, felt good about the marriage, expecting that 'now she would be taken care of.' However, their opinions began to change as time went on. In one daughter's words:

For my mother it was very hard. She somehow expected a little more. She found out later on that the husband she married didn't really have anything. He had debts too because he had bought a farm. She worked very hard on the farm. He was a widower with two children. It didn't work out too well with the children either. When they got married she asked her husband to tell the children to take everything that's theirs so that when she comes in she knows what is ours. He says he did but when she was there things disappeared all the time.[54]

In another case, a widow who lived in Ontario and whose first husband had been arrested during the Stalin purges met a man who was from the same village in the Soviet Union. At the age of seventy she married him, and the couple moved to British Columbia. According to one of her three daughters, 'It turned out very sad. He was everything we girls had feared. He didn't look after her. All he wanted was a housekeeper.' When it became apparent that her health was in danger, the daughters retrieved their mother from British Columbia and took legal action to prevent her second husband from trying to take her back.[55] The sentiments expressed in these two stories and evident in other accounts indicate that, for some widows, the decision to remarry brought neither emotional nor financial comfort – an especially sad ending to their lives, given the many other tragedies they had faced.

In choosing to remarry, with or without knowledge of a first spouse's death, some widows may have been trying to create a 'normal' family, either one that existed in memories of the past or one that emulated the families of their relatives and neighbours in Canada. In a society that viewed the husband as the proper 'head of the family,' widows may also have been attempting to escape from the anomalous gender roles they had assumed following the death or disappearance of spouses. It seems ironic, given the wartime experiences that saw most widows care for their families to almost heroic proportions, but women themselves and the people who surrounded them seemed to place a high priority on the necessity of a male caregiver. The increasing tolerance toward remarriage points to a desire on the part of the church's officials and members to incorporate widows and their children into a traditional family structure of which the husband was properly the head. Mennonites, after all, took their prescriptive cues for gender roles from biblical passages regarding male headship in the universal order and also in the home. The widow who remarried ceased to be a sexual threat and was also viewed as less likely to become a financial or emotional burden on the community. The self-sufficiency and independence modelled by women who had delivered themselves and their families from horrendous wartime situations may have posed a dilemma, if not an actual threat, to the notions of familial hierarchy held by Canadian Mennonites.

In some households, families were re-created through unexpected and almost miraculous reunions with missing family members. Following the death of Stalin in 1953 and the subsequent amnesty for prisoners of war in the Soviet Union, some women in Canada began to receive news from husbands who had managed to stay alive in the gruelling conditions of the hard labour camps. The British Columbia Provincial Relief Committee reported in March 1954 of one recent example in which a 'supposed' widow from Greendale had received news from her husband, who had been missing for thirteen years.[56] In the case of Lena, a widow with two young children who arrived in Canada in 1948, the reunification had elements of the miraculous. As a young woman, Lena had many opportunities to remarry in Canada but, lacking confirmation of her husband's fate, she chose not to. After fifteen years, Lena received news one Easter morning that he was still living in the Soviet Union. Jacob had not remarried either, and so the two began corresponding. Lena began a sixteen-year campaign lobbying the Canadian government and writing endless appeals to have him emigrate. After several occasions when Jacob's permit to leave the Soviet Union was denied at the last minute, Lena began to lose hope. Ironically, the final telegram of confirmation never reached Lena, and so one night in the early 1970s she was awakened by a telephone call that announced Jacob's arrival at the Vancouver airport. They were reunited after a separation of over thirty years.

Although some couples reunited in this manner found that after such a long separation they were no longer compatible, Lena insists that she and Jacob simply resumed what had been a very happy marriage.

Undoubtedly there were adjustments to make, especially in the area of gender roles, which had been altered when Lena became head of the family in Jacob's absence. Lena continued to do all the business because her husband spoke no English and she was thirty years ahead of him in acculturating to Canadian society. Within the household, she frequently found herself interrupted while doing 'male' tasks, such as hammering a nail, by her husband, who would step in and ask, 'What am I here for?'[57]

Another means of restoring the family was through organized reunification efforts. Shortly after the war ended, the Mennonite Central Committee established a tracing service to help North American Mennonites locate missing relatives and bring about reunions. The service's brief, but numerous case files contained 15,000–17,000 names of missing persons and were cross-referenced with the tracing services of other organizations. The service remained active well into the 1960s. An MCC employee said that, initially, those working with the tracing service would be very excited when they located a lost one and would immediately send telegrams to both sides of the family. Later they became more low-key when they realized that such news created mixed emotions, especially when new marriages had occurred and children had been born of those new unions.[58] In some cases, the decision was made not to reunite. In a few cases, a husband and wife, separated for possibly thirty years, found that reunification was a problem, even if neither had remarried. In one instance, a woman living in Canada travelled to Germany to be reunited with her husband, who had emigrated there from the Soviet Union. They were together several weeks, but decided that they had 'drifted too far apart' and were 'not compatible any longer.' In another case, great happiness accompanied the reunification of a couple in Canada, but about a year later they separated, one remaining in Winnipeg while the other moved to Ontario. The couple, both in their sixties, found that 'each had learned to cope on his and her own' and 'living together just didn't work out anymore.'[59] The happiness of other reunion efforts was hampered by the death of one spouse just prior to or shortly following the meeting, or by situations in which joining one's spouse in Canada meant leaving one's adult children behind in the Soviet Union.

Despite the mixed experiences that the postwar immigrants had with remarriage and reunification, marriage remained the ideal state and an important goal for most never-married adults, both men and women. Although their widowed mothers may have represented an oddity in postwar Canadian society, the adult children who arrived after the war seemed eager to establish the kind of normal family unit that they themselves were robbed of. They were also, however subconsciously, fitting into the patterns of Canadian society. In his study of household formation in postwar Canada, John R. Miron notes that marriage went through a phase of popularity in the period up to the 1960s; during this so-called 'marriage rush,' adults of all ages were increasingly likely to marry.[60] Postwar thinking that idealized the nuclear family may have contributed to as well as reflected the pro-marriage trend.

Although comprehensive data do not exist regarding the marriage rates for Mennonite refugees in Canada, anecdotal and memory sources suggest that single immigrants, both women and men, were relatively quick to marry after establishing themselves in their new homes. For many, romance had already developed during the refugee years in Europe. Mark Wyman observes that 'wholesale weddings' became commonplace in DP camps as a way of compensating for wartime dislocation and to make up for the loneliness and isolation felt by many refugees who had been torn from their family members.[61] Frequently, however, relationships that developed prior to emigration would have to be tested by some type of separation. Some engagements were broken when one party became eligible to emigrate while the other did not. Young Mennonites who had developed relationships with *Reichsdeutsche* (German citizens) were faced with the option of ending the romance or enduring temporary separation in the hopes that the Canadian government's initial closed-door policy toward Germans would change. As a result, the Canadian Mennonite Board of Colonization received occasional correspondence from new immigrants who wished to sponsor fiancés/fiancées who remained in Germany. One young woman who wrote to the board in November 1948 would have to wait two years before Canadian immigration policy changed, thus allowing her intended husband, a German citizen, to immigrate.[62] In cases where a young Mennonite man had served in the German military and was sent to a prisoner-of-war camp, his fiancée would likely precede him to Canada to await his release, sometimes several years later.

Even if the question of German nationality or military service did not separate engaged couples, other circumstances related to immigration rules and requirements could. Couples assigned to different places of work were expected to fulfil their labour contracts and/or obligations to sponsors before they could set up house together. One young man in Alberta, inquiring whether his fiancée, who was on a farm labour contract in a different community in the same province, could be relocated to the same locale, was told by J.J. Thiessen that it would be best if she stayed to fulfil her contract. In the meantime, he said, they could meet and plan for the future, given that they lived not too far apart.[63]

For some single immigrants, whether arriving in Canada with or without immediate family members, marriage offered the chance at beginning a whole family, unlikely to be torn apart by politics or war. One young woman, who immigrated as an orphan with two younger brothers, married at the young age of nineteen, three years after arriving in Canada. Mary Rempel, whose story was told at the outset of this chapter, married early partly to recover a father-figure in her life, a motive she readily admitted. 'I got married so young partly I think out of security. I felt vulnerable all my life since I was five [the year her father was arrested]. And here was a gentleman very much like what I used to know, my Dad. Who I could trust.'[64] Justina also married young, to a man she had met in a DP camp in Germany, two years after arriving with her sister in Canada in 1949. She proudly described her wedding, which she had financed completely on her own. Her wedding dress of lace and pearls cost a week's wages at $15.50, while the cake alone cost $3.50. She also purchased bridesmaid dresses for three of her friends. The bouquet was store-bought and was couriered by bus from Winnipeg to the southern Manitoba town where the wedding was held. In Justina's words: 'I did the whole wedding. I invited the whole church. I think there were 250 people. We had cookies, cheese, buns. I arranged everything. I even gave the ladies in the kitchen some money for all they did. They were very impressed with how far an orphan had come.' Happily married for over forty years, with seven children born in nine years, Justina's memories of marriage are positively correlated with the end of her refugee identity.[65]

The pattern of Justina's wedding fit the societal trends of the 1950s in which dresses, cakes, and flowers were increasingly elaborate and store-bought. However, certain 'modern' wedding practices were difficult, if not impossible, for fatherless refugee women to follow. Katie Dirks Friesen, who immigrated with her mother and sister in 1948, found herself in the middle of a tug-of-war over which man would accompany her down the aisle at her wedding in the spring of 1950. A former employer of Katie's had wanted to act as her father and give Katie away, but her fiancé would not agree to it. Even when the couple were ready to walk into the church, the would-be father was nearby to see if the groom had changed his mind.[66] Whatever examples of female autonomy that Katie had seen or experienced in her family of women undoubtedly paled in this simple but profound reminder of male ownership and dominance on the part of both father and husband.

Anna's memories of marriage are so negative that they are almost completely repressed in her personal narrative. Anna was already married in Germany and arrived in Canada with her husband, separately from her mother and sisters. However, her account of travel and arrival in Canada contains anecdotes that include her mother and sisters, with no reference to her husband at all. Further conversation revealed that she divorced her husband after an abusive and unhappy marriage, and thus her oral life history, while highly personal on many other topics, initially eliminated what was for her the most painful part of her life. Although she moved with her husband to western Canada, and had a daughter there, his abuse made her begin to fear for her life, and so she returned to the community where her family had settled: 'It didn't work out. I was too unhappy. I couldn't manage. I tried my best. There was no way out. After he tried to kill me one night ... there was no way out ... for me to save my child and me, we had to leave.'[67]

As theorists of memory and personal narrative have argued, individuals frequently eliminate from their life story elements that are at variance with the 'social memory' of their communities.[68] In leaving her former husband out of the main text of her narrative, Anna was not only repressing that which was especially painful for her, she was also removing an episode in her life that did not fit the culture of her community. In the 1950s, domestic violence was spoken of little in Mennonite communities, while divorce was altogether proscribed by the church. Anna was quietly allowed to remain in the Mennonite Church, despite her divorce, but her experience marginalized her within that group.

Anna's life was made even more painful when her widowed mother, who had remarried in Canada, experienced a similar pattern of abuse. Within Anna's family, attempts to re-create the kind of family life that had been lost when her father was taken remained elusive, both for her mother and for herself. Her recollections of these years are shaped by her own feelings of failure over a broken marriage, her regret that she was unable to protect her mother from a similar experience, and her awareness that, because of the church's disapproval of divorce, she remained forever outside the normative patterns of family life.

At least in the early years following migration, young adults who married within the Mennonite fold tended to marry persons from the same migrant group. A good indication of the extremely narrow definitions applied to Mennonite exogamy can be found in the fact that marriages between Canadian Mennonites and postwar immigrants were frequently described as 'mixed' marriages, this despite the fact that kinship relations existed, particularly with the Russian immigrants of the 1920s. As a sign of good relations between the two groups, one church history noted that of the seventy-one marriage ceremonies performed between 1956 and 1962, twenty-seven were cases in which 'one marriage partner was a recent immigrant and the other an immigrant of earlier times or a child of the latter.'[69]

Although no comprehensive survey of this form of endogamy exists, one localized study categorized all marriages within the Mennonite community in Leamington, Ontario, between 1952 and 1962. Krista Taves found very little marriage or courtship between Canadian Mennonites and postwar immigrants until the late 1950s. She explains this pattern in part by referring to demography but also suggests that social boundaries and discrimination played a role as well. For example, she cites one incident in which a young Canadian Mennonite man was 'severely discouraged' by his family from pursuing a relationship with a woman because she was a recent immigrant.[70] In the story of the Bergen family by Gerhard Lohrenz, young Henry Bergen wanted to marry his Canadian Mennonite girlfriend, but her parents 'were not overjoyed' by the fact that he was 'just a new immigrant earning 40 cents an hour.'[71] Unease with such 'mixed' marriages had little to do with incompatibility – cultural or economic – at the personal level, but rather reflected a social hierarchy that developed between settled Mennonites and the newcomers.

Whether orphans, unmarried mothers, remarrying widows, or never-married adults, Mennonite immigrant women keenly felt the contrast between their own fragmented family history and the happy and united families that were idealized, if not fully realized, in postwar Canadian society. In aspiring to the ideal, refugees themselves and their sponsoring Mennonite communities sought ways of reconfiguring family life on Canadian terms, which for older immigrants meant recovering family forms remembered from their childhood, and for young immigrants, creating family types that they had hardly known at all. Finding homes for orphans or celebrating weddings of never-married adults was gratifying evidence of successful assimilation. Accepting unmarried mothers with their children, or dealing with the weighty issue of remarriage, was more troublesome and prompted reactions ranging from paternalism, to genuine empathy, to rejection and discrimination. Whatever the individual response, the issue of remarriage in particular reinforced the vast gaps in experience between newcomers and Canadian Mennonites, a divergence that would make itself felt in other areas of church life.

7

Learning to Be Mennonite

As young women in their early twenties, Helena Giesbrecht and her sister immigrated to Canada in 1948, their parents having been delayed in Germany for medical reasons. Helena worked as household help for relatives in southern Manitoba in the first year, and after experiencing a religious conversion at an evangelistic meeting, felt she was ready to be baptized into a Mennonite church. The practice in most Mennonite churches at the time was that after a baptismal candidate had given her testimony before the congregation, someone was called upon to verify her character and suitability for baptism. After Helena had given her testimony of conversion, the minister followed with the customary question, 'Who knows this girl?' Although Helena had requested that her employer (a member of the church) speak on her behalf, apparently he had not shown up that Sunday, and so she was left in the awkward and humiliating position of being without a witness. And even though she was well known in the church by that point, mainly because of her outgoing personality, no one else came forward at the necessary moment. Although the baptism went ahead, the incident confirmed for Helena her status and identity as a 'Russian girl,' a 'Waisenkind' (orphan), and an outsider.[1] Although Helena felt she had already made great progress in adapting to Canadian ways, the experience taught her that she still had much to learn about being a Canadian Mennonite.

This final chapter describes the integration of Soviet and east European immigrants into Mennonite community and church life in the decade and a half following their arrival in Canada. The discussion examines the perceptions that Canadian Mennonites had of the religious condition of the newcomers and the ways in which church life was altered by the inclusion of so many women without men. From the perspective of the immigrants, becoming settled involved the challenge of understanding and accommodating to a variety of church practices and acceptable modes of behaviour. The end result was a hierarchy, within Mennonite church communities, based mainly on period of migration.

Alongside the practical task of making a living, and the emotional one of reconfiguring family life, the postwar Mennonite immigrants faced the challenge of integrating themselves into Canadian society and into the culture and communities of their co-religionists. As refugees, they were certainly not alone in experiencing the impact of Canadian attitudes toward the one and a half million displaced persons and other immigrants that flooded into Canada in the decade after the war. Although many newcomers recalled the welcome and sympathy of Canadians toward the war sufferers, there were also numerous incidents of discrimination and prejudicial attitudes. The pejorative appellation of 'DP,' when used in derision, was especially familiar as a display of the nativist response of some Canadians to postwar immigrants.[2] This label, and the attitudes of contempt and ridicule that accompanied it, was well remembered by Mennonites as well. One Mennonite immigrant remembered being called a 'dumb DP' by one of her own cousins, while another reflected that she always felt like an outsider, regardless of the national context. In Russia, they were set apart as 'the Germans,' she said, while in Germany they were 'the Russians,' and in Canada they became 'the DPs.'[3]

One might expect that the acceptance of Mennonite refugees into their own ethno-religious and familial community would have offered a retreat from the hostilities directed at them by other Canadians, but this was not necessarily the case. As earlier chapters have demonstrated, the relations between Canadian Mennonites and the eight thousand refugees whom they sponsored as immigrants was at times strained and awkward. In a 1959 research paper based on oral interviews with postwar immigrants done in 1951, one analyst wrote: 'It is the preconception of the Canadian Mennonites that these more recent immigrants have very definite characteristics which are difficult to appreciate. As a result of this idea there is some friction between the earlier established Mennonites and those that have arrived more recently.'[4] Friction between different migrations within an ethnic group was not unique to the Mennonites. For instance, within Ukrainian and Lithuanian communities, there were strong ideological divisions between communist sympathizers among earlier migrants and the postwar arrivals, who were anti-

Soviet and even accused of being fascist.[5] At least one individual expressed the opinion that the postwar Mennonite immigrants viewed the Soviet Union in more negative terms – based on their experiences of collectivization and repression – than the earlier migrants, who maintained memories of the 'paradise' that Russia had once been for the Mennonites.[6] For the most part, however, political differences among the Mennonites had more to do with German than Soviet nationalism. In some communities, tensions arose over what was perceived as overly 'pro-German' and 'sometimes pro-Hitler' allegiances on the part of the postwar immigrants, many of whom viewed Germany as their liberator from Soviet oppression.[7] Beyond the ideological discord, the gaps in experience, particularly in the realm of church life, made for moments of misunderstanding on both sides.

Differing historical experience inevitably made for varying degrees of conflict between Canadian Mennonites and the newly arrived refugees from the Soviet Union and eastern Europe, notwithstanding the many blood ties between the two groups. Differences revolved around such issues as language, remarriage, lifestyle, and understandings of church doctrine. The published history of the Niagara United Mennonite Church described the integration of newcomers thus: 'In spite of good cooperation, there occured [sic] at times, differences of opinion and misunderstandings about church policy.'[8] In her study of the relations between second migrant (1920s) and third migrant (post–Second World War) Russian Mennonites in Leamington, Ontario, Krista M. Taves found evidence of a 'hierarchical mentality,' even a class differential between the two groups. She suggested that the Canadian Mennonites were 'incredibly paternalistic' toward the newcomers and were suspicious in particular of the latter's style of religiosity and German nationalism.[9] A young man who arrived in Winnipeg via Paraguay in the mid-1950s characterized the demeanor toward the immigrants in his Mennonite Brethren congregation as one of 'toleration.'[10] And while numerous memory sources suggest that Canadian Mennonites were welcoming and relations generally good, few immigrants minimized the extent to which differences in experience, lifestyle, and religious understanding had to be overcome in order for a harmonious relationship to develop.

Sociologist Raymond Breton has suggested that, 'because of peculiarities of each period of immigration, newcomers may have ideological orientations that are so incompatible with those of the established community that the two segments do not see each other as authentic representatives of the culture.'[11] The relationship between different groups of Mennonite migrants may not have been alienated to this extent, but neither was the encounter akin to 'a big family reunion,' at least not always.[12] While Canadian Mennonites were ready to *take in* the refugees, much as one might take in a lost child, it was perhaps less easy for them to *include* the newcomers, if one uses the criteria of ethnic inclusion described by Raymond Breton. He suggests that these criteria are either denotative, that is, membership comes with the possession of certain traits or characteristics, or normative, meaning that in order to be included one must behave in certain ways in particular circumstances. Although the two groups had in common the traits of ancestry, religious heritage, and familial ties, thus *denoting* the identity of the postwar migrants as Mennonite, the newcomers had much to learn in order to meet the standards of *normativity* of their Canadian co-ethnics.

One of the issues that caused tension between the new immigrants and the Canadian Mennonites was the fact that the former were not as attached to an agricultural lifestyle as their co-religionists thought they should be. Officials with the Canadian Mennonite Board of Colonization (CMBC) in particular became concerned with the rate at which the immigrants left their farm placements as soon as they could, sometimes before their one-year contracts were completed. In 1950, J.J. Thiessen wrote to William T. Snyder, the executive officer of the Mennonite Central Committee in Pennsylvania, saying, 'Our farmers are somewhat hesitant to make applications for farm help because many immigrants have disappointed the sponsors, in not living up to the agreement and leaving the farm for the city. Repeatedly we have admonished our newcomers not to do that, but they find it very hard to live on a lonely farm, far away from city facilities and life.'[13] In part, the tendency of the immigrants to urbanize was attributed to their refugee experience, which saw them on the move for many years and living in crowded camps. According to J.J. Thiessen, 'Having lived in congested areas, they seem to feel lonesome on our scattered farms. It takes time for them to get adjusted and to settle down to a normal life under new conditions.'[14] Expressing similar concerns over immigrants who were tempted to seek their fortunes in the city, the chairman of the British Columbia Provincial Relief Committee said: 'We continue to believe that as Mennonites we do much better when we stay on the land.'[15] With this in mind, the CMBC undertook to explore agricultural opportunities in relatively unsettled regions of British Columbia and Alberta. The board felt that 'the immigrants should at first get acquainted with farming and working conditions in Canada, repay their transportation, and then get settled on the land.'[16] However, given the lack of necessary capital to purchase land, as well as the lack of desire on the part of immigrants either to move to remote areas or, in some cases, to take up farming at all, these settlement plans did not get much past the idea stage.

The expectation that the majority of immigrants would become agriculturalists revealed a misplaced notion on the part of Canadians regarding the skills and aspirations of the newcomers and did not take into account the postwar Canadian economy. First of all, opportunities to get established in farming were costly and limited, whereas urban and industrial jobs were plentiful. Secondly, those men who were adults during the 1930s – already relatively few in number – had experienced farming in terms of collectivization; many were not interested in farming, nor had they the skills and experience to become independent farm operators. Furthermore, while some widows did purchase small berry farms in British Columbia, the expectations of Canadian Mennonites did not address the demography of the migrant group, for whom the family farm enterprise would have been extremely difficult to realize.

Alongside the concern that refugee families were not inclined toward farming lay a general uneasiness, even distrust, of the moral character of many newcomers to Canada. Suspicions about unseemly moral behaviour were directed against the DPs generally, not just the Mennonites. In her discussion of Lithuanian DPs who immigrated to Canada on domestic contracts, Milda Danys quotes H.L. Keenleyside of the Immigration Branch as saying: 'As you know, there have been suggestions that experiences through which some of these women have gone have had a bad effect on their characters and habits.' It was feared that wartime experiences such as 'bombings and famine, the necessity of lying and stealing, the danger of rape, overcrowded living conditions, the humiliations and pressures of the DP camps' might have an adverse affect on the conduct of women as domestics in Canadian homes.[17] Apparently, the moral status of Ukrainian DPs was a concern of officials of the Ukrainian Catholic Church in Canada, who referred specifically to the 'loosening of marital and family ties' among newcomers of that group.[18]

Expressed fears about the moral disposition of Mennonite immigrants were rarely phrased in specific terms. On the one hand, such fears arose from the assumption that the suppression of Christian practice in the Soviet Union for over a decade had resulted in a decay of morals and values. At the same time, vague references to 'wartime experiences' – which likely included bribery, stealing, lying, and sexual encounters, and, for the men, military service – created a general moral cloud over the immigrants. Knowledge of the common-law marriages that existed among the new colonists in Paraguay also contributed to a generalized negative attitude toward the entire postwar migrant group. In his 1950 report, the chairman of the British Columbia Provincial Relief Committee noted that although most of the immigrants had made the committee happy, there were also quite a few difficult cases that had caused considerable frustration, effort, and money, due to some immigrants' immoral lifestyle and demands for government relief.[19]

Many Mennonite churches in Canada during this era held strong positions against forms of behaviour and lifestyle that were seen to follow modern secular trends and were often described as 'worldly.' As the forces of urbanization and assimilation increasingly threatened Mennonite ethno-religious identity, frequent warnings against forbidden practices arose out of efforts to maintain sectarian boundaries between Mennonites and 'the world.' Rigid controls were simultaneously reinforced by the theological influences of evangelical fundamentalism and piety that, as Harvey Neufeldt has pointed out, were especially attractive to Mennonite preachers in the 1950s.[20]

One immigrant, who recalled frequent preaching on such things as dress codes, hair length, silk stockings, and make-up – described as 'the preacher's harping on women's behaviour' – felt that the proscriptions of the day pertained to women more than to men.[21] To the extent that behavioural standards were directed more at women than men, this position was perhaps a gendered reaction to the liberalization of women's roles that had occurred in Canada during wartime. Harvey Neufeldt, analysing the Mennonite community at Yarrow, British Columbia, also suggests that, as a way of regulating sexual behaviour, in their codes of piety 'church leaders, all male, paid special attention to women.'[22] The degree to which a strict stance was held varied between Mennonite conferences and also among individual congregations and according to locale. The Mennonite Brethren tended to be more conservative on matters of external conduct, but there were also some General Conference churches with ministers who were described as 'MB-like' in their outlook.

For women, cut or curled hair, make-up, or any particular dress style deemed immodest, prompted sermonizing, informal discipline, and, in some cases, an official written prohibition from the church hierarchy. Even in an urban congregation like Home Street Mennonite Church, in downtown Winnipeg, two members wrote to their pastor as late as 1961 asking whether it was permissible for women to cut their hair or get a permanent.[23]

Dress was one area in which postwar immigrant women had to adapt quickly to standards acceptable to Canadian Mennonites or risk being criticized and possibly ostracized. Lina Wohlgemut, a young widow with three children, arrived in Canada on a Friday in the late fall of 1949. The next day her sister-in-law, who had immigrated one year earlier, took her shopping for a hat, since it was very important that Lina, as a married woman, 'conform to the church's expected dress code and have her head covered for church the next day.'[24] Even if there was nothing particularly worldly or improper about their dress, some immigrants felt that just being different posed a problem. One young woman felt overwhelmed by all the new things she had to learn in Canada, such as using deodorant and wearing clothes that matched. She said: 'Everybody was criticizing us. We combed our hair differently. When we put on clothes, we thought they were clean, but they didn't match. We were lucky if we had something for the top, the middle, and the bottom. This idea that things had to match ... was so new to us.'[25]

The concern about dress and hairstyles extended to other aspects of lifestyle that provoked comments about immorality and worldliness. J. Wichert, a Canadian minister who worked with Mennonite refugees in Europe, reportedly considered them 'lost to the Mennonite faith' because they 'drank, danced, smoked, and visited theatres.'[26] Certainly, many of the immigrants did follow such practices. Young men, many of whom used tobacco and alcohol in moderation, soon abstained altogether under the prohibitions of Canadian ministers. A British Columbia minister, remembered with fondness by many immigrants, had the reputation for making brief, five-minute visits to newcomers, often while they worked in the berry fields. He would usually ask whether they were 'happy in the Lord,' whether they still smoked, and, if so, when they planned to quit.[27]

Particularly during their several-year sojourn in Germany, many of the immigrants had attended music concerts and theatres and read popular German literature. One young man who considered himself quite culturally experienced – 'I had seen the world' – was shocked to discover that bowling was considered worldly.[28] Even in Germany a widow was chastised before the refugee congregation for attending the cinema with her young son, and more generally for the 'worldly' life that she had followed during the war years.[29] And after immigrating to

Canada, one young man regretfully gave up his trumpet playing, a talent that he had displayed in bands in Moscow.[30]

Another custom practised by the postwar immigrants but generally condemned by Canadian Mennonites was dancing. For most of the immigrants, dancing was something they had grown up with and participated in, especially during their years in Germany. Regardless of whether an individual had a strong sense of religious faith or not, dancing was not something that had been linked to Christian values, the way it had become in North America. Newcomers quickly discovered, however, that even if enjoyed by Canadian Mennonite lay people, dancing was something definitely frowned upon by the leadership, increasingly so in the 1950s. For instance, one woman recalled that at her own wedding a dance was held at a hall in town, following the ceremony and meal at the Mennonite church. The festivities began with traditional Russian Mennonite circle games (folk dances), but just when they had started the first 'real' dance, the minister arrived and then abruptly left. 'He just came at the wrong time,' she said.[31] Although most newcomers found it difficult to understand why dancing was wrong, they conformed to the social limits expected of them if that was required to meet the Canadian Mennonite standard. As one woman recalled, 'I became a Christian here and [not dancing] went with it.'[32] Acquiescence did not come without some chafing, as the following reflection suggests: 'Everything seemed strict to me because we weren't used to it. We loved dancing and all these kind of things. In Germany every weekend we went dancing and [in Canada] that was strictly taboo. All kinds of things were taboo that I couldn't understand why.'[33]

The growing opposition to dancing and other vices in this era was reflected in numerous official warnings issued by congregations and conferences. In 1954 the United Mennonite Conference of Ontario sent a message to churches expressing concern about participation in such worldly practices as dancing, use of alcohol and tobacco, attendance at movies, and the inordinate use of cosmetics.[34] The same year an Ontario Mennonite Brethren congregation listed abstinence from drinking, smoking, dancing, and theatre attendance as prerequisites for its baptismal candidates.[35] In 1961 the Conference of Mennonites in Canada observed that dancing, particularly in connection with weddings and other special occasions, had become a problem in some locales.[36]

That the growing problem of dancing was referred to numerous times in the records of one Winnipeg congregation with a high percentage of immigrants suggests that there may have been a connection between the postwar migrants and prohibitions against dancing. The tensions over the issue at Sargent Avenue Mennonite Church may have been exacerbated by the fact that the leading ministers in the early years of the congregation had arrived in Canada with the 1920s migrant group while the majority of members up until the mid-1960s were immigrants of the 1940s and 1950s. In 1957, one of the church leaders, Elder J. Toews, reminded the congregation that it had been continually stressed that dancing was a sin, that it had been emphasized in baptismal instruction, and that the issue had come up quite a few times at church council meetings. He asked the congregation to take a firm position against dancing on the part of church members, which the assembled group did. But notably, there were quite a few abstentions on the vote.[37]

In June 1961, two church council meetings at Sargent were devoted entirely to the issue of dancing. It had been learned that a female church member was planning to have a dance at her wedding. In working through this particular case, the council reached the conclusion that members who went ahead and danced, even after a visit from church leaders, would lose their membership. As well, they decided that all members should be prohibited from attending weddings where dances were planned, although there was not complete agreement on this proposition.[38] The hard-line position at Sargent was followed one month later by the Conference of Mennonites in Canada stance against dancing, decided by a vote of five hundred to twenty-six.[39]

If Canadian Mennonites thought of the immigrants as immoral and worldly, then the latter frequently considered their co-religionists in Canada as 'far too conservative,' and the restrictions placed on them as 'out-dated.'[40] One immigrant man resisted obtaining church membership because of what he perceived as the 'holier than thou' attitude on the part of Canadian Mennonites. Of the refugee experience, he said, 'We had gone through rough times, many different stages of life that weren't too pleasant nor too good either.' This he felt was not understood by Canadians.[41] Another individual interviewed in 1951 by historian Cornelius Krahn was reluctant to tell his story because he claimed that the misunderstanding on the part of North Americans was so great that his own experiences were laughed at. His wife had been left behind in Russia, where she died, and in Canada he was now living with a woman whose husband had been sent back to the Soviet Union, his fate unknown. The man was not attending a Mennonite church.[42]

For the most part, immigrants who wanted to be part of Mennonite churches in Canada quietly altered their behaviour to conform to the ways of their hosts and helpers. Speaking retrospectively, the son of one widow expressed bitterness over the way in which his mother and other women were condemned for their conduct; clearly, he wished that they had had the strength to rebel.

The women ... whether it was silk stockings, the hair, the length of skirts ... those were the themes of preaching and sermonizing at the time. Which we who had come from Europe found very strange. I'm always amazed at my mother and other women ... they were so different and yet they never rebelled against any of this. They even taught us young people to submit nicely, after all, this is Canada, this is the Mennonite church here, they no doubt must be right, this must be the way of the Lord.[43]

While the Canadian Mennonites considered the conduct and morality of the newcomers to be reflective of religious ignorance, for their part the immigrants considered themselves to be people of strong faith. While most readily admitted that they lacked a formal church upbringing, the memory sources of postwar immigrants attest to a strong personal faith in a supreme being, expressed in informal ritual, such as prayer and song, that was suffused with the traditional forms of Mennonitism. The religious values held by the postwar migrants were ones shaped by the struggle for survival and the need to cling to hope for the future, rather than ones shaped by the influences of evangelicalism and fundamentalism, with its anti-modernism and ethical legalism, that had come to permeate North American Mennonitism. Furthermore, the generation of immigrants that had grown up prior to the closure of churches beginning in 1928 were neither ignorant in basic Christian beliefs nor in terms of specific Mennonite doctrine. In some areas of Soviet Mennonite settlement, a few churches had actually remained open until 1935.

The tumultuous events that hit Soviet Mennonites during the 1930s, particularly the arrests and exiles, and the family losses that resulted, undoubtedly caused a spiritual crisis for many individuals. As well, the secularization of education and the disintegration of other Mennonite cultural institutions removed religion from its former central place in community life. Even though official accounts emphasize the disintegration of Mennonite culture and religion in the years following the Bolshevik Revolution, one could argue that personal religious belief may have actually experienced a revival during the years when formal religious institutions and practices were suppressed. Rather than becoming a godless people, as was implied by their co-religionists in North America, Soviet Mennonites may have developed a more fervent inner faith quite different from a religion of rote belief. Historian Sheila Fitzpatrick has observed that the mass closing of churches, the burning of icons, and the arrest of priests that accompanied collectivization in the Soviet Union, 'effected an instantaneous revival of Orthodox piety' among the peasantry. Later on in the 1930s, she argues, religion became less Orthodox but evolved into a mix of Old Belief, sectarianism, and folk religion: 'peasants developed their own homemade religious observances.'[44] Similarly, Pamela Klassen has argued that Mennonites who came out of Ukraine during the war developed a 'domestic religion' that was based on stories, relationships, and informal ritual.[45] Soviet Mennonites came to rely on the most foundational rituals, such as prayer, song, and Bible-reading, as manifestations of their religious belief.

The memory sources of immigrants offer reflective and anecdotal evidence of the way in which the events and experiences in their lives prompted the deepening of an already existing religious faith, or a dramatic conversion experience, or the sense that some form of providence was operating in their lives. For instance, Elizabeth recalled that she became a Christian when she was unexpectedly reunited with her family in the Warthegau in 1944, after a separation of two years.[46] Such a fortuitous happening in the midst of war confirmed for her the existence of a more gracious power than fate. In the baptismal testimonies of young adults wanting to join Canadian Mennonite churches, it was not uncommon to find statements of faith gained in moments of adversity experienced during the refugee sojourn. For instance, Katie Wiebe related in her testimony before the Elmwood Mennonite Brethren Church in Winnipeg that she had been converted while fleeing the Red Army in Germany.[47] In a similar testimony at Virgil (Ontario) Mennonite Brethren Church, Annie Petkau declared that in her hard experiences during the flight across Europe she had repeatedly seen God's protecting hand. During the same service, Katie Petkau confirmed how she had been conscious of God's saving hand during times of great danger. She also stated that she had found peace with God through the urging and example of her mother.[48]

Besides attesting to the existence of religious belief in their lives, the memory sources of postwar immigrants are replete with references, like that above, to the teaching and example of mothers in the development of religious faith. Katie Friesen's description of her mother is typical:

My brother and I had a devoted Christian mother, who by her example and instruction radiated the love of Christ. She passed her faith on to us. She taught us to love and pray and gave us her very best. I can still see her standing in the corner of the room by the shelf on which a kerosene lamp stood, reading from the Bible and her book of meditations. After blowing out the light, she would kneel and pray at length and then join me in bed. She instructed us concerning the special celebrations of the church: Christmas, Easter, Pentecost, and Thanksgiving.[49]

Women had taken significant initiative and leadership in maintaining at least minimal religious practice within their communities during their latter years in Ukraine and through the years of displacement from their homes.[50] Although Mennonite leaders paid homage to the important role that mothers had played in the religious development of their children, the concern about the religious decay of the immigrants suggests that the teaching provided by mothers did not measure up to that offered by the institutional church. Perhaps because women were ministering mainly to children, the elderly, and each other, and not to very many adult men, their spiritual leadership was not taken seriously.

The fear on the part of some Canadian Mennonites that the immigrants were lost to the spiritual life did not seem to be born out by their lack of interest in joining churches. Reporting to the annual meeting of the British Columbia Provincial Relief Committee, J.J. Thiessen commented on the gratifying involvement of immigrants, including young people, in church life, from preaching on the part of ministers, to directing choirs, to teaching Sunday school. He further observed: 'The refugees have gone through difficult experiences and our churches could learn much from them.'[51] At the official level, Canadian Mennonite churches warmly welcomed the newcomers. When new immigrants first attended the Niagara United Mennonite Church, they were 'greeted from the pulpit, followed by a sincere welcome and an expression of God's blessing for a new start in life.'[52] At the Leamington United Mennonite Church, services included a public recognition and special hymn sung in honour of each new arrival.[53] As for the immigrants, organized church life offered a sense of belonging to a group where at least the language, if not much else, was familiar. One young woman recalled that church life was 'all new to me,' yet she attended a Winnipeg church regularly because, as a live-in domestic, she felt isolated and lonely. At the church, she said, 'at least I got to know somebody, could talk to somebody, it's very lonely if you can't speak English.'[54]

That postwar immigrants were eager to become bona fide members of Mennonite churches is suggested by the rate at which they seized the opportunity to become baptized when the ritual was offered. Already during the years of the German occupation in Ukraine, large baptisms were performed by the few Mennonite ministers available.[55] Similarly, many refugees received baptism from North American Mennonite clergy in Germany and Holland, and some attended and received baptism in German Lutheran and Evangelical churches. The next opportunity came in Canadian churches, where a substantial number of newcomers were baptized within a few years of arrival. The first baptismal group at the newly formed Sargent Avenue Mennonite Church on 12 July 1949 consisted of one man and ten women.[56] And while baptism was frequently a sincere declaration of new-found religious faith, it also functioned as a ritual of inclusion and a badge of Mennonitism.

The practice of baptism itself raised to the surface differences in understanding around the concept of Mennonitism. One aspect of Canadian church life that was relatively foreign, or perhaps irrelevant, to the immigrant population was the strong denominational boundaries between Mennonite Brethren (MB) and General Conference (GC) Mennonite churches. The immigrants had already been introduced to some of the tensions between the two groups in Germany and Paraguay, and also their competition for members among the newcomers, but the differences became even more clear in North America. One young widow, Justina, recalled that during the years of the German occupation in the Soviet Union, the Mennonite Brethren and *Kirchliche*, as the General Conference was known in Russia, met together in homes for worship services. At that time, Justina had been baptized according to the Mennonite Brethren method of total immersion in water. When she settled in Coaldale, Alberta, the Mennonite Brethren Church was insistent that she become a member there because she had been baptized as an MB. But her sponsoring relatives, who 'had done so much for me,' were members of the General Conference Church, and since 'it was good enough for them it was good enough for me,' Justina said.[57] Her immersion baptism was not an obstacle to joining the GC church, which practised the baptismal method whereby the candidate was sprinkled on the head with water. The converse, however, was problematic, and in most cases *Kirchliche* Mennonites who wished to join an MB church in Canada had first to be rebaptized by immersion.

In a similar situation, Katie began taking catechism classes at a General Conference church because she felt most comfortable there. But because her uncle/employer was Mennonite Brethren, the MB church in the same community thought she should be baptized there. As a result, the GC church she was attending did not want to baptize Katie, so as not to offend the MBs. As for Katie, she recalled her confusion over the denominational boundaries by saying, 'I don't know why it should be that one group thinks it is holier than the other.'[58] Becoming an 'official' Mennonite thus meant not only submitting to the formal ritual of baptism, but also gradually learning to understand the distinctive practices that existed within Canadian Mennonitism.

Those congregations that received a substantial number of postwar refugees soon experienced unprecedented rates of church growth. At the Niagara United Mennonite Church, the membership almost doubled in the early 1950s; 'almost every family' in the church had relatives in Europe whom they sponsored as immigrants. This church alone accepted eighty individuals in thirty-two family units in the decade following the war. In anticipation of the sudden influx of new members, the church undertook to construct a new church building with a seating capacity of a thousand.[59] At the Coaldale Mennonite Church in Alberta the 'most immediate impact' of the inflow was that the church building completed only a decade earlier became inadequate in size, necessitating first an expansion and several years later a completely new structure.[60] Cornelia Lehn states that the 3,014 Mennonite DPs who settled in British Columbia in the years 1947 to 1961 had a 'tremendous impact' on the Mennonite community, many churches in the Fraser Valley doubling in membership with the influx.[61]

Accompanying the general growth in church membership was the creation of a sex imbalance in some congregations. For instance, an Ontario minister visiting First Mennonite Church in Calgary in 1959 remarked that 'the great majority of those present at the service consisted of women and girls who had found work in this large city.'[62] At the Sargent Avenue Mennonite Church in 1952, there were 36 adult men and 63 women; two decades later the ratio had changed only slightly, there being 169 men and 251 women members in 1971.[63] And at the Niagara United Mennonite Church, during the years 1947 to 1950,

78 women over the age of fifteen were received as members compared to only 37 men.[64]

Despite the fact that a female majority quickly resulted from the influx of postwar immigrants, this did not bring about a dramatic increase in women's roles in church life. The Canadian Mennonite churches that the immigrant community joined were ones in which women's roles were clearly delineated. During this era, women could not be ordained and serve as ministers, nor could they hold other leadership positions within the administrative and pastoral structure of the church, be it as deacon, treasurer, or member of church council. Although most churches – except those belonging to ultra conservative groups – accepted the presence of women at congregational meetings, in many Mennonite churches women could not yet vote at those meetings, and thus were barred from formal participation in decision-making processes. In fact, some scholars have interpreted the 1950s as a regressive phase in women's leadership opportunities, citing in particular the 1957 decision by the Mennonite Brethren conference to change the existing 'ordination' of women as missionaries to a less formal and less authoritative process of 'commissioning.'[65] For the most part, women's roles were 'subordinate' and 'supportive' ones, as Gloria Neufeld Redekop has observed.[66] Women participated in church life mainly through teaching Sunday school – but only to women and children – in mission work, and in church choirs.

The question of women's official participation in church decision making via the franchise was one that was on the agenda of numerous Canadian Mennonite congregations in the decades following 1950. At this point, there was significant variation among Mennonite conference groups and also among individual congregations regarding women's presence at and participation in meetings of the church membership, and whether they could cast a vote at those meetings. In 1958 Ontario minister N.N. Fransen circulated a questionnaire to seventy churches, posing the question: 'Do the Sisters of your church have full franchise?' Of forty-six responses, twenty-one answered yes and twenty-five no. In some churches, Fransen found that women could attend congregational meetings, but vote only in elections for church leaders – that is, for the bishop, ministers, Sunday school superintendent – but not when financial matters were being decided. In other churches the opposite was true. In his conclusions, Fransen conceded that recognition should be given to the fact that in some households women, specifically widows, were the supporters of their families and therefore should have the right to speak on behalf of their families in church matters.[67]

By mid-century women held the franchise in a larger percentage of General Conference Mennonite congregations than among the Mennonite Brethren, where progress was slower. Disparity in practice existed within provinces and even within regions. In the Niagara Peninsula, women at the Vineland United Mennonite Church received the right to vote on all matters in 1936, whereas at the nearby Niagara United Mennonite Church women obtained full voting rights at members' meetings only in 1962, despite the fact that both churches were General Conference.[68] With 100 more women than men in a membership of 694, the delay at Niagara may speak for itself![69] While a comprehensive survey of practices in Canadian Mennonite congregations would be necessary for firm conclusions, evidence from the churches investigated for this study suggests that the influx of women without men into some congregations may have hastened the coming of the female franchise. On the one hand, the significantly higher number of women than men in a congregation may have generated some fear over a 'women's voice' suddenly becoming a factor in church votes. Yet it is more probable that the extension of women's rights within many congregations beginning in the mid to late 1950s may have been stimulated by the recognition that the hegemony of men over decision making had effectively and completely excluded the voices of the many female-headed families that joined Canadian Mennonite churches during that decade.

First Mennonite Church in Saskatoon faced the dilemma of other urban Mennonite churches that received a large number of single women and widows during the postwar migration. The demographic bulge of women highlighted the contradiction, which had existed in some churches for many years, whereby a self-supporting woman, possibly with dependants, was required to pay full church dues yet had no voice in the decision-making process. In 1947, the suggestion of a male member at First Mennonite that women be allowed to attend the congregational meetings, called *Brüderschaft*, or brotherhood, was not considered. The following year, after serving supper to the brotherhood, women were allowed to sit in for the presentation of reports. In 1949, the concern was again raised that widowed and single women who were members had no one to speak for them. The only concession made at this point was that women could attend the annual reporting session, so long as they did not participate in the discussion of issues or the decision making. Thus, the 1950s saw a division of congregational meetings into two sessions: a first evening of reporting, to which all members were invited, and a second evening to set the budget and make decisions, at which only the male membership was present. Despite several petitions from women's societies within the church, it wasn't until 1964 that First's constitution was amended to allow women to attend and vote at congregational meetings. The discrimination inherent in the church's past practice, and the fear of taking the step toward equal rights, is highlighted when one considers that of a total membership of 478, 198 were men and 280 were women, of whom 113 were single or widowed.[70]

At Sargent Avenue Mennonite Church, where the membership in the 1950s consisted mainly of postwar immigrants, it seemed only natural that women would have full rights. Responding to N.N. Fransen's questionnaire on the topic, one of Sargent's ministers replied: 'Since we have a number of Sisters who provide for their families and also support the church financially, it was natural and practical that they also have the vote.'[71] This reasoning was reiterated more directly in a 1971 review of the status of women at Sargent. The recorder wrote: 'Since our first *Brüderschaft* (brotherhood or members' meeting) it was always taken for granted that women would be present with full voting rights. The fact that we had so many women who had lost their husbands in the Second World War necessitated such an attitude. Besides that, we had always had a number of other widows in the church who wouldn't have been taken into consideration had they not had the vote.'[72]

The presence of immigrant widows was cited as one factor in a difficult struggle over women's rights at the West Abbotsford Mennonite Church in British Columbia. In 1951, a church split was narrowly avoided, one of the issues being the authority of the *Gemeindeberatung*, in which women participated, vis-à-vis the *Brüderschaft*, which was the domain of the men. The senior minister, Heinrich M. Epp, was supportive of women's greater involvement, arguing that a woman's presence could have a positive influence on an 'impetuous' husband, and furthermore, 'the participation of the sisters was also especially helpful for the many immigrant women in the raising of their older children.'[73] By a vote of ninety-seven to twenty, the members favoured the primacy of the congregational meeting over the brotherhood. Although Epp's statement lacks context in the church's published history, one can speculate that he recognized the problem of denying a meaningful voice in church affairs to women who were economic providers as well as moral and spiritual guides for their families.

An immigrant widow who became a member at West Abbotsford recalled having the same rights as men, although she said it wasn't normal for the women to talk at church meetings and so she kept quiet most of the time.[74] Other memory sources confirm that a variety of conventions existed across the country. At the Waterloo-Kitchener United Mennonite Church, in Ontario, women went to congregational meetings and voted alongside the men; one young immigrant woman recalled attending meetings soon after she arrived and quickly being voted onto church committees.[75] At the Coaldale Mennonite Brethren Church, women attended church meetings, sitting on the opposite side of the sanctuary from the men; they did not speak and had no vote. The son of an immigrant widow recalled the discrepancy with amazement: 'The women of course had no vote, no say. It was just the men who spoke and decided. What amazed me was that when there were these meetings, the women would always be there. They would come. They would simply sit there, quietly, nicely [and] listen to what was going on.'[76]

To what extent immigrant women themselves were eager to participate equally with men in church decision making is difficult to assess. Because older women had not been part of formal church life for two decades and younger women possibly not at all, church activity at any level was new and welcome. Some women found it enough to attend Sunday services, while others became Sunday school teachers or joined choirs. There were so many church women working as domestics in Vancouver in the 1950s that the Mennonite Brethren congregation in that city found it necessary to start a women's choir.[77] The primary outlet for women's church activity, however, was within their own organizations, often called sewing circles (*Naehvereine*) or mission societies. For Canadian Mennonite women, women's societies had become a kind of 'parallel' church in which they held authority and, for the most part, autonomy.[78]

Like the congregations themselves, women's organizations within Mennonite churches grew and flourished during the war as well as in the aftermath of the postwar migration. Historians have described the 1940s through the 1960s as a 'golden era' and a 'flowering' for Mennonite women's organizations, as women mobilized to send material and financial relief to the many war sufferers on the European continent.[79] At some churches, immigrant women were absorbed into existing societies, and the strength in numbers of those groups increased as a result. Often, an immigrant woman's first introduction to Canadian church life was through the local *Frauenverein* (women's society). Maria Reimer was welcomed by the Waterloo-Kitchener *Frauenverein* shortly after her arrival in the spring of 1947. In writing about the special evening arranged for her and another immigrant, Maria said her pen could scarcely convey the feelings that overwhelmed her on that evening. The women presented each newcomer with a 'beautifully-wrapped bundle' full of useful presents.[80] For her, the integration into the existing women's group was a warm statement of welcome.

In other locales, new groups were formed specifically to accommodate the recent arrivals. Frances Swyripa has demonstrated that with the influx of displaced persons into the Ukrainian-Canadian community, new women's organizations were formed with markedly different ideological platforms from prewar associations.[81] For Mennonite women, the difference was not so much ideological as one of culture and experience. Many Canadian churches were beginning to make the transition from German to English during the 1950s; the influx of refugee women meant that new sewing or mission circles were created to accommodate the language needs of the newcomers. For instance, at the Niagara United Mennonite Church, a third society, called *Missionsverein* (mission society), was founded in 1952, primarily with immigrant women as members.[82] This women's group eventually became the largest in number and also in income, due mainly to its food catering service.[83]

Some of the impetus for immigrant women starting their own societies may have also come from their exclusion, for whatever reason, from pre-existing women's groups. This is suggested by the experience of one woman interviewed by Krista Taves: 'our Vereins (women's groups) are all from after World War II. Some from Paraguay and some from Russia. We started these Vereins in the 1950s. I can't remember being invited to the Vereins so we started our own.'[84] While exclusion from or discomfort in joining pre-existing women's societies may have been partial factors that prompted immigrant women to form their own groups, their desire for fellowship among themselves was likely a stronger pull. Common language and, more importantly, common experience brought immigrant women together in a context where they could empathize with one another's past tragedies and current struggles of adaptation. At Sargent Avenue Mennonite Church, the first *Frauenverein*, formed in 1951, continued in 1975 to be composed mainly of older-generation, postwar immigrant women, notwithstanding the expansion of the church membership with Mennonites from other backgrounds and the subsequent creation of additional women's groups. A church history notes: 'In this society there are especially many women who have lost their husbands, many from the Second World War.'[85]

Raymond Breton suggests that with the arrival of new immigrant waves, an existing ethnic collectivity may have to formulate new 'incorporative myths' that will create new 'bases of belongingness.'[86] Further research that explores the impact of the postwar immigrants from the perspective of Canadian Mennonites is necessary to understand fully how the ethnic collectivity was altered by the inclusion of newcomers. Perhaps the most significant effect of the postwar immigrants on formal church life was in the area of language, as their presence delayed for a number of years the shift in some congregations from German to English. For the most part, however, it seems that the postwar immigrants accommodated themselves to the existing ethnic myths and altered their behaviour and/or patterns of thinking in order to meet the criteria of inclusion. One immigrant woman reflected that her entire life seemed to have been one of adapting to the norms of the society around her. She commented: 'So many times in Russia we had to learn how to get along with the Russians. When the Germans came we had to learn the proper German and how to behave. When we came all the way to Germany we had to learn so many other things. And here we came to Canada and there were new things to learn again! It seemed to me that there had been so many years and a continual series of things for us to learn because we were forever so backward and we couldn't catch up with the world.'[87] Alongside the recognition that there were many things to learn in order to conform, came the sense, expressed by numerous immigrants, that they were inferior to Canadian Mennonites and indeed, Canadians generally. Feelings of backwardness and inferiority arose from a variety of circumstances and situations in the immigrants' lives: the limited education possessed by many, the lack of formal religious training, the extreme poverty and history of material deprivation, and the lack of work and language skills for Canadian life.

The lack of educational credentials that immigrants possessed on arrival resulted from thwarted opportunity, not from a lack of ambition. Rural education in the Soviet Union was expanded during the 1930s, so that children were receiving seven mandatory years of primary education at the end of the decade, compared with four years at the beginning.[88] Despite this improvement 'in principle,' not all Mennonite children seemed to have benefited. During the decade, some school-aged children had to stay home with younger siblings while their mothers worked on the collective farm. The arrest of her father in 1938 meant that one young woman's plans to attend university in Zaporozhe were put aside, since she was the eldest and now had to help provide for her family.[89] The war itself disrupted the education of many individuals, especially those attending high school and university at a distance from their homes. Although refugees placed their children in school whenever they stopped long enough during their journey to the West, education remained sporadic for close to a decade following their departure from Ukraine.

The fact that children were behind Canadian standards academically was painfully evident for some. On arrival in Canada, one sixteen-year-old girl was placed into Grade 1, along with her thirteen-year-old brother. Because she was so big, she had to sit at the teacher's desk. Fortunately, private tutoring allowed her to quickly advance to the Grade 8 class.[90] The increased emphasis on parochial education by Canadian Mennonites in the immediate postwar years heightened the immigrants' awareness of their own lack of schooling. The existence of Mennonite high schools in many communities – nine were established between 1944 and 1950[91] – provided immigrant youth with a comfortable environment in which to renew their education. If the postwar immigrants were somewhat behind educationally when they arrived in Canada, many quickly caught up by attending high school, Bible school, and university.[92]

For the women without men, there were many added reasons to feel of lesser value than their Canadian Mennonite counterparts. For some women, embarrassment occurred over something as simple as not knowing how to cook traditional Mennonite foods.[93] For widows, the lack of a husband, a provider, and the proper 'head' of the family, gave rise to the sense that they ranked somewhat lower in value than others within the community. And in some cases, even the lack of a father induced feelings of worthlessness, as the following example poignantly illustrates. While working at a printing company in Winnipeg, Susie avoided the students from the nearby Mennonite high school who came to meet their fathers after work. Although she was a peer, she felt inferior to the students, having lost both a father and a step-father in the course of her young life.[94]

Learning to be a Canadian and a Mennonite meant many things to the postwar Mennonite immigrants: being baptized, grasping denominational differences, performing the rites of formal church life, and adhering to the standards of Christian conduct that prevailed in a particular locale. For the most part, the newcomers acquiesced and conformed to expectations, even if they didn't fully understand or agree with the prescriptions and admonitions that prevailed. After years of turmoil and instability, most immigrants were eager to be settled and secure, which also meant fitting in as much as possible. Women in particular found ways of reconciling, even if only in outward appearances, the incongruity of their pre-migration lives and their Canadian lives as women subordinate within their churches and communities.

Conclusion

The story of Maria Redekop Wall, told briefly at the outset of this study, bears many similarities to that of Faduma Abdi, a refugee from Somalia. Faduma, whose story is told in *Safe Haven: The Refugee Experience of Five Families*, was pregnant when she immigrated to Canada in 1989 with two small children.[1] Her husband had been abducted and imprisoned because of his activities in the Somalian democratic movement. He was released, but died during his escape from the country. Faduma settled in Toronto, and in 1991 was fortunately reunited with her three older children , who had been detained in Somalia.

Both Maria and Faduma escaped settings fraught with wartime chaos and sought safety and stability for their families in Canada. Both were abruptly separated from their husbands and became widows, although Maria never learned the actual date or place of her spouse's death. Both faced the stigma of being single parents in a society that values whole, nuclear families. They faced varying degrees of discrimination based on their status as immigrants, Faduma's experience being compounded by racial intolerance. Both women found supportive networks within their respective ethnic and religious communities in Canada. As new immigrants, Maria and Faduma faced similar challenges: learning a new language, adapting to Canadian culture, and making a living for their families. In the latter respect their experiences diverged, as Maria arrived in Canada during a postwar economic boom, while Faduma immigrated on the heels of a recession. Thus, Maria's grown children were easily employed, and she was able to purchase a small berry farm. Faduma, on the other hand, received social assistance to support her family of six. Both Maria and Faduma considered Canada to be a 'safe haven,' but neither woman shed her refugee identity completely, as memories of tragedy in their homelands and sadness over the loss of husbands continued.

The purpose of comparing these two women, separated by over fifty years of history, is to illustrate how this case study of Mennonite immigrants of the 1940s and 1950s is applicable beyond the particular historical circumstances of the Second World War. Indeed, one is struck by the similar narratives of war refugees in different eras and locales. The experience of Mennonite women refugees from Ukraine and eastern Europe was shaped by their identity as Mennonites, but they also shared much in common with women of other religions and nationalities who were victims of the same world events. In their identities as *Volksdeutsche* (ethnic Germans), Mennonite families experienced the impact of purges, exiles, and deaths in ways similar to other Soviet Germans. As refugees fleeing the advance of the Red Army, first in Ukraine and later in eastern Europe, Mennonite women experienced the terror of sexual violence that all German women on the eastern front feared. Their experience of dislocation in cramped refugee camps resembled that of thousands of other displaced persons in the aftermath of the war.

Mennonites represented less than 1 per cent – 0.7 to be precise – of the total number of immigrants arriving in Canada in the years 1947 to 1955. When compared with the close to two million individuals who were part of a massive postwar immigration up to 1960, their numbers are even more minute. Yet their experience represents a microcosm of the circumstances surrounding the lives of many postwar newcomers in Canada and can be compared with other migrant groups of this era. The histories of Lithuanian and Ukrainian refugees, for instance, reveal a number of commonalities with Mennonites: violent wartime uprooting from their homes, followed by anxious and debilitating years of displacement, and the subsequent uphill battle to overcome their DP identity in Canada. Like many other immigrants, not all of them refugees, who sought new opportunities in Canada in the postwar era, Mennonites faced the challenges of becoming Canadian. This meant finding their place within the postwar economic order, which was not too hard, and establishing a position in the social order, which was more difficult. More studies of particular ethnic and religious groups within the postwar influx are needed to illustrate the varied ways in which disparate groups adapted to Canadian society and how the host society, in turn, changed because of the migrants.

Certain aspects of their identity and experience differentiated Mennonite refugees from other immigrants. The predominance of female-headed families among Mennonite postwar immigrants in fact has closer parallels with contemporary refugee movements than with other displaced person groups of the Second World War. A close comparison of more recent refugee movements and the Mennonite migration after the Second World War might reveal interesting parallels of family fragmentation and gender-role transformation. Numerous people interviewed for this study remarked that they saw their own histories played back as they watched news out of Bosnia-Herzegovina in the early 1990s.

As members of a small, ethno-religious community, Mennonite refugees may have faced less isolation and a greater sense of belonging to an identifiable community than immigrants who did not have a similar sense of group identiy. Mennonite women and their children were rarely alone in their refugee sojourn. They shared food, shelter, advice, and comfort with small groups composed mainly of relatives and neighbours from their villages. As refugees came into contact with Mennonite relief workers in Europe, they were immediately made aware that they were part of something distinguishable from the mass of displaced humanity that needed assistance at the end of the war. Similarly, their absorption into familiar and familial Mennonite cultures in both Paraguay and Canada undoubtedly helped to alleviate the alienation of resettlement.

At the same time, learning to be Mennonite was not without trials and tribulations. For the generation of young adults and children who had grown up during the decline of formal church life in the Soviet Union, many of the rituals and doctrines of North and South American Mennonites were foreign. Almost all refugees claimed a strong religious faith based on fundamental beliefs in a protecting God, faith that was for many moulded by the teachings of mothers and grandmothers. But denominational divisions and strict associations of outward conduct with Christian belief had to be learned, even if the rationale for them was not understood.

Established Mennonites in both Canada and Paraguay reacted to a perceived lack of religion among the immigrants with a program of rehabilitation that was frequently attended by paternalism and sometimes outright judgment. The immigrants in turn felt inferior to their hosts and struggled to fit in. The reception of the newcomers was thus a double-edged sword in which sincere empathy and welcome material assistance were accompanied by the development of a social hierarchy within Mennonite communities.

At the bottom of this hierarchy, even within the migrant group itself, were female-headed families. Families lacking husbands and fathers were considered heroic on the one hand but weak and burdensome on the other. Fears that widows and children would become economically dependent were for the most part not borne out. Yet these families were discomforting because they portrayed loss and tragedy and because they were an aberration from the idealized nuclear family of the post-war era. Even as they adapted to the norms and standards of Mennonite church life, many fragmented immigrant families attempted to re-create family life as they remembered it, or as they thought it should be.

The demographics of the Mennonite migrant group changed over time, according to evolving circumstances and to the creation of new family forms as births, deaths, and marriages altered the look of any one household. Despite the ongoing presence of 'some' adult men, sources that document the period, whether immediate or based in memory, share a pervasive sense that a community of women and children without men appeared during the Soviet era and persisted through resettlement in Canada and Paraguay. The striking number of families that lacked husbands, fathers, and grown sons overwhelmed the existence of families that were 'intact.' The psychological impact of losing so many men in a relatively small community was immense. That absent fathers and husbands were idealized, while sons were raised to fill their fathers' shoes, suggests the ideological form of families changed little, even if the immediate functions of family members did. More questions could be asked in this respect. For instance, was the long-term behaviour of daughters transformed through the modelling and example of their widowed mothers? Daughters (and some sons) interviewed for this study expressed sadness and sometimes even rage about the way in which their mothers, viewed within the family as strong and capable, were put down by structures and attitudes within the Mennonite community. Yet, anecdotal evidence suggests that daughters married eagerly, some quite young, and did not try to emulate their mothers' self-sufficiency by remaining single.

While families themselves were fragmented and reconfigured, traditional gender roles were also tested. Mennonite women experienced the erosion of a male presence in their families, and for a time became accustomed to communities in which women and children predominated. This was especially true in Paraguay, where the sex imbalance was most obvious and persistent because of the immigrants' isolation from other Mennonite colonists. Despite women's numeric predominance, the overall patriarchal social order was unchanged. Without fathers, husbands, and sons, women assumed roles normally assigned to the opposite sex. Women became breadwinner, protector, moral and spiritual guide, rescuer and strategist. In the context of an unchanged gender order, however, women were frequently reminded of their place. During wartime, women's vulnerability was heightened by their fears, and lived experiences, of sexual harassment and rape. Mennonite women in displaced person camps were soon reminded of their place in the religious order by their ineligibility for sanctioned leadership and the devaluation of their role in raising Christian children. As well, their own wartime heroism paled alongside the adulation given to male relief workers, who were viewed as the refugees' rescuers. In Canada and Paraguay, the rehabilitation of refugees emphasized the weakness of female-headed families and juxtaposed the structure of refugee families against the strong, male-headed family that was normative.

Women without husbands had to negotiate through a community terrain in which certain social stigmas were attached to both their sex and marital status and, at the same time, a personal terrain of independence and self-sufficiency that derived from their experience of being the family head. Mennonite women refugees were of a generation that offered little resistance to prevailing gender norms. They were also part of a community that valued acquiescence, submission, and humility, particularly on the part of women.[2] The self-sacrifice they demonstrated in caring for their families and their meekness in the midst of Mennonite officialdom were normative behaviour for mothers and women in the church. Their boldness, courage, and personal autonomy, on the other hand, were an aberration. The value that women themselves attached to their aloneness and independence varied but was inevitably influenced by a patriarchal social system in which women without men were regarded mainly with pity.

Women's behaviour and their self-perception were also shaped by their personal circumstances and individual personality. It is easy to make the mistake of interpreting the experience of Mennonite women refugees and their families as homogeneous, particularly given their membership in an ethno-religious group that valued internal conformity. The events that swept them across Europe and over the Atlantic were common, but families had different responses to their specific circumstances. One woman may have faced a situation with submission and resignation while another, under the same circumstances, may have been defiant and rebellious. Disparate responses on the part of parents in turn influenced the next generation's interpretation and memory of those events. The experiences of individuals and families were further shaped by the postwar communities that became their homes. Closer comparison of the Mennonite culture and the socio-economic situation within particular regions of the country is necessary to understand how the experience of an immigrant in British Columbia's Fraser Valley was different from, or similar to, that of a person settling in Ontario's Niagara Peninsula.

As well, the histories of those refugee families who first went to South America diverged markedly from their relatives and neighbours who migrated to Canada. The most fundamental difference was in the sheer difficulty of making a home in the wilderness and finding the means to subsist in the Volendam jungle or Neuland Chaco, in contrast to settlement in Canada. Because they were settled in new villages in new colonies, the Paraguayan refugees continued for the most part as a separate community, unlike those immigrating to Canada. As a result, the supportive communities of women so important in sustaining the refugees throughout their sojourn were maintained for a longer period of time. Families arriving in Paraguay despaired over the hardships that lay before them. Yet, it could be that women's strength was enhanced by the common experience that drew them together and the support they shared. A detailed study of the evolution in social norms within the villages of Paraguay as the male–female ratio diminished would offer fascinating insights into the history of gender-role transformation.

If the families who immigrated to Paraguay experienced hardship, the families 'left behind' in the Soviet Union attempted to survive at the most basic levels. The women and families whose lives are analysed in this study represent only a small proportion of Soviet Mennonites living in Ukraine at the outset of the Second World War. In comparison to the 12,000 men, women, and children who immigrated to North and South America, approximately 23,000 were killed or went missing on the warfront or were repatriated to the Soviet Union. Thousands more Mennonites remained in the eastern Soviet Union in 1941, when entire settlements and villages were evacuated prior to the arrival and occupation by German forces.

The Mennonites who were repatriated and those who never left the country were resettled in the far north and east of the Soviet Union, especially the Republic of Kazakhstan. Historian John B. Toews describes this diaspora as consisting 'mainly of women and children, occasionally accompanied by aging grandparents or middle-aged men disabled by disease.'[3] The postwar lives of Soviet Mennonites were infinitely more difficult than those who emigrated, including even the families that scraped out a living in the jungle and bush of Paraguay. The exiles and those repatriated were sentenced to hard labour in work camps or were simply dropped off freight trains to eke out an existence in remote, sparsely populated areas. Within a few years, many had died of illness or starvation.

Following Nikita Khrushchev's program of de-Stalinization in the mid-1950s, Mennonites along with other exiled minorities received amnesty and permission to relocate, although they were not allowed to return to their former homes in Ukraine. At the same time, Soviet Mennonites established contact with relatives in the West, and hopes for reunification were slowly rekindled. Migration on a small scale began in the 1960s, as individuals in Canada petitioned for the admittance of spouses or other close family members. The bulk of the out-migration was to Germany, beginning in the early 1970s. By the mid-1990s, close to a hundred thousand Mennonites from the former Soviet Union had settled in Germany.

The stories of the *Aussiedler* (those who emigrated from the Soviet Union to Germany beginning in the 1960s) are increasingly being told, and much is being learned about the immediate postwar experiences of Mennonites in the Soviet Union. A comprehensive study of the group that 'remained behind' would offer a fascinating point of comparison for understanding the postwar lives of Mennonite women in Canada and Paraguay. Even more than the families who emigrated, the Mennonites in the Soviet diaspora were almost exclusively women, children, and the elderly. This was especially the case in the early postwar years, as surviving adult males served harsh terms in Soviet prisoner-of-war camps. The narratives of those who emigrated to the West are inevitably tempered by a degree of 'survivor's guilt' in light of the much more difficult postwar lives of those who remained behind. The Soviet memoir material that does exist suggests that adult women were almost superhuman in sustaining their families at a material level, and that they took leadership in perpetuating basic cultural and religious rituals.[4] The history of these Soviet Mennonite families together with the stories of those who immigrated to Canada and Paraguay, as well as the stories of women like Faduma, highlight a significant pattern in the history of war and revolution, whereby women play a central and crucial role in maintaining families and keeping alive basic ingredients of the culture.

Several conclusions can be drawn from this study of women without men that might, with further exploration, be applicable to women refugees and immigrants of other groups and in other historical eras. First of all, the wartime experiences of women are very gender-specific, a fact even more pronounced within female-headed families. War heightens the vulnerability of women as targets of sexual violence; it also destroys their homes and tears apart their families. Yet war also breaks down some social boundaries and frees women to behave in response to a situation, rather than in accordance with gender limitations. Examples from this study include women rescuing their menfolk from prisoner-of-war camps or challenging repatriation officers. The stories of Mennonite refugee families exhibit the complex dichotomy of women as victims of the times but heroines of their own lives.

Dichotomies and ambiguity also characterize their experiences as immigrants to a new land, where women simultaneously find opportunities and are confronted with barriers. Immigration offers safety and stability, particularly for refugees, and hope that their children will have a better future. Yet, the immigrant widow with children also stands outside social norms in her role as wage-earner and as family head. In societies where immigrants and single parents are near the bottom of the socio-economic hierarchy, such women are potentially the subjects of double discrimination.

Maria Redekop Wall died in 1974. Her six children, all married and with many grandchildren of their own in the 1990s, prosper in their upper-middle-class Mennonite communities in British Columbia. The households of their offspring represent the diversity of Canadian families in the late twentieth century: single adults; nuclear units with several children; common-law couples with no children; families with step-parents and step-children resulting from divorce; and single parents. Their values and activities are oriented toward hard work, family, church, and community. After fifty years in Canada, their primary community remains other Mennonite families who immigrated as refugees after the Second World War. Although they are 'ordinary' Canadians, their pre-migration lives continue to dominate their memories and story telling. Central to their reminiscences is the loss of their father and their subsequent identity as a fatherless family led by Maria Wall, a refugee widow who successfully led them to a new land.

Appendix

The statistics in Table 1 are drawn from questionnaires distributed to villages with a German-speaking population in 1942–3. The surveys, conducted under the direction of Dr Karl Stumpp, were completed mainly in villages on the west side of the Dnieper River. The seventeen villages in this sample were chosen because they represented a range of demography and also because the numbers were the most accurate. In some village reports, the number of German men, women, and children do not add up to the number given for total German population. I chose those that were closest, but in some cases I altered the total slightly to make the addition correct. These village surveys are contained in a collection called 'Captured German War Documents,' originally deposited with the Library of Congress in Washington, DC. The microfilm copies that I used are at the Mennonite Archives of Ontario, Waterloo, Ontario.

Table 1
Population Statistics for Selected Villages in Mennonite Settlements West of the Dnieper River, c. 1942

Settlement/ village	German population	No. of men	No. of women	No. of children	No. of families without male head	
Chortitza						
Adelsheim	407	77	128	202	38/112	(34%)
Alexanderfeld	546	76	172	298	68/137	(50%)
Blumengart	256	40	73	143	21/62	(34%)
Neuendorf	1,629	294	450	885	133/399	(33%)
Neuhorst	159	29	35	95	5/32	(16%)
Rosengart	475	66	148	261	61/121	(50%)
Schoenhorst	1,008	177	291	540	97/240	(40%)

Table 1 (*continued*)

Settlement/ village	German population	No. of men	No. of women	No. of children	No. of families without male head	
Yazykovo						
Hochfeld	199	15	62	122	45/57	(79%)
Nikopol						
Blumenfeld	232	33	77	122	35/67	(52%)
Steinau	227	40	65	122	30/64	(47%)
Baratov & Shlakhtin						
Gnadental	501	86	148	267	86/129	(67%)
Neu-Chortitza	470	77	143	250	59/116	(51%)
Zagradovka						
Altonau	520	31	164	325	112/132	(85%)
Neuhalbstadt	467	79	132	256	59/122	(48%)
Nikolaifeld	366	74	120	172	37/89	(42%)
Orloff	601	109	175	317	50/156	(32%)
Tiege	451	39	156	256	96/125	(77%)
Average % families without male heads	49%					

The totals that I have arrived at in Table 2 for all three years differ by approximately ten (plus or minus) from the standard numbers given in Canadian Mennonite Board of Colonization records and in a variety of published sources (for instance Epp, *Mennonite Exodus*). The discrepancy may be due to a number of factors: in some cases I eliminated from the database registers that had too little information to be useful; in a few cases I eliminated from the database immigrants who had arrived in Canada from destinations other than Paraguay or Europe, but who are included in official CMBC tabulations; and in a few cases individuals appeared on more than one record and, although I tried to account for this, I may have missed some for which insufficient information appears on the form.

Table 2
Mennonites Immigrating to Canada by Sex, 1947–1949

Sex	1947	1948	1949	Total
Female	314 (59%)`	2,224 (58%)	875 (57.4%)	3,413 (58%)
Male	220 (41%)	1,613 (42%)	647 (42.4%)	2,480 (42%)
Unknown	2	1	3 (0.2%)	6
Total	536	3,838	1,525	5,899

Table 3
Adult Immigrants to Canada by Age and Sex, 1948

Age	Female (%)	Male (%)	Total
20–29	540 (62%)	326 (38%)	866
30–39	325 (75%)	107 (25%)	432
40–49	303 (69%)	134 (31%)	437
50–59	201 (72%)	80 (28%)	281
60–	124 (77%)	37 (23%)	161
Unknown	21 (53%)	19 (47%)	40
Total	1,514 (68%)	703 (32%)	2,217

In Table 4, I define an individual as widow (widower) on the following basis: if, under the question regarding marital status, it was explicitly stated or indicated that the spouse was missing; if a woman is listed without a spouse (with or without children) and a maiden name appears in brackets or if she is designated *Frau*; or if a woman is accompanied by children with the same surname but no father is listed.

In this table, the number of those listed as married is an odd number and therefore does not represent an equal number of men and women. In some cases spouses appeared on separate forms for a variety of reasons – one may have been detained in Europe for processing reasons or a couple may have arrived a different times. It is possible that one-half of the couple may not have been sponsored by the CMBC and therefore would not appear in their records, or that marital status was assumed to be single among groups of male contract workers when in fact some may have been married.

Table 4
Mennonites Immigrating to Canada as Defined by Position within the Family, 1947–1949

Family Position	Sex	1947	1948	1949	Totals
Children	f	57	533	224	814 (47%)
(under age 16)	m	74	627	225	926 (53%)
	u*	1	0	3	4
		132	1,160	452	1,744
% of total		25%	30%	30%	30%
Young adults	f	32	183	45	260 (50%)
(age 16 to 19)	m	24	186	48	258 (50%)
	u	1	1	0	2
		57	370	93	520
% of total		11%	10%	6%	9%
Single adults	f	78	547	210	835 (61%)
(age 20 & older)	m	55	332	158	545 (39%)
	u	0	0	0	0
		133	879	368	1,380
% of total		25%	23%	24%	23%
Widows		94	592	210	896
(with dependants					
under age 16)		(40)	(313)	(98)	(451)
% of total		18%	15%	14%	15%
Widowers		19	98	33	150
(with dependants					
under age 16)		(0)	(6)	(2)	(8)
% of total		4%	3%	2%	3%
Married		88	723	365	1,176
% of total		16%	19%	24%	20%
Divorced		0	3	2	5
Unknown		13	13	2	28
Total		536	3,838	1,525	5,899

*u = unknown

Notes

Introduction

1 Information about Maria Redekop Wall is in Paul Born, 'Family History: The Borns' (unpublished paper, n.d.).

2 Statistic from Canada Employment and Immigration Commission, quoted in Reg Whitaker, *Canadian Immigration Policy since Confederation* (Ottawa: Canadian Historical Association 1991), Table I, p. 2

3 The sex imbalance among Mennonite displaced persons was quite different than for other DP communities. For instance, almost two-thirds of Ukrainian adults immigrating to Canada from 1947 to 1951 were male. See Ihor Stebelsky, 'Ukrainian Population Migration after World War II,' in *The Refugee Experience: Ukrainian Displaced Persons after World War II*, ed. Wsevolod Isajiw et al. (Edmonton: Canadian Institute of Ukrainian Studies Press 1992). Among Polish refugees immigrating during the same years, there were three times as many men as women. See Henry Radecki with Benedykt Heydenkorn, *A Member of a Distinguished Family: The Polish Group in Canada* (Toronto: McClelland and Stewart 1976), 33–4.

4 Linda Peavy and Ursula Smith, *The Gold Rush Widows of Little Falls: A Story Drawn from the Letters of Pamelia and James Fergus* (St Paul: Minnesota Historical Society 1990), 55

5 The title of this book is, in part, a play on the title of immigration historian Robert Harney's 1978 article 'Men without Women,' an important study of Italian male migrants in Canada at the turn of the century. See Robert F. Harney, 'Men without Women: Italian Migrants in Canada, 1885–1930,' in *The Italian Immigrant Woman in North America*, ed. Betty Boyd Caroli et al. (Toronto: Multicultural History Society of Ontario 1978), 78–101.

6 Monica Boyd observes that 'female immigrants have been rendered as invis-

ible or stereotyped' as dependants. See Boyd, 'Immigrant Women in Canada,' in Simon and Brettell, eds., *International Migration*, 45.

7 Caroline B. Brettell and Rita James Simon, 'Immigrant Women: An Introduction,' in *International Migration: The Female Experience*, ed. Rita James Simon and Caroline B. Brettell (Totowa, NJ: Rowman and Allanheld 1986), 3. See also Betty Bergland, 'Immigrant History and the Gendered Subject: A Review Essay,' *Ethnic Forum* 8, no. 2 (1988): 24–39; Donna Gabaccia, 'Immigrant Women: Nowhere at Home?' *Journal of American Ethnic History* 10, no. 4 (summer 1991): 61–87; and Gabaccia, *From the Other Side: Women, Gender, and Immigrant Life in the U.S., 1820–1990* (Bloomington: Indiana University Press 1994); Sydney Stahl Weinberg, 'The Treatment of Women in Immigration History: A Call for Change,' with comments by Donna Gabaccia, Hsia R. Diner, and Maxine Schwartz Seller, *Journal of American Ethnic History* 11, no. 4 (summer 1992): 25–69. A particularly useful and specifically Canadian treatment of the issue is Franca Iacovetta, 'Manly Militants, Cohesive Communities, and Defiant Domestics: Writing about Immigrants in Canadian Historical Scholarship,' *Labour/Le Travail* 36 (fall 1995): 217–52.

8 An important breakthrough was a 1985 conference on women, immigration, and ethnicity sponsored by the Multicultural History Society of Ontario, which resulted in the book *Looking into My Sister's Eyes: An Exploration in Women's History*, ed. Jean Burnet (Toronto: Multicultural History Society of Ontario 1986). This volume, accompanied by a special issue on women and ethnicity in the MHSO's journal, *Polyphony*, was especially significant in its attention to a wide range of ethnic groups represented among female immigrants.

9 Marilyn Barber, 'The Women Ontario Welcomed: Immigrant Domestics for Ontario Homes, 1870–1930,' *Ontario History* 7 (1980): 148–72. Varpu Lindström-Best, *Defiant Sisters: A Social History of Finnish Immigrant Women in Canada* (Toronto: Multicultural History Society of Ontario 1988); Joy Parr, 'The Skilled Emigrant and Her Kin: Gender, Culture and Labour Recruitment,' *Canadian Historical Review* 68, no. 4 (Dec. 1987): 529–51. Black women arriving mainly from the Caribbean have also constituted a significant portion of single women immigrants. See, for instance, Agnes Calliste, 'Race, Gender, and Canadian Immigration Policy: Blacks from the Caribbean, 1900–1932,' *Journal of Canadian Studies* 28, no. 4 (winter 1993–4): 131–48.

10 See, in particular, Franca Iacovetta, *Such Hardworking People: Italian Immigrants in Postwar Toronto* (Montreal: McGill-Queen's University Press 1992). Also three articles by Iacovetta: 'From Contadina to Worker: Southern Italian Immigrant Working Women in Toronto, 1947–62,' in Burnet, ed., *Looking into My Sister's Eyes*; 'Making "New Canadians": Social Workers, Women, and

the Reshaping of Immigrant Families,' in *Gender Conflicts: New Essays in Women's History*, ed. Franca Iacovetta and Mariana Valverde (Toronto: University of Toronto Press 1992), 261–303; and 'Remaking Their Lives: Women Immigrants, Survivors, and Refugees,' in *A Diversity of Women: Ontario, 1945–1980*, ed. Joy Parr (Toronto: University of Toronto Press 1995), 135–67.

11 Ellen Cole, Oliva M. Espin, and Esther D. Rothblum., eds., *Refugee Women and Their Mental Health: Shattered Societies, Shattered Lives* (Binghamton, NY: Harrington Park Press 1992), 2. The authors in this collection of essays offer a variety of definitions, depending on the particular national and political context being explored.

12 Susan Forbes Martin, *Refugee Women* (London: Zed Books 1992), 5. Other sources state that 80 per cent of refugees worldwide are adult women: see the Foreword by Theanvy Kuoch, Sima Wali, and Mary F. Scully in Cole, Espin, and Rothblum, eds., *Refugee Women and Their Mental Health*, xii; Judith Ramirez, 'The Canadian Guidelines on Women Refugee Claimants Fearing Gender-Related Persecution,' *Refuge* 14, no. 7 (Dec. 1994): 3. Several authors have noted the predominance of women and children in refugee movements from Cuba, Cambodia, and Vietnam, for instance. See Silvia Pedraza, 'Women and Migration: The Social Consequences of Gender,' *Annual Review of Sociology* 17 (1991): 303–25.

13 Doreen Indra, 'Gender: A Key Dimension of the Refugee Experience,' *Refuge* 6, no. 3 (Feb. 1987): 3–4; Indra, 'Ethnic Human Rights and Feminist Theory: Gender Implications for Refugee Studies and Practice,' *Journal of Refugee Studies* 2, no. 2 (1989): 221–42. See also the two-part Special Issue on Women Refugees, *Refuge* 14, nos. 7–8 (Dec. 1994–Jan. 1995). There is little historical research on refugee movements in Canada. Those studies that exist are oriented toward government policy and organizational developments rather than the experiences of refugees themselves. Nor has gender been a key consideration. See, for instance, Gerald E. Dirks, *Canada's Refugee Policy: Indifference or Opportunism?* (Montreal: McGill-Queen's University Press 1977); Irving Abella and Harold Troper, *None Is Too Many: Canada and the Jews of Europe, 1933–1948* (Toronto: Lester and Orpen Dennys 1982).

14 Isabel Kaprielian's research into the lives of female refugees from Armenia in the 1920s and Milda Danys's study of Lithuanian displaced persons following the Second World War provide glimpses into the ways in which stresses in the migration and settlement process of refugees were different from those of other immigrants. See Isabel Kaprielian, 'Creating and Sustaining an Ethnocultural Heritage in Ontario: The Case of Armenian Women Refugees,' in Burnet, ed., *Looking into My Sister's Eyes*, 139–53; Milda Danys, *DP: Lithuanian Immigration to Canada after the Second World War* (Toronto: Multicultural His-

tory Society of Ontario 1986). Janice Potter-MacKinnon, in her study of refugee women who came to Canada as Loyalist settlers in the late eighteenth century, significantly places gender at the centre of her analysis as she describes the ways in which traditional relationships and lines of authority were disrupted during the American Revolution. Janice Potter-MacKinnon, *While the Women Only Wept: Loyalist Refugee Women in Eastern Ontario* (Montreal: McGill-Queen's University Press 1993). See also Iacovetta, 'Remaking Their Lives,' 135–67.

15 Potter-MacKinnon, *While the Women Only Wept*, 61, 126–7

16 F. James Davis and Barbara Sherman Heyl, 'Turkish Women and Guestworker Migration to West Germany,' in Simon and Brettell, eds., *International Migration*, 192

17 Sosie Andezian, 'Women's Roles in Organizing Symbolic Life: Algerian Female Immigrants in France,' and Parminder Bhachu, 'Work, Dowry, and Marriage among East African Sikh Women in the United Kingdom,' both in ibid.

18 Theanvy Kuoch, et al., 'Healing the Wounds of the Mahantdori,' in Cole, Espin, and Rothblum, eds., *Refugee Women and Their Mental Health*, 204

19 Royden K. Loewen, *Family, Church, and Market: A Mennonite Community in the Old and the New Worlds, 1850–1930* (Toronto: University of Toronto Press 1993), 96

20 Annemarie Tröger, 'German Women's Memories of World War II,' in *Behind the Lines: Gender and the Two World Wars*, ed. Margaret Randolph Higonnet et al. (New Haven: Yale University Press 1987), 293–4

21 See Iacovetta, 'Manly Militants,' for a discussion of the problem of creating a dichotomy between victimization and agency in historical writing on immigrant women.

22 For historical background on Mennonites in Russia, see, for instance, James Urry, *None But Saints: The Transformation of Mennonite Life in Russia, 1789–1889* (Winnipeg: Hyperion Press 1989); John Friesen, ed., *Mennonites in Russia, 1788–1988: Essays in Honour of Gerhard Lohrenz* (Winnipeg: CMBC Publications 1989). Studies that examine developments within the Mennonite colonies under the Soviet regime include: John B. Toews, *Czars, Soviets and Mennonites* (Newton, KS: Faith and Life Press 1982), chaps. 11–12; John B. Toews, 'Early Communism and Russian Mennonite Peoplehood,' 265–87, and Victor G. Doerksen, 'Survival and Identity in the Soviet Era,' 289–98, both in *Mennonites in Russia*; Harvey L. Dyck and Anne J. Konrad, eds., *Mennonites in the Soviet Inferno* (Kitchener, ON: Pandora Press forthcoming); Colin Peter Neufeldt, 'The Fate of Mennonites in Soviet Ukraine and the Crimea on the Eve of the "Second Revolution" (1927–1929)' (MA thesis,

University of Alberta, 1989). The experience of the Mennonites is similar to that of other German colonists in the Soviet Union. Useful for a broader perspective is Ingeborg Fleischhauer and Benjamin Pinkus, eds., *The Soviet Germans: Past and Present* (London: C. Hurst 1986).

23 Frank H. Epp's 1962 history of the Canadian Mennonite Board of Colonization examines the organization that facilitated the immigration of Mennonites to Canada from the Soviet Union from the 1920s until 1960. Useful as an institutional history, Epp's book is, however, uninformed by the methods and questions of social or women's history and is written from a parochial perspective. See *Mennonite Exodus: The Rescue and Resettlement of the Russian Mennonites since the Communist Revolution* (Altona, MB: D.W. Friesen 1962). George K. Epp's 1987 article on Mennonite immigration to Canada after the Second World War is important, albeit brief and inadequate in documentation. See 'Mennonite Immigration to Canada after World War II,' *Journal of Mennonite Studies* 5 (1987): 108–19.

24 T.D. Regehr's 1996 volume on the history of Mennonites in Canada from 1939 to 1970 contains material on postwar immigration but as a survey history leaves out a good deal, particularly about women's roles. See *Mennonites in Canada, 1939–1970: A People Transformed* (Toronto: University of Toronto Press 1996), in particular chap. 4, 'Refugee Immigrants.' See also Regehr's article about one mythic episode in the Mennonite refugee experience: 'Anatomy of a Mennonite Miracle: The Berlin Rescue of 30–31 January 1947,' *Journal of Mennonite Studies* 9 (1991): 11–33.

25 For accounts by and about Mennonite relief and immigration workers, see especially Peter Dyck and Elfrieda Dyck, *Up from the Rubble: The Epic Rescue of Thousands of War-Ravaged Mennonite Refugees* (Scottdale, PA: Herald Press 1991); Herbert Klassen and Maureen Klassen, *Ambassador to His People: C.F. Klassen and the Russian Mennonite Refugees* (Winnipeg: Kindred Press 1990).

26 First-person accounts by postwar Mennonite immigrants include: Henry H. Winter, *A Shepherd of the Oppressed: Heinrich Winter, the Last Aeltester of Chortitza* (Leamington, ON: the author 1990); Susanna Toews, *Trek to Freedom: The Escape of Two Sisters from South Russia during World War II*, trans. Helen Megli (Winkler, MB: Heritage Valley Publications 1976); Maria Foth, *Beyond the Border: Maria's Miraculous Pilgrimage* (Burlington, ON: G.R. Welch 1981); Katie Friesen, *Into the Unknown* (Steinbach, MB: the author 1986); Helene Latter, *I Do Remember* (Morden, MB: Walter F. Latter 1988); Katharina Ediger, *Under His Wings: Events in the Lives of Elder Alexander Ediger and His Family* (Kitchener, ON: the author 1994). These are just a sampling of English-language publications; there are more in both English and German.

Examples of fiction include: Barbara C. Smucker, *Henry's Red Sea*

(Scottdale, PA: Herald Press 1955); Helen Good Brenneman, *But Not For-saken: A Vivid Story about the Tragic Experiences of a Russian Mennonite Refugee Family* (Scottdale, PA: Herald Press 1954); Ingrid Rimland, *The Wanderers: The Saga of Three Women Who Survived* (St Louis, MO: Concordia House 1977); Florence Schloneger, *Sara's Trek* (Newton, KS: Faith and Life Press 1981). Also of note are various semi-fictional collections by Mennonite historian Gerhard Lohrenz: *The Odyssey of the Bergen Family* (Winnipeg: the author 1978), *Stories from Mennonite Life* (Winnipeg: the author 1980), *The Lost Generation and Other Stories* (Winnipeg: the author 1982).

27 A notable exception to the dominant portrayal of Mennonite refugee women is a 1994 book by Pamela E. Klassen, who documented, through the use of oral interview and videotape, the religious lives of two Russian Mennonite women who had immigrated to Canada following the Second World War. Klassen's study is overtly feminist in its methodology and perspective and thus highlights the particular experiences of these refugee women as women in a patriarchal community. See *Going By the Moon and the Stars: Stories of Two Russian Mennonite Women* (Waterloo: Wilfrid Laurier University Press 1994). For other scholarly works about the history of Canadian Mennonite women, see, for instance, Frank H. Epp and Marlene G. Epp, 'The Diverse Roles of Ontario Mennonite Women,' in Burnet, ed., *Looking into My Sister's Eyes*; three articles by Marlene Epp: 'Women in Canadian Mennonite History: Uncovering the "Underside",' *Journal of Mennonite Studies* 5 (1987): 90–107; 'The Mennonite Girls' Homes of Winnipeg: A Home Away from Home,' *Journal of Mennonite Studies* 6 (1988): 100–14; and 'Carrying the Banner of Nonconformity: Ontario Mennonite Women and the Dress Question,' *Conrad Grebel Review* 8, no. 3 (fall 1990): 237–57; Frieda Esau Klippenstein, '"Doing What We Could": Mennonite Domestic Servants in Winnipeg, 1920s to 1950s,' *Journal of Mennonite Studies* 7 (1989): 145–66; Gloria Neufeld Redekop, *The Work of Their Hands: Mennonite Women's Societies in Canada* (Waterloo: Wilfrid Laurier University Press 1996).

28 Epp, *Mennonite Exodus*, 397

29 Sheila Fitzpatrick, *Stalin's Peasants: Resistance and Survival in the Russian Village after Collectivization* (New York: Oxford University Press 1994), 221. Fitzpatrick states that the 'grab bag family' was not at all uncommon in the Soviet Union during the 1930s. Annemarie Tröger, 'Between Rape and Prostitution: Survival Strategies and Chances of Emancipation for Berlin Women after World War II,' in *Women in Culture and Politics: A Century of Change*, ed. Judith Friedlander et al. (Bloomington: Indiana University Press 1986), 101–2

30 Daniel Bertaux and Paul Thompson, eds., *Between Generations: Family Models, Myths, and Memories*, International Yearbook of Oral History and Life Stories Series, vol. 2 (Oxford: Oxford University Press 1993), 2

31 Diana Gittins, *The Family in Question: Changing Households and Familiar Ideologies* (London: Macmillan 1985), 4
32 See review essay by Cynthia R. Comacchio, 'Beneath the "Sentimental Veil": Families and Family History in Canada,' *Labour/Le Travail* 33 (spring 1994): 279–302.
33 Ida Blom, 'The History of Widowhood: A Bibliographic Overview,' *Journal of Family History* 16, no. 2 (1991): 191–210
34 Arlene Scadron, ed., *On Their Own: Widows and Widowhood in the American Southwest, 1848–1939* (Urbana: University of Illinois Press 1988), x, 310
35 Bettina Bradbury has done pioneering research on widowhood in the Canadian setting, emphasizing the numerous strategies widows adopted to sustain themselves and their families. See 'Surviving as a Widow in Nineteenth-Century Montreal,' *Urban History Review* 17, no. 3 (Feb. 1989): 148–60; *Working Families: Age, Gender, and Daily Survival in Industrializing Montreal* (Toronto: McClelland and Stewart 1993), especially chap. 6; 'The Fragmented Family: Family Strategies in the Face of Death, Illness, and Poverty, Montreal, 1860-1885,' in *Childhood and Family in Canadian History*, ed. Joy Parr (Toronto: McClelland and Stewart 1982), 109–28. On widows in Europe, see for instance, Barbara J. Todd, 'The Remarrying Widow: A Stereotype Reconsidered,' in *Women in English Society, 1500–1800*, ed. Mary Prior (London: Methuen 1985), 54–92. Olwen Hufton, 'Women without Men: Widows and Spinsters in Britain and France in the Eighteenth Century,' *Journal of Family History* 9, no. 4 (winter 1984): 355–76.
36 See, for instance, Klassen, *Going By the Moon and the Stars*; Ruth Linden, *Making Stories, Making Selves: Feminist Reflections on the Holocaust* (Columbus: Ohio State University Press 1993); Julie Cruikshank, *Life Lived Like a Story: Life Stories of Three Yukon Native Elders* (Lincoln: University of Nebraska Press 1990). For examples of a feminist approach to doing oral history, see Daphne Patai and Sherna Berger Gluck, eds., *Women's Words: The Feminist Practice of Oral History* (New York: Routledge 1991). Although I did not, as collaborative methods might demand, provide narrators with the opportunity to either edit their initial stories or my interpretations of them, I did offer, and many individuals accepted, copies of their own interview on tape. Many immigrants viewed the telling of their stories as the partial completion of a task that they had 'always meant to do' and also valued the taped interview as something to pass on to future generations.
37 Susan Geiger, 'What's So Feminist about Doing Women's Oral History?' *Journal of Women's History* 2, no. 1 (spring 1990): 175–6
38 James Fentress and Chris Wickham, *Social Memory* (Cambridge, MA: Blackwell 1992), 2
39 Passerini's best-known work is *Fascism in Popular Memory* (Cambridge: Cam-

bridge University Press 1987). See also 'Women's Personal Narratives: Myths, Experiences, and Emotions,' in *Interpreting Women's Lives: Feminist Theory and Personal Narratives*, ed. Personal Narratives Group (Bloomington: Indiana University Press 1989), 189–97. Her work is described in Geiger, 'What's So Feminist?' 174.

40 See for instance Jean Peneff, 'Myths in Life Stories,' in *The Myths We Live By*, ed. Raphael Samuel and Paul Thompson (London: Routledge 1990).

41 The term 'memory sources' is similar to the descriptor 'subjective documents,' which Virginia Yans-McLaughlin uses for personal data such as 'autobiographies, life histories, letters, oral narratives, interviews, and court records.' See 'Metaphors of Self in History: Subjectivity, Oral Narrative, and Immigration Studies,' in *Immigration Reconsidered: History, Sociology, and Politics*, ed. Virginia Yans-McLaughlin (New York: Oxford University Press 1990), 254.

42 Fentress and Wickham, *Social Memory*, xi

43 Ibid., 7

44 Concerning the existence of 'social memory' within a society or community, see, for instance, Paul Connerton, *How Societies Remember* (Cambridge: Cambridge University Press 1989).

45 Louis Dupré, 'Alienation and Redemption of the Self in Time and Memory,' in *Transcendent Selfhood: The Loss and Rediscovery of the Inner Life* (New York: Seabury 1976), 74. One study that focuses on the importance of historical understanding to Mennonite self-definition is Rodney Sawatsky, 'History and Ideology: American Mennonite Identity Definition through History' (PhD diss., Princeton University 1977). Another Mennonite historian suggests that 'Mennonites have been a history-formed people.' See James C. Juhnke, 'Mennonite History and Self Understanding: North American Mennonitism as a Bipolar Mosaic,' in *Mennonite Identity: Historical and Contemporary Perspectives*, ed. Calvin Wall Redekop and Samuel J. Steiner (Lanham, MD: University Press of America 1988), 84.

46 Joan Ringelheim, 'Gender and Genocide: A Split Memory,' in *Gender and Catastrophe*, ed. Ronit Lentin (London: Zed Books 1997), 18–33

47 Billie Melman, 'Gender, History and Memory: The Invention of Women's Past in the Nineteenth and Early Twentieth Centuries,' *History and Memory* 5, no. 1 (spring–summer 1993): 5–41

Chapter 1: When the Men Went Away

1 So as to respect my informants' desire for confidentiality, I refer to the interviews by number only and use pseudonyms in the text. Interview 8

2 On the history of Mennonites in Imperial Russia and the Soviet Union, see, for instance, John Friesen, ed., *Mennonites in Russia, 1788–1988: Essays in Honour of Gerhard Lohrenz* (Winnipeg: CMBC Publications 1989); James Urry, *None But Saints: The Transformation of Mennonite Life in Russia, 1789–1889* (Winnipeg: Hyperion Press 1989).

3 Harvey L. Dyck, trans. and ed., *A Mennonite in Russia: The Diaries of Jacob D. Epp, 1851–1880* (Toronto: University of Toronto Press 1991), 48. A study of one Mennonite community where the family was central is Royden K. Loewen, *Family, Church, and Market: A Mennonite Community in the Old and the New Worlds, 1850–1930* (Toronto: University of Toronto Press 1993).

4 John B. Toews, 'Childbirth, Disease, and Death among the Mennonites in Nineteenth-Century Russia,' *Mennonite Quarterly Review* 60, no. 3 (July 1986): 450–68

5 These events are described in numerous sources. See, for instance, John B. Toews, 'Early Communism and Russian Mennonite Peoplehood,' in Friesen, ed., *Mennonites in Russia*, 265–87; John B. Toews, *Czars, Soviets, and Mennonites* (Newton, KS: Faith and Life Press 1982); Dietrich Neufeld, *A Russian Dance of Death: Revolution and Civil War in the Ukraine*, trans. and ed. Al Reimer (Winnipeg: Hyperion Press 1977); Gerald Peters, trans. and ed., *Diary of Anna Baerg, 1916–1924* (Winnipeg: CMBC Publications 1985). A good fictional treatment is Al Reimer, *My Harp Is Turned to Mourning* (Winnipeg: Hyperion Press 1985).

6 For discussions of de-kulakization and collectivization in Mennonite settlements, see for instance, Toews, *Czars, Soviets, and Mennonites*, chaps. 11–12; Toews, 'Early Communism'; and Victor G. Doerksen, 'Survival and Identity in the Soviet Era,' 289–98, in Friesen, ed., *Mennonites in Russia*; Colin Peter Neufeldt, 'The Fate of Mennonites in Soviet Ukraine and the Crimea on the Eve of the "Second Revolution" (1927–1929)' (MA thesis, University of Alberta 1989); Colin P. Neufeldt, 'Through the Fires of Hell: The Dekulakization and Collectivization of the Soviet Mennonite Community, 1928–1933,' *Journal of Mennonite Studies* 16 (1998): 9–32. General studies in English include Robert Conquest, *The Harvest of Sorrow: Soviet Collectivization and the Terror-Famine* (Edmonton: University of Alberta Press in Association with the Canadian Institute of Ukrainian Studies 1986); Sheila Fitzpatrick, *Stalin's Peasants: Resistance and Survival in the Russian Village after Collectivization* (New York: Oxford University Press 1994).

7 Benjamin Pinkus, 'From the October Revolution to the Second World War,' in *The Soviet Germans: Past and Present*, ed. Ingeborg Fleischhauer and Benjamin Pinkus (London: C. Hurst 1986), 46–7

8 Toews, *Czars, Soviets, and Mennonites*, 153

9 Interview 22
10 See, for instance, Conquest, *Harvest of Sorrow*; Fitzpatrick, *Stalin's Peasants*.
Published personal acounts of conditions in Mennonite communities during
the 1930s include: John B. Toews, trans. and ed., *Letters from Susan: A
Woman's View of the Russian Mennonite Experience (1928–1941)* (North Newton, KS: Bethel College 1988); Jacob A. Neufeld, *Tiefenwege: Erfahrungen und
Erlebnisse von Russland-Mennoniten in zwei Jahrzehnten bis 1949* (Virgil, ON:
the author 1958).
11 Interview 17
12 See Conquest, *Harvest of Sorrow*, chap. 12.
13 Interview 6
14 Maria Martens Bargen to 'Dear Children Franz and Liese Bargen,' spring
1933 and 2 Feb. 1932, in *From Russia with Tears: Letters from Home and Exile,
1930–1938*, ed. Peter F. Bargen, trans. Anne Bargen (Calgary, AB: the authors
1991), 351–2
15 Interview 23
16 Interview 20
17 Robert Conquest, *The Great Terror: A Reassessment* (London: Pimlico 1992),
257
18 'World War II (Soviet Union),' *Mennonite Encyclopedia* (Scottdale, PA: Herald
Press 1990), 5: 941–2. George K. Epp states that 'By 1940 close to 50% of Mennonite families in Russia were without the head of the household.' The
source of his statistics is unclear. See 'Mennonite Immigration to Canada
after World War II,' *Journal of Mennonite Studies* 5 (1987): 110. A study of the
Baratov-Schlakhtin colonies northwest of Chortitza notes that about one-half
of the men had been arrested and exiled. The percentage of female-headed
families in three villages in these colonies just prior to the Second World War
was: Steinfeld – 46 per cent, Gruenfeld – 89 per cent, Neu-Chortitza – 51 per
cent. John Friesen, *Against the Wind: The Story of Four Mennonite Villages*
(Winnipeg: Henderson Books 1994), 95, 148 n. 40.
19 Fitzpatrick, *Stalin's Peasants*, 218
20 Anny Penner Klassen Goerzen with Anne Klassen Suderman and Susan
Thiessen Klassen, *Anny: Sheltered in the Arms of God. A True Story of Survival
in Russia* (Fort St James, BC: the author 1988), 159
21 Interview 16
22 Interview 10
23 Helene Dueck, Letter to T.D. Regehr, 16 March 1989. I am grateful to Dr T.D.
Regehr for sharing this correspondence with me. Dueck's published memoir
is: *Durch Trübsal und Not* (Winnipeg: Centre for Mennonite Brethren Studies
1995).

24 This unknown woman is quoted by the narrator in Interview 10.

25 Goerzen, *Anny*, 154

26 Gerhard Lohrenz, *The Odyssey of the Bergen Family* (Winnipeg: the author 1978), 11–12

27 Interview 13

28 Based on recent research in Soviet archives, historian Harvey L. Dyck has discovered that a very high proportion of men arrested in 1937–8 were shot at local NKVD prisons within months of their arrest.

29 Goerzen, *Anny*, 159–60

30 Maria Unger's report on her experiences was written in 1947 and quoted in C.A. DeFehr, *Memories of My Life Recalled for My Family* (Altona, MB: D.W. Friesen 1967), 99–101.

31 Interview 8

32 Letter from Liese Martens Regehr (Soviet Union) to 'Dearly Beloved Children and Grandchildren, all of you and Benjamin Klassens' (Canada), 25 Feb. 1938. In Bargen, ed., *From Russia with Tears*, 115

33 Interview 24

34 Susanna Toews recalls that during the purges of 1937–8 many women were also taken but most were eventually released and were able to recover their children. See *Trek to Freedom: The Escape of Two Sisters from South Russia during World War II*, trans. Helen Megli (Winkler, MB: Heritage Valley Publications 1976), 17.

35 Lohrenz, *Lost Generation*, 129–52. A note to the story of Anna states that it is a true story and was first published in German in 1974.

36 Fitzpatrick, *Stalin's Peasants*, 221; Annemarie Tröger, 'Between Rape and Prostitution: Survival Strategies and Chances of Emancipation for Berlin Women after World War II,' in *Women in Culture and Politics: A Century of Change*, ed. Judith Friedlander et al. (Bloomington: Indiana University Press 1986), 101–2

37 Interview 10

38 Agatha Loewen Schmidt, *Gnadenfeld, Molotschna, 1835–1943* (Kitchener: the author 1989), 51

39 Interview 23

40 Interview 17

41 Katie Friesen, *Into the Unknown* (Steinbach, MB: the author 1986), 36

42 George K. Epp, 'Mennonite Immigration to Canada after World War II,' *Journal of Mennonite Studies* 5 (1987): 111

43 Interviews 24 and 2

44 David Hildebrand, 'The Hildebrands: A Family Genealogy (1841–1984)' (research paper, Mennonite Heritage Centre n.d.), 11–12. For a description

(with photographs) of the Dnieper dam and its destruction in 1941, see Robert S. Kreider, 'World War II Comes to the Chortitza,' *Mennonite Life* 39, no. 2 (June 1984): 11–17.

45 Interview 11

46 'World War II (Soviet Union),' *Mennonite Encyclopedia*, 5: 942

47 Friesen, *Into the Unknown*, 42–3

48 The statistics about the Mennonite population are from T.D. Regehr, *Mennonites in Canada, 1939–1970: A People Transformed* (Toronto: University of Toronto Press 1996), 81, Table 4.1. The statistic of 55,000 Mennonites deported by the Soviets is taken from reports Regehr obtained in the Weierhof Mennonitische Forschungsstelle. According to Ingeborg Fleischhauer, of a prewar population of about one million, approximately 650,000–700,000 Soviet Germans were deported from the European to the Asian part of the Soviet Union prior to the German retreat in 1943. Fleischhauer, '"Operation Barbarossa" and the Deportation,' in Fleischhauer and Pinkus, eds., *Soviet Germans*, 87.

49 Epp, 'Mennonite Immigration to Canada,' 112. A standard treatment of the German occupation of parts of the Soviet Union during the Second World War is Alexander Dallin, *German Rule in Russia, 1941–1945: A Study of Occupation Policies*, 2nd rev. ed. (Boulder, CO: Westview Press 1981). Focusing specifically on the Ukraine is Bohdan Krawchenko, 'Soviet Ukraine under Nazi Occupation, 1941–44,' in *Ukraine during World War II: History and Its Aftermath*, ed. Yury Boshyk (Edmonton: Canadian Institute of Ukrainian Studies 1986), 15–37. On the ethnic German population, see Ingeborg Fleischhauer, 'The Ethnic Germans under Nazi Rule,' in Fleischhauer and Pinkus, eds., *Soviet Germans*, 92–102.

50 Interview 10

51 Schmidt, *Gnadenfeld*, 33

52 Henry H. Winter was one such minister who returned from prison to the Chortitza settlement and resumed his work under the occupation. He is mentioned often in oral and written memoirs, and his autobiography contains numerous photographs of baptisms conducted in 1942–3. The majority of the baptismal candidates are women. See Henry H. Winter, *A Shepherd of the Oppressed: Heinrich Winter, the Last Aeltester of Chortitza* (Leamington, ON: the author 1990).

53 Numerous memoirs, both oral and written, recall the 'wonderful' all-female choirs. See for instance, Jennifer Polle, 'Katherine Unger Polle: From Nicopol, Ukraine to Vancouver, B.C.' (research paper, Mennonite Heritage Centre 1990), 4; Schmidt, *Gnadenfeld*, 34; Friesen, *Into the Unknown*, 45–6.

54 Letter, Dueck to Regehr, 13

55 Schmidt, *Gnadenfeld*, 35. This is confirmed in J.C. Krause, *Gnadenfeld. Molot-schna, Sued-Ruszland, 1835–1943: Erinnerungen aus guter und schwerer Zeit* (Yarrow, BC: the author 1954), 13.
56 Interview 8
57 For a brief description of German attempts to privatize agriculture in Ukraine, see Gerhard Fast, 'Mennonites of the Ukraine under Stalin and Hitler,' *Mennonite Life* 2, no. 2 (April 1947): 18–24, 44.
58 Letter, Dueck to Regehr, 12
59 John Friesen, *Against the Wind: The Story of Four Mennonite Villages* (Winnipeg: Henderson Books 1994), 99
60 Interview 10
61 Interview 6
62 Schmidt, *Gnadenfeld*, 34
63 Letter, Dueck to Regehr, 12
64 This incident is referred to in correspondence between two historians of the Russian Mennonite experience. See Letter to David Rempel from I.G. Neufeld, 21 Feb. 1974, in David G. Rempel Collection, Thomas Fisher Rare Books, University of Toronto. I am grateful to E. Reginald Good for pointing out this document to me.
65 Interview 23. The German program of foreign labour recruitment, which included the *Ostarbeiter* is described in detail in Ulrich Herbert, *Fremdarbeiter: Politik und Praxis des 'Auslaender-Einsatzes' in der Kriegswirtschaft des Dritten Reiches* (Berlin: Verlag J.H.W. Dietz Nachf. 1985). According to German statistics, by May 1945 the total numer of Soviet *Ostarbeiter* in Germany was 2.8 million, of whom about 2.2 were from Soviet Ukraine. Soviet sources claim a much higher total of 4 million Soviets forced to work in Germany. See Wsevolod W. Isajiw, Yury Boshyk, and Roman Senkus, eds., *The Refugee Experience: Ukrainian Displaced Persons after World War II* (Edmonton: Canadian Institute of Ukrainian Studies Press 1992), 19, nn 27, 29.
66 Pamela E. Klassen, *Going By the Moon and the Stars: Stories of Two Russian Mennonite Women* (Waterloo: Wilfrid Laurier University Press 1994), 44
67 Interview 13
68 Interview 10
69 Ingrid Rimland, *The Wanderers: The Saga of Three Women Who Survived* (St Louis, MO: Concordia 1977), 124
70 Interview 25
71 Schmidt, *Gnadenfeld*, 35. Orest Subtelny notes that 'many Ukrainians expected things to improve under German rule,' and anticipated the abolition of collective farms and establishment of Ukrainian self-government. See 'Ukrainian Political Refugees: An Historical Overview,' in Isajiw, Boshyk,

and Senkus, eds., *Refugee Experience*, 11. The treatment of the Ukrainian population under Nazi occupation is also thoroughly discussed in Boshyk, ed., *Ukraine during World War II.*

72 Story of Anna in Lohrenz, *Lost Generation*, 134–5.

73 Fleischhauer, 'The Ethnic Germans under Nazi Rule,' in Fleischhauer and Pinkus, eds., *Soviet Germans*, 98

74 See, for instance, the story of a Jewish woman being shot, in Toews, *Trek to Freedom*, 20. Also Interviews 19 and 24.

75 Cornelius Krahn interview with Mary Fast, 1951. Mennonite Library and Archives (MLA), Bethel College, North Newton, Kansas.

76 Friesen, *Into the Unknown*, 68–9

77 From Mennonite Exodus notes, chap. 23 (NE-37), in Frank H. Epp Collection, Mennonite Archives of Ontario (MAO), Waterloo, Ontario. See also Interview 14.

78 Letter, Dueck to Regehr, 9

79 This painting is owned by me. Another of Schmidt's paintings, *Exodus II*, which depicts the trek out of the Ukraine in 1943, has been described as an 'icon' that has become part of the Mennonite 'collective consciousness.' See 'Conrad Grebel College acquires a Mennonite "Icon",' *Mennonite Reporter* (28 Nov. 1994): 10.

80 Friesen, *Into the Unknown*, 37

81 Interview 9

82 Interview 10

83 Agnes Thiessen, 'My Story' (unpublished manuscript 1986). This written memoir was translated by Thiessen's granddaughter and kindly shared with me by Linda Huebert Hecht.

84 One man from the Chortitza colony stated that in his village just two Mennonites that he knew of joined the Communist Party, but that was 'enough to destroy everything.' He claims that one of these betrayed his own brothers-in-law. Interview 24. Similar claims are made in Interviews 9, 14, and 28. Colin Neufeldt has examined Mennonite involvement in Communist Party organizations and in de-kulakization. See 'Through the Fires of Hell,' 9–32.

85 Fitzpatrick, *Stalin's Peasants*, chap. 9

86 Alden Braul, 'A History of the Goetz (Goetzke) Family' (research paper, Mennonite Heritage Centre 1984), 42

87 Interview 25

88 Ibid.

89 Ibid.

90 Interview 19

91 Interview 1

92 Interview 10

93 Maria Parrino, 'Breaking the Silence: Autobiographies of Italian Immigrant Women,' *Storia Nord Americana* 5, no. 1 (1988): 137–58

94 For a thoughtful and intriguing discussion of the role of martyrdom in Mennonite stories and self-perception, see Magdalene Redekop, 'Escape from the Bloody Theatre: The Making of Mennonite Stories,' *Journal of Mennonite Studies* 11 (1993): 9–22.

95 The biographies were compiled by Aaron A. Toews and published in 1949. The English translation is Toews, *Mennonite Martyrs: People Who Suffered for Their Faith, 1920–1940*, trans. John B. Toews (Winnipeg and Hillsboro, KS: Kindred Press 1990).

96 Katharina Ediger, *Under His Wings: Events in the Lives of Elder Alexander Ediger and His Family* (Kitchener: the author 1994)

97 For reflections on the question of whether Mennonite victims of Stalinist oppression were martyrs, see Rudy Wiebe, 'Flowers for Approaching the Fire: A Meditation on *The Bloody Theatre, or Martyrs Mirror*,' *Conrad Grebel Review* 16, no. 2 (spring 1998): 110–24; Harry Loewen, '"Can the Son Answer for the Father?": Reflections on the Stalinist Terror,' *Journal of Mennonite Studies* 16 (1998): 76–90.

98 Cornelius J. Dyck, *An Introduction to Mennonite History*, 3rd ed. (Scottdale, PA: Herald Press 1993), 189

99 Friesen, *Against the Wind*, 107

Chapter 2: Leaving Home, Becoming Refugees

1 Otto Klassen, producer, *The Great Trek*, Faith and Life Communications of the Conference of Mennonites in Manitoba, Winnipeg, 1991)

2 Letter, Helene Dueck to T.D. Regehr, 16 March 1989, 20

3 Edith Annchen Berg, 'Eine Reisebeschreibung,' *Die Vereinsglocke* (Oct. 1948): 8

4 Interview 26

5 Interview 9

6 Doreen Indra, 'Gender: A Key Dimension of the Refugee Experience,' *Refuge* 6, no. 3 (Feb. 1987): 3–4

7 Letter, Dueck to Regehr, 15

8 Interview 13

9 Letter, Dueck to Regehr, 23

10 Ingrid Rimland, *The Wanderers: The Saga of Three Women Who Survived* (St Louis, MO: Concordia 1977), 144

11 Letter, Dueck to Regehr, 16

12 See Jacob A. Neufeld, *Tiefenwege: Erfahrungen und Erlebnisse von Russland-Mennoniten in zwei Jahrzehnten bis 1949* (Virgil, ON: the author 1958).
13 Susanna Toews, *Trek to Freedom: The Escape of Two Sisters from South Russia during World War II*, trans. Helen Megli (Winkler, MB: Heritage Valley Publications 1976), 28
14 Herta Janzen, untitled written memoir, 8
15 Katie Friesen, *Into the Unknown* (Steinbach, MB: the author 1986), 57
16 Agnes Thiessen, 'Our Deliverance from Russia during World War II' (unpublished manuscript, n.d.). I am grateful to Linda Huebert Hecht for giving me a copy of this memoir.
17 Neufeld, *Tiefenwege*, 163, translation by T.D. Regehr
18 Interview 27
19 Interview 8
20 Erwin Strempler, 'Uprooted, But Not without Opportunity to Go On,' *Der Bote*, no. 38 (13 Oct. 1993), 22–3.
21 Interview 27
22 Mary Krueger, 'An Unforgettable Childhood Experience,' *EMMC Recorder* 26, no. 2 (Feb. 1989): 7
23 See Ingeborg Fleischhauer, 'Ethnic Germans under Nazi Rule,' in *Soviet Germans Past and Present*, ed. Ingeborg Fleischhauer and Benjamin Pinkus (London: C. Hurst 1986), 101.
24 Berg, 'Eine Reisebeschreibung,' Part 2, 6
25 These statistics are from T.D. Regehr, 'Polish and Prussian Mennonite Displaced Persons, 1944–50,' *Mennonite Quarterly Review* 66 (April 1992): 247. A detailed discussion of Prussian Mennonites during the Second World War is Horst Gerlach, 'The Final Years of Mennonites in East and West Prussia, 1943–45,' *Mennonite Quarterly Review* 66 (April and July 1992): 221–46, 391–423. Gerlach states that in 1941 there were about ten thousand Mennonites in East and West Prussia; of these, about nine hundred were killed in action and about seven hundred were murdered or died during the flight west or in Polish or Soviet camps (421). A more general history is Peter J. Klassen, *A Homeland for Strangers: An Introduction to Mennonites in Poland and Prussia* (Fresno, CA: Center for Mennonite Brethren Studies 1989). See also Bruno Ewert, 'Four Centuries of Prussian Mennonites,' *Mennonite Life* 3, no. 2 (April 1948): 10–18. By the end of the war there were only about two hundred Mennonites left in these regions.
26 Regehr, 'Polish and Prussian Mennonite,' 254. Regehr footnotes William I. Schreiber, *The Fate of the Prussian Mennonites* (Goettingen: Goettingen Research Committee 1955).
27 Erland Teichroeb, 'Die Flucht: Prussian Mennonites Flee Their Homeland' (research paper, Mennonite Heritage Centre, Winnipeg, 1987), 17

28 Interview 5

29 The expulsion of Germans from eastern Europe in the latter months of the war is well told in Alfred M. deZayas, *Nemesis at Potsdam: The Expulsion of the Germans from the East*, 3rd ed. (Lincoln: University of Nebraska Press 1989). deZayas claims that approximately fifteen million Germans were displaced from their homes as a result of the Soviet occupation of eastern Europe in the winter of 1944–5.

30 Michael R. Marrus, *The Unwanted: European Refugees in the Twentieth Century* (New York: Oxford University Press 1985), 301

31 These events are told in more detail in Regehr, 'Polish and Prussian Mennonite'; Gerlach, 'The Final Years of Mennonites'; and deZayas, *Nemesis at Potsdam*.

32 A detailed recollection of the flight west in the winter of 1945, with many references to the severe cold and snow, is Elisabeth Wiens, *Schicksalsjahr 1945: Erlebnisse nach Tagebuchnotizen* (Niagara-on-the-Lake: the author 1993); also, Elizabeth Wiens, 'Flucht vom Weichseltal 1945,' *Mennonitische Geschichtsblaetter* 38 (1981): 7–22. See also the memoir of a Mennonite woman originally from Breslau, in eastern Germany: Margaret L. Dick, *From Breslau to America* (Wichita, KS: the author 1992).

33 Wiens, *Schicksalsjahr 1945*, 28–9.

34 Marga Siemens, 'Schweres Schicksal einer jungen Frau,' *Der Bote* 24 (5 March 1947): 3

35 For instance Interview 13. In this memory source, a young woman found her mother and sisters when she practically stumbled over them at a railway station, awaiting transport to the West. The story of Katie Dirks Friesen is very similar, as told in her autobiography, *Into the Unknown*, chap. 5. Edith Annchen Berg was reunited with her family just prior to her evacuation from school. See 'Eine Reisebeschreibung,' 14.

36 Friesen, *Into the Unknown*, chap. 5

37 Interview 13

38 Irene Peters, 'Meine Erlebnisse in Deutschland,' *Menno-Blatt* 18 (July 1947): 7

39 Recollections of Anna Heide Retzlaff written at the age of eighty-two. In Agatha Loewen Schmidt, *Gnadenfeld, Molotschna, 1835–1943* (Kitchener: the author 1989), 72

40 Interview 28

41 Fleischhauer,'The Ethnic Germans under Nazi Rule,' 101–2. Fleischhauer notes that the loss of life on the transport east was 15 to 30 per cent.

42 Mark R. Elliott, *Pawns of Yalta: Soviet Refugees and America's Role in Their Repatriation* (Urbana: University of Illinois Press 1982), 82. Other discussions of repatriation include Nikolai Tolstoy, *Victims of Yalta* (London: Hodder and

Stoughton 1977) and Nicholas Bethell, *The Last Secret: Forcible Repatriation to Russia, 1944–1947* (London: Deutsch 1974).

43 T.D. Regehr, *Mennonites in Canada, 1939–1970: A People Transformed* (Toronto: University of Toronto Press 1996), 81

44 Elsie Pauls, 'My Family and My Daily Work,' *George Street Journal* 4, no. 6 (Feb. 1993): 13

45 Interview 10

46 Interview 7

47 Interview 13

48 'A Letter from Germany,' *War Sufferers' Relief Bulletin* 2, no. 5 (July 1946): 6 The letter is signed 'Agnes and children.'

49 Interview 27

50 Eve Kolinsky, *Women in Contemporary Germany: Life, Work and Politics*, rev. ed. (Providence, RI: Berg 1993), 26–8. For a detailed discussion of the Soviet occupation of Germany, see Norman M. Naimark, *The Russians in Germany: A History of the Soviet Zone of Occupation, 1945–1949* (Cambridge: Belknap Press of Harvard University Press 1995).

51 Interview 19

52 Edna Schroeder Thiessen's story is analysed by Angela Showalter, 'Growing Up in a Crumbling World: World War II Poland as Remembered by a Mennonite Woman' (research paper, Goshen College, Goshen, IN, 1995), 26, 32.

53 Harry Loewen, 'From Russia to Canada: My Mother Was Betrayed by the Church,' *Mennonite Reporter*, 1 Oct. 1990, 9

54 David Hildebrand, 'The Hildebrands: A Family Genealogy (1841–1984)' (research paper, Mennonite Heritage Centre, Winnipeg, n.d.), 16–17

55 Interview 25

56 Interview 27

57 Interview 10

58 Several sources suggest that Soviet soldiers were incited to rape in part by the literary propaganda of Soviet writer Ilya Ehrenburg. See, for instance, de Zayas, *Nemesis at Potsdam*, 65–6. One first-person account observes that Soviet soldiers, in explaining their assault on German territory and civilians, would recite a seemingly rehearsed list of German atrocities against their people, implying that there was a systematic element in their attacks. See 'Report of Johanna Dueck, formerly of Marienburg, West Prussia, on the Death of the Marienburg Mennonite Home for the Elderly, known as "Helenenheim,"' in Horst Penner, *Die ost- und westpreussischen Mennoniten in ihrem religioesen und sozialen Leben in ihren kulturellen und wirtschaftlichen Leistungen* (Kirchheimbolanden: the author 1987), 2: 142.

59 Annemarie Tröger cites statistics of German women raped, which vary from

twenty thousand to half a million. See 'Between Rape and Prostitution: Survival Strategies and Chances of Emancipation for Berlin Women after World War II,' in *Women in Culture and Politics: A Century of Change*, ed. Judith Friedlander et al. (Bloomington: Indiana University Press 1986), 99. See also Tröger, 'German Women's Memories of World War II,' in *Behind the Lines: Gender and the Two World Wars*, ed. Margaret Randolph Higonnet et al. (New Haven: Yale University Press 1987), 285–9. Barbara Johr estimates that two million women were raped in the aftermath of war, 12 per cent of whom died as a result. See 'Die Ereignisse in Zahlen,' in *BeFreier und Befreite: Krieg, Vergewaltigungen, Kinder*, ed. Helke Sander and Barbara Johr (Munich: Verlag Antje Kunstmann 1992), 59. Included in Johr's estimate are women in the German population in the expelled territories, the population in the Soviet zone of occupation, and in greater Berlin. Norman Naimark acknowledges that Johr's statistics are possible, but says the number is 'more likely in the hundreds of thousands.' See *Russians in Germany*, 133. See also the special issue, 'Berlin 1945: War and Rape – "Liberators Take Liberties",' *October* 72 (spring 1995).

60 Ruth Seifert, 'War and Rape: A Preliminary Analysis,' in *Mass Rape: The War against Women in Bosnia-Herzegovina*, ed. Alexandra Stiglmayer (Lincoln: University of Nebraska Press 1994), 57

61 A more detailed discussion of Mennonite refugees and rape is in my article, 'The Memory of Violence: Soviet and East European Mennonite Refugees and Rape in the Second World War,' *Journal of Women's History* 9, no. 1 (spring 1997): 58–87.

62 Helene Dueck, 'Refugee Family Scattered in War-time Trek,' *Christian Info News*, July 1993, 20

63 Interview 5

64 Letter dated 6 Feb. 1949. Quoted in C.P. Toews, Heinrich Friesen, and Arnold Dyck, *The Kuban Settlement*, trans. Herbert Giesbrecht (Winnipeg: CMBC Publications and Manitoba Mennonite Historical Society 1989), 90.

65 Recollections of Anna Heide Retzlaff, in Schmidt, *Gnadenfeld*, 72. Ruth Harris, in her study of the First World War testimonies of French women, also observed a rhetorical style in which as little as possible was said about the assault itself. See 'The "Child of the Barbarian": Rape, Race, and Nationalism in France during the First World War,' *Past and Present* 141 (Nov. 1993): 170–206.

66 Recollections of Susanna Janzen Wiens, in Schmidt, *Gnadenfeld*, 65

67 Showalter, 'Growing Up,' 27–8

68 Cornelius Krahn interview with Mary Fast, c1951, Mennonite Library and Archives, Bethel College, North Newton, Kansas.

69 Psychiatrist Vera Folnegovic-Smalc, who has studied wartime rape in Croatia and Bosnia-Herzegovina, found that the psychiatric consequences for secondary victims (observers) were sometimes greater than for primary victims. See 'Psychiatric Aspects of the Rapes in the War against the Republics of Croatia and Bosnia-Herzegovina,' in Stiglmayer, ed., *Mass Rape*, 174.

70 'Report of Johanna Dueck,' 141–5

71 The story of Helene Hamm is told near the beginning of the memoir of Helene Berg, an elderly refugee from the Ukraine, who was resident in the home for the elderly for close to a year. Berg's story is almost identical in detail to that of Johanna Dueck. See *Unsere Flucht: Erinnerungen von Frau Helene Berg, frueher Halbstadt, Sued-Russland* (Baden, Germany 1947).

72 Naimark, *Russians in Germany*, 86

73 Interview 17

74 Tröger, 'Rape and Prostitution,' 102; Atina Grossmann, 'A Question of Silence: The Rape of German Women by Occupation Soldiers,' *October* 72 (spring 1995): 54–5

75 Interview 28

76 Rimland, *The Wanderers*, 196. In an interview following the publication of her novel, the author of *The Wanderers* acknowledged the 'compromising survival-tactics' made by her mother (the heroine), admitting that she owed her life to those compromises. See Mary M. Enns, 'Ingrid Rimland Turns to Face the Forces That Shaped her Life,' *Mennonite Mirror* 8, no. 5 (Jan. 1979): 6.

77 Gerhard Lohrenz, *The Odyssey of the Bergen Family* (Winnipeg: the author 1978), 92–3

78 Written memoir of a refugee woman (name withheld) given to the author.

79 Interview 28

80 The idea of 'master narratives' as applied to German women's stories of rape is discussed by Gertrud Koch, 'Blood, Sperm, and Tears,' *October* 72 (spring 1995): 35–6.

81 Hildebrand, 'The Hildebrands,' 15

82 Grossmann, 'A Question of Silence,' 60.

83 Jacob A. Neufeld, a refugee from Gnadenfeld, Molotschna, suggests that frequently people did not picture what was imminent for them in the Soviet Union. See *Tiefenwege*, 230.

84 One man described how a group of Mennonite men, married and single, were voluntarily repatriated from an American prisoner-of-war camp because they believed that they would be reunited with their families. Interview 14. In another instance, a Mennonite woman went to a repatriation camp but then returned to the farm where she was employed, heeding the warnings of the French POWs who were also working there. For her, 'It was

a very hard decision,' vindicated when she later learned that all the Mennonites who had willingly returned had been sent to hard labour in the Asian
republic of Kazakhstan. Her memoir suggests a certain freedom in the com-
ings and goings from repatriation camps, which further reinforces the notion
that some returnees went willingly. Interview 17. Other Mennonites were
more suspicious and resisted the 'carrots' that Soviet officials dangled in the
form of hopes that they would see exiled family members. Interview 8.

85 Neufeld, *Tiefenwege*, 229

86 See, for instance, Cornelius Ryan, *The Last Battle* (New York: Simon and
Schuster 1966); Naimark, *Russians in Germany*, 86.

87 Peter Dyck, a Mennonite Central Committee relief worker in postwar
Europe, observed that while there were a lot of suicides among other refugees and Germans, there were few among the Mennonites. See Robert Kreider, ed., *Interviews With Peter J. Dyck and Elfrieda Klassen Dyck: Experiences in
Mennonite Central Committee Service in Europe, 1941–1949* (Akron, PA: Mennonite Central Committee 1988), 378. One person interviewed was aware
that there were suicides among Mennonites faced with repatriation in the
Munich area, though he didn't have any specific details. Interview 19. Walter
Gering, a relief worker who visited Mennonites in Danish camps for displaced persons, wrote about refugees receiving news of missing loved ones
who had committed suicide. See 'With Prussian Mennonites in Denmark,'
Mennonite Life 2, no. 4 (Oct. 1947): 14. Horst Gerlach also makes a general reference to suicides among Prussian Mennonites in 'The Final Years of Mennonites,' 419.

88 Friesen, *Into the Unknown*, 83

89 Dick, *From Breslau to America*, 71

90 I first heard this story told by Dr George K. Epp at a symposium on Mennonites in Canada during the Second World War, held in Winnipeg in 1987. He
was reportedly told the story in confidence by a Mennonite refugee woman.

91 Interview 25. The memoir of a Prussian Mennonite man corroborates this
form of suicide; he describes how one of his aunts jumped with her baby into
a lake to escape constant raping: Horst Gerlach, *Nightmare in Red* (Carol
Stream, IL: Creation House c1970), 32.

92 See especially Johr, 'Die Ereignisse in Zahlen,' in Sander and Johr, eds.,
BeFreier und Befreite; Grossmann, 'A Question of Silence.' Also Atina Gross-
mann, *Reforming Sex: The German Movement for Birth Control and Abortion
Reform, 1920–1950* (New York: Oxford University Press 1995), chap. 8.

93 Interview 28

94 Interview 2

95 Norman Naimark says that 'Many women ... chose to go ahead and have

their babies,' but acknowledges that no data are available on the number of occupation babies – called *Russenkinder* – born in the Soviet zone. See *Russians in Germany*, 124. Stuart Liebman and Annette Michelson state that 'many thousands' of such children were born. See 'After the Fall: Women in the House of the Hangmen,' *October* 72 (spring 1995): 9. Barbara Johr estimates that 5 per cent (1,156) of babies born in Berlin from September 1945 to August 1946 were *Russenkinder*. See 'Die Ereignisse in Zahlen,' 54.

96 Cornelius Krahn interview with Mrs Micka, 1951, Mennonite Library and Archives, Bethel College, North Newton, Kansas.

97 Interview 28

98 Friesen, *Into the Unknown*, 52

99 This particular statement was made by C.F. Klassen, a Canadian Mennonite who worked with refugees in postwar Europe. See 'Mennonite Refugees – Our Challenge,' in *Proceedings of the Fourth Mennonite World Conference* (3–10 Aug. 1948), 183. The Berlin rescue story has been described thoroughly elsewhere. See, for instance, Frank H. Epp, *Mennonite Exodus: The Rescue and Resettlement of the Russian Mennonites since the Communist Revolution* (Altona, MB: D.W. Friesen 1962), 376–9; Peter Dyck and Elfrieda Dyck, *Up from the Rubble: The Epic Rescue of Thousands of War-Ravaged Mennonite Refugees* (Scottdale, PA: Herald Press 1991); Herbert Klassen and Maureen Klassen, *Ambassador to His People: C.F. Klassen and the Russian Mennonite Refugees* (Winnipeg: Kindred Press 1990). The first fictional treatment of the postwar Mennonite refugees centred around the Berlin events: Barbara Smucker, *Henry's Red Sea* (Scottdale, PA: Herald Press 1955). A critical assessment of the historiography of the Berlin story is T.D. Regehr, 'Anatomy of a Mennonite Miracle: The Berlin Rescue of 30–31 January 1947,' *Journal of Mennonite Studies* 9 (1991): 11–33.

100 Interview 28

101 Agatha Schmidt describes how during the famine of 1932–3 in the Ukraine, a woman 'thoroughly shrouded to conceal her identity' appeared with a freshly baked loaf of bread, left it on the table, and disappeared. See Schmidt, *Gnadenfeld*, 47. Also, Ben Stobbe tells the story of how his father was visited by an angel who urged him to continue his flight westward ahead of advancing Soviet troops in Poland in January 1945, at a moment when there seemed no hope of escape: 'The "Prompt",' *George Street Journal* 4, no. 6 (Feb. 1993): 14–15. A very similar story is that of Annie (Fehderau) Bartsch, who says she was woken at night by a voice saying 'Away!' – instructing her to flee to the American zone. See Katharina Ediger, *Under His Wings: Events in the Lives of Elder Alexander Ediger and His Family* (Kitchener, ON: the author 1994), 120–1.

102 Interview 6

103 Irmgard Kriese's story is told in Ediger, *Under His Wings*, 98.

Chapter 3: New Homes, New Identities

1 Interview 28
2 Dariusz Stola, 'Forced Migrations in Central European History,' *International Migration Review* 26, no. 2 (summer 1992): 330. See also Michael R. Marrus, *The Unwanted: European Refugees in the Twentieth Century* (New York: Oxford University Press 1985), especially chap. 5.
3 Of the 35,000 Mennonites who had left the Soviet Union, approximately 12,000 remained in Europe after postwar repatriations. Mennonites who had formerly resided in Danzig, Prussia, and northern Poland constituted another 2,000 refugees. The latter statistic is from T.D. Regehr, 'Of Dutch or German Ancestry? Mennonite Refugees, MCC, and the International Refugee Organization,' *Journal of Mennonite Studies* 13 (1995): 7.
4 The history of the Mennonite Central Committee is told in a variety of published sources. See for instance, John C. Unruh, *In the Name of Christ: A History of the Mennonite Central Committee and Its Service, 1920–1951* (Scottdale, PA: Herald Press 1952); 'Mennonite Central Committee, 1920–1970,' special issue of *Mennonite Quarterly Review* 44, no. 3 (July 1970); Frank H. Epp, ed. *Partners in Service: The Story of Mennonite Central Committee Canada* (Winnipeg: Mennonite Central Committee Canada 1983).
5 Siegfried Janzen, 'Das fluechtlingslager Gronau,' *Der Mennonit* (1949): 52–3, 64
6 Walter Gering, 'Displaced Mennonites in Denmark,' *War Sufferers' Relief Bulletin* 2, no. 4 (June 1946): 5–6
7 Robert Kreider, *Interviews with Peter J. Dyck and Elfrieda Klassen Dyck: Experiences in Mennonite Central Committee Service in Europe, 1941–1949* (Akron, PA: Mennonite Central Committee 1988), Attachment 29
8 Gering, 'Displaced Mennonites,' 5–6
9 Frank H. Epp, *Mennonite Exodus: The Rescue and Resettlement of the Russian Mennonites since the Communist Revolution* (Altona, MB: D.W. Friesen 1962), 368
10 Cornelia Lehn, 'Das Lebensbrot,' *Der Bote* 28 (18 July 1951): 3
11 Siegfried Janzen to William Snyder, 4 Nov. 1949. Mennonite Heritage Centre (hereafter MHC), XXII-A.1, Canadian Mennonite Board of Colonization Collection (hereafter CMBC) (166), 1328/981
12 Klassen's heroic status derives in part from his sudden death in 1954 while working in Germany. See Herbert Klassen and Maureen Klassen, *Ambassador to His People: C.F. Klassen and the Russian Mennonite Refugees* (Winnipeg: Kindred Press 1990).

13 Christine Wiebe, 'Cornelius Wall,' in *Something Meaningful for God: The Stories of Some Who Served with MCC*, ed. Cornelius J. Dyck (Scottdale, PA: Herald Press 1981), 194–214

14 Siegfried Janzen to William Snyder, 4 Nov. 1949. MHC, XXII-A.1, CMBC (166), 1328/981

15 Oberschwester Elise Schwarz, 'MCC.-Krankenhaus in Gronau,' *Unser Blatt* 1, no. 5 (15 Dec. 1947):4

16 Cornelius Wall to Orie O. Miller, 31 Aug. 1948. MHC, XXII-A.1, CMBC (163), 1331/996

17 Mrs C. Wall, 'How Prayer Helps,' *MCC Women's Activities Letter* no. 77 (Feb. 1951)

18 Susan B. Peters to 'Helen,' 15 Nov. 1946. Centre for Mennonite Brethren Studies (hereafter CMBS), Susan B. Peters Collection.

19 Martha Bohachevsky-Chomiak, 'The Women's Movement in the DP Camps,' in Wsevolod Isajiw, Yury Boshyk, and Roman Senkus, eds., *The Refugee Experience: Ukrainian Displaced Persons after World War II* (Edmonton: Canadian Institute of Ukrainian Studies Press 1992), 203–4

20 Unruh, *In the Name of Christ*, 190

21 'Mennonite Central Committee, Refugee Section, Report of Siegfried Janzen, Director Gronau Camp, Unit Directors' Conference, Neustadt, French Zone, Germany, November 24–26, 1948.' MHC, XXII-A.1, CMBC (166), 1328/977

22 'Protokoll der Bruderberatung der Mennonitengemeinschaft im Emigr.-Lager Fallingbostel am 30. Mai 1948.' MHC, XXII-A.1, CMBC (163), 1331/996

23 Cornelius J. Dyck, to C.F. Klassen, J.J. Thiessen, Wm. Snyder, 8 July 1948, with 'Statistik der mennonitischen Lagerinsassen in Fallingbostel, aufgeteilt nach Geschlecht und Alter.' MHC, XXII-A.1, CMBC (163), 1331/996

24 Doreen Indra, 'Gender: A Key Dimension of the Refugee Experience,' *Refuge* 6, no. 3 (Feb. 1987): 4

25 Jacob A. Neufeld, *Tiefenwege: Erfahrungen und Erlebnisse von Russland-Mennoniten in zwei Jahrzehnten bis 1949* (Virgil, ON: the author 1958), 239–41

26 Ibid., 239

27 For a biography of Elfrieda Klassen Dyck, see Marion Keeney Preheim, 'Elfrieda Dyck,' in Dyck, ed., *Something Meaningful for God*, 215–57.

28 Kreider, *Interviews*, 203

29 Ibid.

30 Ibid., 196

31 From 'Activities Report, January, February, March, Fallingbostel, Germany.' This report was probably written by an MCC worker, although no name or

date are given. Conrad Grebel College Archives (hereafter CGCA), Frank H. Epp Collection, *Mennonite Exodus* notes, chap. 24

32 J. Wichert, 'Unter den Fluechtlingen,' *Der Bote* 25 (17 March 1948): 2

33 Henry H. Winter, *A Shepherd of the Oppressed: Heinrich Winter, the Last Aeltester of Chortitza* (Leamington, ON: the author 1990), 140

34 'Dear Sisters,' *MCC Women's Activities Letter* no. 38 (1 Sept. 1947): 2

35 Interview 23

36 Mark Wyman, *DP: Europe's Displaced Persons, 1945–1951* (Philadelphia: Balch Institute Press 1989), 109

37 Epp, *Mennonite Exodus*, 385. See Winter, *Shepherd of the Oppressed*, 137–41, for pictures and lists of baptisms in Germany in 1947.

38 Peter J. Dyck to William T. Snyder, 4 Feb. 1948. MHC, XXII-A.1, CMBC (205), 1367/1356

39 Siegfried Janzen, to J.J. Thiessen, 13 June 1948. MHC, XXII-A.1, CMBC (163), 1331/996

40 Lydia and Johann Wichert to J.J. Thiessen, 23 Dec. 1947. MHC, II-A-1.1, Conference of Mennonites in Canada (121), Secretary Correspondence Files

41 Johann and Lydia Wichert to J.J. Thiessen, 18 Feb. 1948. MHC, II-A-1.1, Conference of Mennonites in Canada (121), Secretary Correspondence Files

42 This argument is discussed in detail in Regehr, 'Of Dutch or German Ancestry?' 7–25. See also Epp, *Mennonite Exodus*, chap. 24.

43 Regehr, 'Of Dutch or German Ancestry?' 19

44 C.F. Klassen, Mennonite Central Committee Special Commissioner to Europe, 'Statement Concerning Mennonite Refugees' (1948). MHC, XXII-A.1, CMBC (163), 1325/957

45 Interview 6

46 Interviews 6, 10, and 19

47 Interview 13

48 Interview 1

49 C.F. Klassen to Orie O. Miller and William T. Snyder, 21 Sept. 1948. CMBS, C.F. Klassen Collection, box 2

50 Interview 1

51 Interview 6

52 Marrus, *The Unwanted*, 312–13

53 Quoted in Marie Brunk, 'Chief Concerns of Refugees,' *Gospel Herald* 39, no. 46 (11 Feb. 1947): 992.

54 'Schweres Schicksal einer jungen Frau,' *Der Bote* 24 (5 March 1947): 3. My translation.

55 'Mennonite Central Committee, Refugee Section, Report of Siegfried Janzen, Director Gronau Camp, Unit Directors' Conference, Neustadt, French

Zone, Germany, November 24–26, 1948.' MHC, XXII-A.1, CMBC (166), 1328/977

56 Victor Thiessen, 'Only by the Grace of God: The Story of a Mennonite Family' (research paper, Mennonite Heritage Centre 1978), 58.

57 Siegfried Janzen to William Snyder, 4 Nov. 1949. MHC, XXII-A.1, CMBC (166), 1328/981

58 Interview 17

59 Reg Good interview with Siegfried Janzen, 17 March 1985, CGCA

60 Information from this case is from 'Vermerke ueber alte Londonfaelle.' MHC, XXII-A.1, CMBC (163), 1331/996

61 For a brief summary of Canadian immigration policy for this period, see, for instance, Reg Whitaker, *Canadian Immigration Policy since Confederation* (Ottawa: Canadian Historical Association 1991). Also, Valerie Knowles, *Strangers at Our Gates: Canadian Immigration and Immigration Policy, 1540–1990* (Toronto: Dundurn Press 1992). For immigration policy pertaining to post-war displaced persons, see Milda Danys, *DP: Lithuanian Immigration to Canada after the Second World War* (Toronto: Multicultural History Society of Ontario 1986), chaps. 4–11.

62 The Canadian Mennonite Board of Colonization was established in 1922 with the initial purpose of arranging the emigration of Mennonites from the USSR to Canada. Between the years 1923 and 1930, approximately 21,000 Mennonites entered Canada, assisted by the CMBC and funded mainly on credit with the Canadian Pacific Railway. The organization dissolved in the early 1960s, and its large archival collection was deposited in Winnipeg at the present Mennonite Heritage Centre. The official history of the CMBC is Epp, *Mennonite Exodus.*

63 Epp, *Mennonite Exodus,* 392

64 Doreen Harms, to J.J. Thiessen, 6 Aug. 1954. MHC, XXII-A.1, CMBC (166), 1328/978

65 Ibid.

66 G.R. Gaeddert, to C.F. Klassen, 30 Oct. 1951. MHC, XXII-A.1, CMBC (166), 1328/980

67 Arnold J. Regier, Director, Gronau Unit, to J.J. Thiessen, Canadian Mennonite Board of Colonization, 8 Feb. 1952. MHC, XXII-A.1, CMBC (166), 1328/977

68 Ibid.

69 For a detailed study of Canadian immigration policy toward German nationals and ethnic Germans, see Angelika E. Sauer, 'A Matter of Domestic Policy? Canadian Immigration Policy and the Admission of Germans, 1945–1950,' *Canadian Historical Review* 74, no. 2 (June 1993): 226–63.

Chapter 4: 'Weak' Women in Paraguay

1 Donna Yoder, 'Mennonite Refugees Leave for New Homeland,' *MCC Services Bulletin* 1, no. 1 (March 1947): 1
2 This total is from 'Table 20 – Distribution of Refugees Arriving in South America, 1947–48' in Frank H. Epp, *Mennonite Exodus: The Rescue and Resettlement of the Russian Mennonites since the Communist Revolution* (Altona, MB: D.W. Friesen 1962), 390. Descriptions of the four transports can be found in Peter Dyck and Elfrieda Dyck, *Up from the Rubble: The Epic Rescue of Thousands of War-Ravaged Mennonite Refugees* (Scottdale, PA: Herald Press 1991). The three major sailings that followed the *Volendam* were the *General Heintzelman* (February 1948), the *Charlton Monarch* (March 1948), and the *Volendam II* (October 1948).
3 For background on Mennonite settlements in Paraguay, see, for instance, J. Winfield Fretz, *Pilgrims in Paraguay* (Scottdale, PA: Herald Press 1953); Peter P. Klassen, *Die Mennoniten in Paraguay: Reich Gottes und Reich dieser Welt* (Bolanden-Weierhof, Germany: Mennonitischer Geschichtsverein 1988).
4 William Schroeder and Helmet T. Huebert, *Mennonite Historical Atlas* (Winnipeg: Springfield Publishers 1990), 115
5 J.W. Warkentin, 'Carving a Home Out of the Primeval Forest,' *Mennonite Quarterly Review* 24, no. 2 (April 1950): 143
6 Although the majority of the post–Second World War immigrants to South America settled in the colonies Volendam and Neuland, several hundred made their homes in the other Mennonite colonies in Paraguay. In 1950, 1,200 postwar refugees from Danzig, West Prussia, and Poland established the settlement of El Ombu in Uruguay.
7 J.W. Warkentin, 'Carving a Home Out of Primeval Forest,' *Proceedings of the Fourth Mennonite World Conference* (1948), 196–9; C.A. DeFehr, 'Our Visit to Colony Volendam,' *MCC Services Bulletin* 1, no. 10 (Dec. 1947): 2
8 Interview 8
9 Warkentin, 'Carving a Home Out' (1948), 197–8
10 C.A. DeFehr, 'Our Visit to Colony Volendam,' *MCC Services Bulletin* 1, no. 10 (Dec. 1947): 2. This article also provides descriptive detail of clearing the land and house-building in the new colony. See photo in Epp, *Mennonite Exodus*, 382.
11 'Volendam and Neuland,' *Mennonite Life* 5, no. 1 (Jan. 1950): 28
12 Ella Berg, 'My Visit to the Chaco's New Colony,' *MCC Services Bulletin* 2, no. 4 (June 1948): 2, 6
13 Fretz, *Pilgrims in Paraguay*, 67

14 J. Winfield Fretz, 'Paraguay – Where Women Carry the Heavy End of the Load,' *Canadian Mennonite* 6, no. 50 (18 Dec. 1958): 4–5
15 Interview 8
16 Interviews 1 and 2
17 Report by C.A. DeFehr to 'Dear teachers and College students,' at Goshen College, Goshen, Indiana, 6 Jan. 1948. MHC, XXII-A.1, CMBC (204), 1366/1353
18 Interview 2
19 Cornelius J. Dyck, 'In South America,' *Mennonite Life* 6, no. 4 (Oct. 1951): 28
20 C.A. DeFehr, 'Report of the Work Done in the Past Year in Connection with the Immigrant Group, 2,305 in Number, Which Landed in Buenos Aires, February 22, 1947,' 3. Centre for Mennonite Brethren Studies (CMBS), C.A. DeFehr Collection, box 3
21 John W. Warkentin, 'New Settlers Receive Much Help from Older Colonies in Paraguay,' *MCC Services Bulletin* 1, no. 11 (Jan. 1948): 2; Fretz, *Pilgrims in Paraguay*, 43
22 Vernon Neuschwander, 'Mennonite Settlement in the Chaco,' *MCC Services Bulletin* 1, no. 9 (Nov. 1947): 2
23 'Brueder in Not! Zur Neusiedlung,' *Menno-Blatt* 18, no. 8 (Aug. 1947):4
24 Klassen, *Die Mennoniten in Paraguay*, 188. My translation
25 Raymond Breton, 'Collective Dimensions of the Cultural Transformation of Ethnic Communities and the Larger Society,' in *Migration and the Transformation of Cultures*, ed. Jean Burnet et al. (Toronto: Multicultural History Society of Ontario 1992), 6–7
26 Klassen, *Die Mennoniten in Paraguay*, 189. My translation
27 Interview 1
28 H. Duerksen, to C.A. DeFehr, 9 Nov. 1948. MHC, XXII-A.1, CMBC (205), 1367/1358
29 C.A. DeFehr, to O.O. Miller and Wm. T. Snyder, 28 Oct. 1947. MHC, XXII-A.1, CMBC (205), 1367/1357
30 Jakob Isaak, 'The Settlement in Paraguay from the Point of View of the Colonist,' *Proceedings of the Fourth Mennonite World Conference* (1948), 192–3
31 J.W. Warkentin, 'Carving a Home' (1948), 199
32 C.A. DeFehr to A.A. Wiens, 19 Aug. 1947. MHC, XXII-A.1, CMBC (205), 1367/1357
33 John B. Toews, *With Courage to Spare: The Life of B.B. Janz, 1877–1964* (Hillsboro, KS: Board of Christian Literature of the General Conference of Mennonite Brethren Churches 1978), 135
34 Henry H. Winter, *A Shepherd of the Oppressed: Heinrich Winter, the Last Aeltester of Chortitza* (Leamington, ON: the author 1990), 190

35 *History of Alberta Mennonite Women in Mission, 1947–1977* (n.p., n.d.), 9. Mrs Sawatzky's first name is not provided in the source.

36 'Protokoll No.8 der Gemeinderatssitzung am 16. September 1954' in Protokollbuch No.1 Sitzungen des Gemeinderates der Sargent Avenue Mennonitengemeinde, pp. 20–1. MHC, III-62, Records of Sargent Avenue Mennonite Church, microfilm 191

37 Interview 26

38 Interview 8

39 From Fretz, *Pilgrims in Paraguay*, 105–6. For further description of the Waisenamt system, see Jake Peters, *The Waisenamt: A History of Mennonite Inheritance Custom* (Steinbach, MB: Mennonite Village Museum 1985).

40 'Confidential Report of J.W. Fretz to the Executive Committee of the Mennonite Central Committee on his study trip to South America,' n.d, p. 12. MHC, XXII-A.1, CMBC/CMRIC (208), 1370/1375

41 H. Duerksen to C.A. DeFehr, 9 Nov. 1948. MHC, XXII-A.1, CMBC (205), 1367/1358

42 Interview 26

43 Dyck and Dyck, *Up from the Rubble*, 332. Also, Robert Kreider, *Interviews with Peter J. Dyck and Elfrieda Klassen Dyck: Experiences in Mennonite Central Committee Service in Europe, 1941–1949* (Akron, PA: Mennonite Central Committee 1988), 188

44 Joan Chandler, *Women without Husbands: An Exploration of the Margins of Marriage* (London: Macmillan 1991), 121

45 Peter Dyck quoted in Kreider, *Interviews*, 378

46 C.A. DeFehr to Jakob Kasdorf, 16 Sept. 1948. MHC, XXII-A.1, CMBC, 1367/1358

47 Vernon Neuschwander to C.A. DeFehr, 1 Nov. 1948. MHC, XXII-A.1, CMBC (205), 1367/1358

48 Ibid.

49 Dyck, 'In South America,' 28

50 C.A. DeFehr, 'A Brief Summary of the Refugee Groups which came to Paraguay and Uruguay in 1948 on the Heintzelman, Charlton Monarch, and Volendam' (report given to the annual meeting of the Mennonite Aid Section, Chicago, 30 Dec. 1948), 5

51 Elfrieda Toews Nafziger, *A Man of His Word: A Biography of John A. Toews* (Hillsboro, KS: Kindred Press 1992), 60–1

52 'Confidential Report of J.W. Fretz to the Executive Committee of the Mennonite Central Committee on his study trip to South America,' n.d, p.8. MHC, XXII-A.1, CMBC/CMRIC (208), 1370/1375

53 Interview 26

54 Ibid.
55 From CMBS, C.A. DeFehr Collection, box 3. It is important to remember that these numbers did not include children and other unbaptized church attenders.
56 Interview 1
57 Berg, 'My Visit to the Chaco's New Colony,' 6
58 This incident is described in Dyck and Dyck, Up from the Rubble, 330–1.
59 See Kreider, Interviews, 329–30
60 From minutes of meeting of MCC workers at Frankfurt, Germany, 4 Jan. 1948. MHC, XXII-A.1, CMBC, 1369/1366
61 William T. Snyder, to C.A. DeFehr, 16 Sept. 1948. In MHC, XXII-A.1, CMBC, 1369/1366
62 Dyck and Dyck, Up from the Rubble, 334–5
63 Ibid., 332–40
64 Ibid.
65 Interview 1
66 Peter J. Dyck to C.A. DeFehr, 17 Sept. 1948. MHC, XXII-A.1, CMBC, 1367/1358
67 Isaak, 'The Settlement in Paraguay,' 192
68 'Auszug aus dem Protokoll der Predigerkonferenz der Mennoniten von Sued-Amerika, abgehalten vom 14.–17. Juli 1949 in Fernheim, Dorf Karsruhe, Chaco, Paraguay.' CMBS, Canadian Conference of Mennonite Brethren Churches Collection, box 1, Board of Spiritual and Social Concerns, B220
69 Ibid.
70 For instance, Dyck and Dyck, Up from the Rubble, 341–2; Interview 26
71 P.C. Hiebert, to C.A. DeFehr, 11 Sept. 1948. MHC, XXII-A.1, CMBC, 1367/1358
72 Elfrieda Dyck, to C.A. DeFehr and A.W. Warkentin, 29 July 1948. CMBS, C.A. DeFehr Collection, box 3
73 C.A. DeFehr, to P. Dyck, 27 July 1948. CMBS, C.A. DeFehr Collection, box 3
74 C.A. DeFehr, to J.A. Warkentin, 11 June 1948. CMBS, C.A. DeFehr Collection, box 3
75 C.A. DeFehr, 'Ein kurzer Ueberblick, betreffs der Immigranten-Gruppen, die im Jahre 1948 mit den Schiffen: Heintzelmann, Charlton Monarch und Volendam nach Paraguay und teilweise nach Uruguay gekommen sind,' 9 Dec. 1948. CMBS, C.A. DeFehr Collection, box 3
76 Interview 1. Similar sentiments are expressed in Interviews 24 and 26.
77 Ingrid Rimland, The Wanderers: The Saga of Three Women Who Survived (St Louis, MO: Concordia 1977), 233–4
78 Interview 8

79 Fretz, *Pilgrims in Paraguay*, 62–4
80 Interview 26
81 J. Winfield Fretz, 'Mennonite Aid Section, Report of the Chairman to MCC Annual Meeting,' 8 Jan. 1948. MHC, XXII-A.1, CMBC (205), 1367/1356
82 Report of C.A. DeFehr to 'Dear teachers and College students'
83 Rie Hoogeveen, 'From Paraguay to Germany,' *Mennonite Life* 18, no. 3 (July 1963): 123. In the article it is not explicitly stated, but is nevertheless implied, that most of the 583 were postwar immigrants to Paraguay.
84 Minutes of the Meeting of MRF (Mennonite Resettlement Finance), 1 Jan. 1948, Goshen, IN. MHC, XXII-A.1, CMBC (204), 1366/1353
85 Cornelius J. Dyck, 'The Chaco Mennonite Colonies,' *MCC Services Bulletin* 3, no. 10 (Dec. 1949): 3
86 Interview 1
87 Peter J. Dyck to C.F. Klassen, 28 Aug. 1948. MHC, XXII-A.1, CMBC (205), 1367/1356
88 George K. Epp, 'Mennonite Immigration to Canada after World War II,' *Journal of Mennonite Studies* 5 (1987): 116. Rie Hoogeveen states that 1,690 persons left Neuland and Volendam mainly for Canada between 1951 and 1956. See 'From Paraguay to Germany,' 122.
89 Klassen, *Die Mennoniten in Paraguay*, 161
90 Interview 8
91 Hoogeveen, 'From Paraguay to Germany,' 122
92 Interview 1
93 Peter Derksen, referred to in Klassen, *Die Mennoniten in Paraguay*, 162
94 This sentiment is expressed in Interviews 1, 24, and 26.
95 Interview 2
96 Interview 24

Chapter 5: Becoming Settled in Canada

1 Herta Janzen, unpublished memoir, 5–6
2 Victor Thiessen, 'Only by the Grace of God: The Story of a Mennonite Family' (research paper, Mennonite Heritage Centre, Winnipeg, 1978), 59
3 Debbie Kirkpatrick, 'The Story of Mrs. Suse Rempel and Her Family' (research paper, Mennonite Heritage Centre, Winnipeg, 1979), 44
4 'Mitteilungen einer Immigrantin,' *Der Bote* 24 (12 Nov. 1947): 3
5 See, for instance, Franca Iacovetta, *Such Hardworking People: Italian Immigrants in Postwar Toronto* (Montreal: McGill-Queen's University Press 1992); Milda Danys, *DP: Lithuanian Immigration to Canada after the Second World War* (Toronto: Multicultural History Society of Ontario 1986).

6 See, for instance, Silvia Pedraza, 'Women and Migration: The Social Consequences of Gender,' *Annual Review of Sociology* 17 (1991): 313. Donna Gabaccia demonstrates the centrality and continuity of labour, both waged and
   unwaged, in the lives of immigrant women. See *From the Other Side: Women,
   Gender, and Immigrant Life in the U.S., 1820–1990* (Bloomington: Indiana University Press 1994).
7 Franca Iacovetta, 'Making "New Canadians": Social Workers, Women, and
   the Reshaping of Immigrant Families,' in *Gender Conflicts: New Essays in
   Women's History*, ed. Franca Iacovetta and Mariana Valverde (Toronto: University of Toronto Press 1992), 263. See also the essays in Joy Parr, ed., *A
   Diversity of Women: Ontario, 1945–1980* (Toronto: University of Toronto Press
   1995).
8 Anne Bargen, 'Conversation with Mothers: Too Gifted to Become a Mere
   Housewife?' *Canadian Mennonite*, 7 Sept. 1956, 2
9 Anne Bargen, 'Conversation with Mothers: A Man Can Build a House, but It
   Takes a Woman to Make a Home,' *Canadian Mennonite*, 1 Feb. 1957, 4
10 See, for instance, Paul Erb, 'Editorial: Church Service for Women,' *Gospel
   Herald* 52, no. 4 (17 Jan. 1959): 75; Elaine Sommers Rich, 'Woman's Place in
   the World,' *Mennonite Life* 12, no. 1 (Jan. 1957): 42–3.
11 For instance, Oscar Burkholder, 'Why Christian Married Women Work,'
   Canadian Mennonite, 21 Jan. 1955, 7.
12 Royden Loewen, 'Rurality, Ethnicity, and Gender Patterns of Cultural Continuity during the "Great Disjuncture" in the R.M. of Hanover, 1945–1961,'
   Journal of the Canadian Historical Association 4, n.s. (1993): 161–82
13 See Franca Iacovetta, 'Remaking Their Lives: Women Immigrants, Survivors,
   and Refugees,' in Parr, ed., *A Diversity of Women*, 135–67.
14 'Canadian Mennonite Immigration,' *MCC Services Bulletin* 4, no. 6 (Aug.
   1950): 2
15 Memo from Anne Giesbrecht, MCC Gronau, to CMBC Saskatoon, 22 Sept.
   1952. MHC, XXII-A.1, CMBC (166), 1328/977
16 Interviews 9 and 14
17 Interview 23
18 Katie Friesen, *Into the Unknown* (Steinbach, MB: the author 1986), 127
19 Interview 17
20 Several studies of the Mennonite Girls' Homes have been done. See, for
   instance, Marlene Epp, 'The Mennonite Girls' Homes of Winnipeg: A Home
   Away from Home,' *Journal of Mennonite Studies* 6 (1988): 100–14; Frieda Esau
   Klippenstein, '"Doing What We Could": Mennonite Domestic Servants in
   Winnipeg, 1920s to 1950s,' *Journal of Mennonite Studies* 7 (1989): 145–66.
21 Cornelia Lehn, *Frontier Challenge: A Story of the Conference of Mennonites in*

B.C. (Clearbrook, BC: Conference of Mennonites in British Columbia 1990), 92

22 C.L. Dick, *The Mennonite Conference of Alberta: A History of Its Churches and Institutions* (Edmonton: Mennonite Conference of Alberta 1980), 76

23 The function of the Girls' Homes as an institution of control over young women in the city has been suggested by Harvey Neufeldt. See 'Creating the Brotherhood: Status and Control in the Yarrow Mennonite Community, 1928–1960,' in *Canadian Papers in Rural History*, vol. 9, ed. Donald H. Akenson (Gananoque, ON: Langdale Press 1994), 226–7.

24 From Andrew R. Shelley, 'An Evaluation of Mennonite Social Welfare Institutions,' in *Proceedings of the Ninth Conference on Mennonite Educational and Cultural Problems*, 18–19 June 1953 (n.p., n.d.), 46

25 Correspondence between J.J. Thiessen and Anne Luise Regier in the summer of 1948, as well as similar correspondence with other domestic workers is in MHC, XXII-A.1, CMBC (163), 1331/999.

26 J.J. Thiessen, to Mrs K. Dixon, 28 Oct. 1948. MHC, XXII-A.1, CMBC (163), 1331/999

27 J.J. Thiessen, 'Report on Canadian Immigration and Resettlement,' to the Annual Meeting of the Mennonite Aid Section, 30 Dec. 1948, 3

28 Donald H. Avery, *Reluctant Host: Canada's Response to Immigrant Workers,1896–1994* (Toronto: McClelland and Stewart 1995), 165

29 Interview 9

30 Interview 17

31 Friesen, *Into the Unknown*, 126–9

32 Jennifer Polle, 'Katherine Unger Polle: From Nicopol, Ukraine to Vancouver, B.C.' (research paper, Mennonite Heritage Centre, 1990), 20

33 Interview 13

34 Interview 17

35 Interview 6

36 Ibid.

37 'In Memoriam: Agnes Klassen-Harder,' *George Street Journal* 4, no. 4 (Dec. 1992): 11

38 Interview 14

39 Interview 28

40 Interview 1

41 Interview 10

42 Frank H. Epp, *Mennonite Exodus: The Rescue and Resettlement of the Russian Mennonites since the Communist Revolution* (Altona, MB: D.W. Friesen 1962), 395, 401

43 Interview 19

44 Quoted in *25th Anniversary, Niagara United Mennonite Church, 1938–1963* (Virgil, ON: Niagara United Mennonite Church 1963), 45.

45 Correspondence between J.J. Thiessen and C.F. Shoubridge, Chief, Finance Branch, IRO, 22 and 31 July 1950. MHC, XXII-A.1, CMBC/CMRIC (194), 1363/1308

46 Helen Block, Elsie Krueger, Aganeta Andres, to Hector Allard, 9 Feb. 1950. MHC, XXII-A.1, CMBC/CMRIC (19), 1353/1130

47 C.F. Shoubridge for Hector Allard, to J.J. Thiessen, 6 March 1950. MHC, XXII-A.1, CMBC/CMRIC (19), 1353/1130

48 See correspondence regarding Bertha Braun and family from 1949 to 1961 in MHC, XXII-A.1, CMBC/CMRIC (191), 1353/1135.

49 Interview 25

50 Interview 13

51 Friesen, *Into the Unknown*, 132

52 For instance, Veronica Strong-Boag, 'Home Dreams: Women and the Suburban Experiment in Canada, 1945–60,' *Canadian Historical Review* 72, no. 4 (Dec. 1991): 471–504. Also, John R. Miron, *Housing in Postwar Canada: Demographic Change, Household Formation, and Housing Demand* (Montreal: McGill-Queen's University Press 1988).

53 Interview 1

54 Friesen, *Into the Unknown*, 129

55 *25th Anniversary, Niagara United Mennonite Church*, 45

56 Ibid.

57 Interview 11

58 N. Isaak to J.J. Thiessen, 19 May 1949; J.J. Thiessen to N. Isaak, 23 May 1949. MHC, XXII-A.1, CMBC (176), 1339/1044

59 'Einladung' to the annual meeting of the B.C. Provincial Relief Committee. MHC, XXII-A.1, CMBC (207), B.C. Hilfskomitee, 1369/1371

60 'Protokoll der Jahresversammlung des B.C. Provincialen Hilfskomitees abgehalten am 29. Oct. 1949 in der Kirche zu West Abbotsford,' p. 12. MHC, XXII-A.1, CMBC (207), 1369/1371. This fund is also referred to in Epp, *Mennonite Exodus*, 446.

61 Anny Penner Klassen Goerzen, with Anne Klassen Suderman and Susan Thiessen Klassen. *Anny: Sheltered in the Arms of God. A True Story of Survival in Russia* (Fort St James, BC: the author 1988), 220

62 A.A. Toews, 'Bericht des Vorsitzenden des Hilfswerkes in B.C. fuer die Vertreter-Versammlung am 11. Nov. 1950.' MHC, XXII-A.1, CMBC (207), 1369/1371

63 'Bericht des Vorsitzenden des B.C. Provinzialen Hilfskomitees, Rev. A.A.

Toews, auf der V.-Versammlung in Clearbrook am 11. Oktober 1951.' MHC, XXII-A.1, CMBC (207), 1369/1371

64 'Bericht vom Provinzialen Hilfskomitee in B.C.,' 6 March 1954. 'Protokoll der V.V. des Provinzialen Mennonitischen Hilfswerkes von B.C., abgehalten in der Kirche zu West Abbotsford am 16. Oktober 1954.' MHC, XX-16, H.M. Epp Collection (2), v.583

65 'Protokoll der Beratung des Executivekomitees des menn. Hilfswerk in Br. Columbien, abgehalten am 23. September 1950.' MHC, XXII-A.1, CMBC (207), 1369/1371

66 'Protokoll der Executive–Sitzung des BC Hilfswerkes am 20-1-1951.' MHC, XXII-A.1, CMBC (207), 1369/1371

67 N.N. Driedger, *The Leamington United Mennonite Church: Establishment and Development, 1925–72* (Leamington, ON: n.p. 1973), 94

68 Goertzen, *Anny*, 222

69 Interview 10

70 Interview 28

71 Friesen, *Into the Unknown*, 126

72 David Ewert, *A Journey of Faith: An Autobiography* (Winnipeg: Centre for Mennonite Brethren Studies 1993), 115

73 'Bericht des Gemeinderates der Schoenwieser Gemeinde auf der Jahresbruderschaft der Gemeinde, abgehalten am 12. Oktober 1947 in der Kirche zu Winnipeg.' MHC, Records of First Mennonite Church, Winnipeg, microfilm 193

74 Minutes of Brotherhood meeting, 27 Dec. 1950, Niagara United Mennonite Church. MHC, III-11, Records of Niagara United Mennonite Church, microfilm 158

75 'Protokoll der Jahresversammlung des B.C. Provincialen Hilfskomitees abgehalten am 29. Oct. 1949 in der Kirche zu West Abbotsford,' p. 12. MHC, XXII-A.1, CMBC (207), 1369/1371

76 Gudrun L. (Wohlgemut) Mathies, 'Refugee Pilgrimage: A Story of God's Care; Lina (Heinrich) Wohlgemut: From Poland to Canada,' *Ontario Mennonite History* 13, no. 1 (March 1995): 13

77 'Protokoll der Vorberatsitzung abgehalten am 19ten Okt. 1949,' and 'Protokoll der Gemeinderatsitzung am 13. November 1949.' CMBS, Virgil MB Church records, microfilm 28

78 'Protokoll No. 94, Der Jaehrlichen Gemeindeberatung am. 5.6.& 9. Oct. 1952.' CMBS, Scott St. MB Church records, microfilm 26

79 Peter D. Zacharias, *Footprints of a Pilgrim People: Story of the Blumenort Mennonite Church* (Gretna, MB: Blumenort Mennonite Church 1985), 139.

Although Zacharias refers to a ten–year residency requirement, the 1951 leg-islation actually stipulated that a recipient of the old age pension must have been a Canadian resident for twenty years. See Dennis Guest, *The Emergence of Social Security in Canada* (Vancouver: University of British Columbia Press 1980), 145.

80 Guest, *Emergence of Social Security*, 133

81 'Protokoll der Jahresversammlung des B.C. Provincialen Hilfskomitees abge-halten am 20. Oct. 1949 in der Kirche zu West Abbotsford,' p. 6. MHC, XXII-A.1, CMBC (207), 1369/1371

82 Mathies, 'Refugee Pilgrimage,' 14

83 Interview 11

84 Iacovetta, 'Remaking Their Lives,' 137

85 Robert Kreider, *Interviews with Peter J. Dyck and Elfrieda Klassen Dyck: Experiences in Mennonite Central Committee Service in Europe, 1941–1949* (Akron, PA: Mennonite Central Committee 1988), 469

86 Interview 1

87 Mary K. Roberson, 'Birth, Transformation, and Death of Refugee Identity: Women and Girls of the Intifada,' in *Refugee Women and Their Mental Health: Shattered Societies, Shattered Lives*, ed. Ellen Cole, Oliva M. Espin, and Esther D. Rothblum (Binghamton, NY: Harrington Park Press 1992), 39

88 Interview 13

89 Interview 11

90 John Funk, 'Interlacing Family History with WWII' (research paper, Menno-nite Heritage Centre, Winnipeg, n.d.), n. 48

91 Patricia K. Robin Herbst, 'From Helpless Victim to Empowered Survivor: Oral History as a Treatment for Survivors of Torture,' in Cole, Espin, and Rothblum, eds., *Refugee Women*, 146

92 Interview 25

93 Dyck, quoted in Kreider, *Interviews*, 467

94 'Sargent Avenue Mennonitengemeinde 1971,' by Jacob Rempel, p. 58. MHC, III-62, Records of Sargent Avenue Mennonite Church, microfilm 190

95 All information concerning this case is from correspondence in MHC, XXII-A.1, CMBC (170), 1332/1004.

96 J.J. Thiessen to George F. Davidson, Deputy Minister of Immigration, 3 Aug. 1961. MHC, XXII-A.1, CMBC (170), 1332/1004

97 George F. Davidson, Deputy Minister of Immigration, quoted by J.J. Thies-sen in correspondence to C.A. DeFehr, A.A. Wiens, A.A. Wall, 20 Sept. 1961. MHC, XXII-A.1, CMBC (170), 1332/1004

98 Michael D. Roe, 'Displaced Women in Settings of Continued Armed Con-flict,' in Cole, Espin, and Rothblum, eds., *Refugee Women*, 93

99 Kay Reimer, 'Learning What It Means to Belong – Emigrating to Canada,'
    Mennonite Mirror (June 1988): 17
100 Interview 16
101 Kreider, *Interviews*, 379

Chapter 6: Re-creating Families

1 Annalee Gölz, 'Family Matters: The Canadian Family and the State in the
   Postwar Period,' *left history* 1 (fall 1993): 9–49
2 For a discussion of familism, see Veronica Strong-Boag, '"Their Side of the
   Story": Women's Voices from Ontario Suburbs,' in *A Diversity of Women:
   Ontario, 1945–1980*, ed. Joy Parr (Toronto: University of Toronto Press 1995),
   52–3. Most of the essays in this collection make reference to gender and fam-
   ily ideology in the postwar era. See also Mona Gleason, 'Psychology and the
   Construction of the "Normal" Family in Postwar Canada, 1945–60,' *Canadian
   Historical Review* 78, no. 3 (Sept. 1997): 442–77.
3 Joy Parr, 'Introduction,' in *A Diversity of Women*, 4
4 Elizabeth Heineman, 'Complete Families, Half Families, No Families at All:
   Female-Headed Households and the Reconstruction of the Family in the
   Early Federal Republic,' *Central European History* 29, no. 1 (1996): 19–60
5 For the role of psychologists in idealizing the postwar family, see Mona Lee
   Gleason, *Normalizing the Ideal: Psychology, Schooling, and the Family in Postwar
   Canada* (Toronto: University of Toronto Press 1999). On the role of social
   workers, see Franca Iacovetta, 'Making "New Canadians": Social Workers,
   Women, and the Reshaping of Immigrant Families,' in *Gender Conflicts: New
   Essays in Women's History*, ed. Franca Iacovetta and Mariana Valverde
   (Toronto: University of Toronto Press 1992), 261–303.
6 John F. Peters, 'Traditional Customs of Remarriage among Some Canadian
   Mennonite Widow(er)s,' *Journal of Mennonite Studies* 10 (1992): 119
7 Margaret Little, 'The Blurring of Boundaries: Private and Public Welfare for
   Single Mothers in Ontario,' *Studies in Political Economy* 47 (summer 1995):
   100–1
8 See correspondence between J.J. Thiessen and A.L. Jolliffe on the following
   dates: 5 July 1949, 19 Sept. 1949, 4 Oct. 1949, 27 Feb. 1950, 6 March 1950.
   National Archives of Canada (NA), RG 76, vol. 855, file 544–22.
9 J.J. Thiessen to A.L. Jolliffe, 28 Sept. 1949. MHC, XXII-A.1, CMBC, 1328/982
10 C.F. Klassen to J.J. Thiessen, 1 July 1949. MHC, XXII-A.1, CMBC (166), 1328/
    983
11 J.J. Thiessen to C.F. Klassen, 14 July 1949. MHC, XXII-A.1, CMBC (166),
    1328/983

12 William T. Snyder to C.F. Klassen, 29 Sept.1949. Snyder is referring to A. MacNamara, Deputy Minister of Labour. MHC, XXII-A.1, CMBC, 1328/982

13 Telegraph, J.J. Thiessen to C.F. Klassen, 5 Oct. 1949. MHC, XXII–A.1, CMBC (166), 1328/983

14 A.L. Jolliffe to J.J. Thiessen, 4 Oct. 1949. MHC, XXII-A.1, CMBC, 1328/982

15 See J.J. Thiessen to A.L. Jolliffe, 27 Feb. 1950; J.J. Thiessen to C.E.S. Smith, acting director of immigration, 6 March 1950. NA, RG 76, vol. 855, file 554–22

16 There are approximately five thousand forms for the post–Second World War period. Because of their deteriorating condition, they were microfilmed circa 1990, sets of which are deposited at the Mennonite Heritage Centre (MHC), Winnipeg, and the Manitoba Archives. See Canadian Mennonite Board of Colonization Collection, RG XXII A1, vols. 3403–12, MHC microfilms 553–68.

17 These cases are found in a search of the Register of Members (Verzeichnis der Glieder der Winnipeg [Stadtmission] Mennoniten Missionsgemeinde), Kirchenbuch nos. 1–4, Sargent Avenue Mennonite Church, Winnipeg, Manitoba. MHC, III-62, microfilms 190–1.

18 This example is from the family register of Clearbrook Mennonite Brethren Church, Clearbrook, British Columbia. CMBS, Clearbrook MB Church records, microfilm 57, BD512.

19 Case file contained in MHC, XXII-A.1, CMBC/CMRIC (191), 1353/1135

20 Interview 28

21 'Protokoll der Beratung des Executivekomitees des menn. Hilfswerk in Br. Columbien, abgehalten am 23. September 1950.' MHC, XXII-A.1, CMBC (207), 1369/1371

22 Interview 6

23 Pamela E. Klassen, *Going By the Moon and the Stars: Stories of Two Russian Mennonite Women* (Waterloo: Wilfrid Laurier University Press 1994), 36–9

24 Annemarie Tröger, 'Between Rape and Prostitution: Survival Strategies and Chances of Emancipation for Berlin Women after World War II,' in *Women in Culture and Politics: A Century of Change*, ed. Judith Friedlander, Blanche Wiesen Cook, Alice Kessler-Harris, and Carroll Smith-Rosenberg (Bloomington: Indiana University Press 1986), 114–15

25 Interview 6

26 Joan Chandler, *Women without Husbands: An Exploration of the Margins of Marriage* (London: Macmillan 1991), 90

27 Klassen, *Going By the Moon and the Stars*, 47

28 Interview 28

29 Klassen, *Going By the Moon and the Stars*, 46–7

30 Interview 11

31 Klassen, *Going By the Moon and the Stars*, 45–6
32 Tröger, 'Between Rape and Prostitution,' 115
33 Anny Penner Klassen Goerzen, *Anny: Sheltered in the Arms of God. A True Story of Survival in Russia* (Fort St James, BC: the author 1988), 222
34 Klassen, *Going By the Moon and the Stars*, 27
35 Katie Friesen, *Into the Unknown* (Steinbach, MB: the author 1986), 34
36 Interview 9
37 Interview 1
38 Interview 10
39 'Protokoll einer Sitzung des Fuersorgekomitees der kanadischen Konferenz, 1 & 2 Januar 1948, Winnipeg.' CMBS, Canadian Conference of Mennonite Brethren Churches Collection, box 1, Board of Spiritual and Social Concerns, B220
40 Ibid.
41 See J. Winfield Fretz, *Pilgrims in Paraguay* (Scottdale, PA: Herald Press 1953); also Peter Dyck and Elfrieda Dyck, *Up from the Rubble: The Epic Rescue of Thousands of War–Ravaged Mennonite Refugees* (Scottdale, PA: Herald Press 1991), chap. 15.
42 Frank H. Epp,.*Mennonite Exodus: The Rescue and Resettlement of the Russian Mennonites since the Communist Revolution* (Altona, MB: D.W. Friesen 1962), 453
43 *Conference of Mennonites in Canada Yearbook* (1949), 10–11
44 Copy (n.d.) of a letter from C.C. Penner to 'das Fuersorgekom. der Can. Konf.' CMBS, Canadian Conference of Mennonite Brethren Churches Collection, box 1, Board of Spiritual and Social Concerns, B220
45 'Protokoll der Sitzungen des Fuersorgekomitees der Kanadischen M.B. Konferenz, abgehalten in den Tagen von 27. Juli–3. Aug 1950.' CMBS, Canadian Conference of Mennonite Brethren Churches Collection, box 1, Board of Spiritual and Social Concerns, B220
46 *Jubilee Issue of the Waterloo–Kitchener United Mennonite Church, 1924–1974* (Waterloo, ON: Waterloo–Kitchener United Mennonite Church c1975), 39–40
47 Correspondence between N. Fransen and J.J. Thiessen, 18 and 22 March 1948. MHC, XXII-A.1, CMBC (175), 1337/1036
48 The story of Anna (not her real name) is pieced together from brief entries in the Family and Member Registers, and also church council minutes of Sargent Avenue Mennonite Church. MHC, III-62, microfilm 190 and 191
49 Minutes, Gemeindestunde (Congregational meeting), 9 Jan. 1966, Niagara United Mennonite Church. MHC, III-11, Niagara United Mennonite Church Records, microfilm 158
50 Minutes, Bruderberatung of Niagara United Mennonite Church, 21 Oct.

1951, MHC, III-11, Niagara United Mennonite Church Records, microfilm 158

51 'Protokoll der Jahresbruderschaft der Schoenwieser Gemeinde, abgehalten den 12. Oktober 1959 in der Kirche an Alverstone, Winnipeg.' MHC, III-59, First Mennonite Church Records, microfilm 193

52 This case is outlined in correspondence from 'Ingrid' (no name given on copy of letter) to J.J. Thiessen, 1 March 1959; and G.G. Neufeld to J.J. Thiessen, 18 March 1959. MHC, vol. 1021, G.G. Neufeld, Conference of Mennonites in Manitoba Collection (1958–1960). I am grateful to Anna Epp Ens for pointing out this correspondence to me.

53 'Sargent Avenue Mennonitengemeinde.' MHC, III-62, microfilm 190

54 Interview 13

55 Interview 16

56 'Bericht Vom Provinzialen Hilfskomitee in B.C.,' 6 March 1954. MHC, XX-16, H.M. Epp Collection (2), v.583

57 Interview 11

58 Robert Kreider, *Interviews with Peter J. Dyck and Elfrieda Klassen Dyck: Experiences in Mennonite Central Committee Service in Europe, 1941–1949* (Akron, PA: Mennonite Central Committee 1988), 187–8

59 Both of these cases are described by Peter Dyck in ibid., 188.

60 John R. Miron, *Housing in Postwar Canada: Demographic Change, Household Formation, and Housing Demand* (Montreal: McGill-Queen's University Press 1988), 8

61 Mark Wyman, *DP: Europe's Displaced Persons, 1945–1951* (Philadelphia: Balch Institute Press 1989), 111

62 See correspondence between Hilda Froese and J.J. Thiessen, 5 and 8 Nov. 1948. MHC, XXII-A.1, CMBC (175), 1337/1036

63 Richard Bartel to J.J. Thiessen, n.d., 1948, and J.J. Thiessen to Richard Bartel, 6 Aug. 1948. MHC, XXII-A.1, CMBC (170), 1332/1001

64 Interview 25

65 Interview 17

66 Friesen, *Into the Unknown*, 133

67 Interview 16

68 See, for instance, James Fentress and Chris Wickham, *Social Memory* (Cambridge, MA: Blackwell 1992); Raphael Samuel and Paul Thompson, eds., *The Myths We Live By* (New York: Routledge 1990).

69 *25th Anniversary, Niagara United Mennonite Church, 1938–1963* (Virgil, ON: Niagara United Mennonite Church 1963), 44

70 Krista M. Taves, 'The Reunification of Russian Mennonites in Post–World War II Canada,' *Ontario Mennonite History* 13, no. 1 (March 1995): 6

71 Gerhard Lohrenz, *The Odyssey of the Bergen Family* (Winnipeg: the author 1978), 106

Chapter 7: Learning to Be Mennonite

1 Interview 17. Although Helena wasn't in reality an orphan, her arrival without parents gave her that identity in the eyes of the Canadian Mennonite community that received her.
2 These attitudes were experienced by other immigrant groups, such as Lithuanians: see Milda Danys, *DP: Lithuanian Immigration to Canada after the Second World War* (Toronto: Multicultural History Society of Ontario 1986); Ukrainians: see Wsevolod Isajiw, Yury Boshyk, and Roman Senkus, eds., *The Refugee Experience: Ukrainian Displaced Persons after World War II* (Edmonton: Canadian Institute of Ukrainian Studies Press 1992); Italians: see Franca Iacovetta, *Such Hardworking People: Italian Immigrants in Postwar Toronto* (Montreal: McGill-Queen's University Press 1992); see also Mark Wyman, *DP: Europe's Displaced Persons, 1945–1951* (Philadelphia: Balch Institute Press 1989).
3 Interviews 28 and 13
4 Bernhard Ratzlaff, 'Experience of the Mennonites of the Ukraine during and after the German Occupation' (research paper, Mennonite Library and Archives, North Newton, KS 1959), 1. This paper is based almost exclusively on interviews by American historian Cornelius Krahn with postwar immigrants in 1950–1.
5 Lubomyr K. Luciuk, 'Unintended Consequences in Refugee Resettlement: Post–War Ukrainian Refugee Immigration to Canada,' *International Migration Review* 20, no. 2 (summer 1986): 467–82
6 Interview 14
7 Regarding the Coaldale, Alberta community, see C.L. Dick, *The Mennonite Conference of Alberta: A History of Its Churches and Institutions* (Edmonton: Mennonite Conference of Alberta 1980), 43. See also Krista M. Taves, 'The Reunification of Russian Mennonites in Post–World War II Canada,' *Ontario Mennonite History* 13, no. 1 (March 1995): 1–7.
8 *25th Anniversary, Niagara United Mennonite Church, 1938–1963* (Virgil, ON: Niagara United Mennonite Church 1963), 44
9 Taves, 'Reunification of Russian Mennonites,' 1–7
10 Interview 1
11 Raymond Breton, 'Collective Dimensions of the Cultural Transformation of Ethnic Communities and the Larger Society,' in *Migration and the Transformation of Cultures*, ed. Jean Burnet et al. (Toronto: Multicultural History Society of Ontario 1992), 6–7

12 Henry Paektau describes the encounter between Russian Mennonite immigrants of the 1920s and the postwar refugees as a family reunion, although he does recognize the existence of some 'discomfort' in the relationship. See 'Separation or Integration? The Russian Mennonite Immigrant Community in Ontario, 1924–45' (PhD thesis, University of Western Ontario 1986), 379.

13 J.J. Thiessen to William T. Snyder, 6 May 1950. MHC, XXII-A.1, CMBC (166), 1328/975

14 J.J. Thiessen, 'Report on Canadian Immigration and Resettlement,' to the Annual Meeting of the Mennonite Aid Section, 30 Dec. 1948, p. 3

15 A.A. Toews, 'Bericht des Vorsitzenden des Hilfswerkes in B.C. fuer die Vertreter-Versammlung am 11. Nov. 1950.' MHC, XXII-A.1, CMBC (207), B.C. Hilfskomitee, 1369/1371

16 'Canadian Mennonite Immigration,' MCC Services Bulletin 4, no. 6 (Aug. 1950): 2

17 Danys, DP, 132

18 Alexander Baran, 'The Ukrainian Catholic Church,' in Isajiw, Boshyk, and Senkus, eds., The Refugee Experience, 154

19 A.A. Toews, 'Bericht des Vorsitzenden.' MHC, XXII-A.1, CMBC (207), B.C. Hilfskomitee, 1369/1371

20 Harvey Neufeldt, 'Creating the Brotherhood: Status and Control in the Yarrow Mennonite Community, 1928–1960,' in Canadian Papers in Rural History, vol. 9, ed. Donald H. Akenson (Gananoque, ON: Langdale Press 1994). Richard Kyle argues that fundamentalism was the strongest theological influence on Mennonite Brethren in North America during the years 1940 to 1960. See 'North American Mennonite Brethren at Mid-Century: Ecclesiological Developments,' in Bridging Troubled Waters: Mennonite Brethren at Mid-Twentieth Century, ed. Paul Toews (Winnipeg: Kindred Productions 1995), 193–212. See also T.D. Regehr, Mennonites in Canada, 1939–1970: A People Transformed (Toronto: University of Toronto Press 1996).

21 Harry Loewen, 'From Russia to Canada: My Mother Was Betrayed by the Church,' Mennonite Reporter 20, no. 19 (1 Oct. 1990): 9

22 Neufeldt, 'Creating the Brotherhood,' 225–26

23 Dennis Stoesz, The Story of Home Street Mennonite Church: 1957–1982 (Winnipeg, MB: Home Street Mennonite Church 1985), 36. At this same church, women did not receive full voting rights until 1968, when after a motion in favour won by only one vote.

24 Gudrun L. (Wohlgemut) Mathies, 'Refugee Pilgrimage: A Story of God's Care; Lina (Heinrich) Wohlgemut: From Poland to Canada,' Ontario Mennonite History 13, no. 1 (March 1995): 13

25 Interview 16

26 Wichert's statement was recalled by an individual interviewed by Krista Taves. See 'Reunification of Russian Mennonites,' 3.

27 Interview 7

28 Interview 19

29 Loewen, 'From Russia to Canada,' 9

30 Bruno Fast, 'Recollections of a Refugee,' *Mennonite Brethren Herald* 22, no. 13 (July 1983): 6

31 Interview 13

32 Interview 28

33 Interview 27

34 Marlene Epp, 'Research Findings from Mennonite History: To Dance or Not to Dance,' *Mennonite Reporter* 18, no. 6 (14 March 1988): 8

35 'Aussprache der Taufkand. am 28. Aug. 1954.' CMBS, Records of Scott St Mennonite Brethren Church, microfilm 26

36 Epp, 'Research Findings,' 8

37 'Protokoll No. 23 der Sargent Avenue Mennoniten Gemeinde am 14. Juni 1957.' MHC, III-62, Records of Sargent Avenue Mennonite Church, microfilm 190

38 'Protokoll No. 104-6, 105-7 der Sitzung des Gemeinderates am 2. und 18. Juni 1961.' In Protokollbuch No. 4 der Sitzungen des Gemeinderates der Sargent Avenue Mennoniten Gemeinde. MHC, III-62, Records of Sargent Avenue Mennonite Church, microfilm 191

39 'Protokoll No. 196-8 der Sitzung des Gemeinderates am 14. Juli 1961.' In ibid.

40 Victor Thiessen, 'Only By the Grace of God: The Story of a Mennonite Family' (research paper, Mennonite Heritage Centre 1978), 61

41 Interview 14

42 Cornelius Krahn interview with J.B., 1951. Mennonite Library and Archives, North Newton, KS

43 Interview 19

44 Sheila Fitzpatrick, *Stalin's Peasants: Resistance and Survival in the Russian Village after Collectivization* (New York: Oxford University Press 1994), 6–7

45 Pamela E. Klassen, *Going By the Moon and the Stars: Stories of Two Russian Mennonite Women* (Waterloo: Wilfrid Laurier University Press 1994)

46 Interview 23

47 'Protokoll der Gemeindestunde am 23. Mai 1949.' CMBS, Records of Elmwood Mennonite Brethren Church, microfilm 92, BC 522

48 'Protokoll der Gemeindeberatung Oktober 5, 1949.' CMBS, Records of Virgil Mennonite Brethren Church, microfilm 28, BD 518

49 Katie Friesen, *Into the Unknown* (Steinbach, MB: the author 1986), 27

50 See also my article, '"My Mom Was a Preacher": Female Religion in the Soviet Era,' *Sophia* 5, no. 1 (winter 1995): 14–15.

51 'Protokoll der Jahresversammlung des B.C. Provincialen Hilfskomitees abgehalten am 29. Oct. 1949 in der Kirche zu West Abbotsford.' MHC, XXII-A.1, CMBC (207), B.C. Hilfskomitee, 1369/1371

52 *25th Anniversary*, 43

53 N.N. Driedger, *The Leamington United Mennonite Church: Establishment and Development, 1925–1972* (Leamington, ON: n.p. 1973), 77

54 Interview 27

55 For instance, in August 1943, a Reverend Boldt baptized thirty young people in the village of Gnadenfeld, Molotschna. Agatha Loewen Schmidt, *Gnadenfeld, Molotschna, 1835–1943* (Kitchener, ON: the author 1989), 35. Also see Henry H. Winter, *A Shepherd of the Oppressed: Heinrich Winter, the Last Aeltester of Chortitza* (Leamington, ON: the author 1990) for numerous photographs of baptisms in 1942–3 in the Chortitza settlement and also in Germany and Holland in the postwar years. For instance, in the first baptism that occurred under the German occupation in 1942, 99 people were baptized, of which about 75 were women and 24 were men (p. 66).

56 'Protokollbuch.' MHC, III–62, Sargent Avenue Mennonite Church records, microfilm 190

57 Interview 28

58 Interview 6

59 *25th Anniversary*, 7, 43–44.

60 Dick, *Mennonite Conference of Alberta*, 42. Similar expansion occurred in other Canadian churches of Russian Mennonite origin. See for instance, *Jubilate: 60 Years First Mennonite Church, 1926–1986* (Winnipeg: First Mennonite Church 1991), 132; Driedger, *Leamington United Mennonite Church*, 75–7.

61 Cornelia Lehn, *Frontier Challenge: A Story of the Conference of Mennonites in B.C.* (Clearbrook, BC: Conference of Mennonites in British Columbia 1990), 90

62 Winter, *Shepherd of the Oppressed*, 175

63 'Protokoll und Tagebuch der Sargent Avenue Mennoniten Gemeinde #1' (1952 statistics) and 'Sargent Ave Mennonitengemeinde 1971' (1971 statistics). MHC, III-62, Sargent Avenue Mennonite Church Records, microfilm 190

64 *25th Anniversary*, 45

65 Gloria Neufeld Redekop, *The Work of Their Hands: Mennonite Women's Societies in Canada* (Waterloo: Wilfrid Laurier University Press 1996), 58

66 Ibid.

67 N.N. Fransen, 'Stimmberechtigung der schwestern in unsern gemeinden im

licht der Bibel und unsere praxis, gelesen in Winnipeg, 13. Jan. 1959.' CGCA, Mennonites in Canada Files (1950 – Women)

68 *50th Anniversary Highlights of the Vineland United Mennonite Church, 1936–1986: Reflect, Rejoice, Renew* (Vineland, ON: Vineland United Mennonite Church 1986), 88; *The Niagara United Mennonite Church, 1938–1988: 50th Anniversary* (Virgil, ON: Niagara United Mennonite Church 1988), 35

69 Statistics from 1963 Annual Report. MHC, III-11, Records of Niagara United Mennonite Church, microfilm 158

70 Esther Patkau, *First Mennonite Church in Saskatoon, 1923–1982* (Saskatoon: First Mennonite Church 1982), 104–5. Membership statistics are for the year 1964.

71 'Protokoll No. 67-26 der Sitzung des Gemeinderates am 5. Dezember 1958,' in Protokollbuch No. 2 der Sitzungen des Gemeinderates der Sargent Ave Mennoniten Gemeinde. MHC, III-62, Records of Sargent Avenue Mennonite Church, microfilm 191

72 'Frauen in der Gemeinde,' from 'Sargent Ave Mennonitengemeinde 1971.' MHC, III-62, Records of Sargent Avenue Mennonite Church, microfilm 190

73 David F. Loewen, *Living Stones: A History of the West Abbotsford Mennonite Church, 1936–1986* (Abbotsford, BC: West Abbotsford Mennonite Church 1987), 61

74 Interview 11

75 Interview 13

76 Interview 19

77 Noted by Doreen Klassen, 'From "Getting the Words Out" to "Enjoying the Music": Musical Transitions among Canadian Mennonite Brethren,' in Toews, ed., *Bridging Troubled Waters*, 231

78 The idea of women's organizations functioning as a parallel church to the formal congregation is suggested by Gloria Neufeld Redekop, 'Canadian Mennonite Women's Societies: More Than Meets the Eye,' in Toews, ed., *Bridging Troubled Waters*, 165–74. See also Redekop, *Work of Their Hands*. Redekop also credits Katie Funk Wiebe, 'Women in the Mennonite Brethren Church,' in *Your Daughters Shall Prophesy: Women in Ministry in the Church*, ed. John E. Toews, Valerie Rempel, and Katie Funk Wiebe (Winnipeg: Kindred Press 1992).

79 Gladys V. Goering, *Women in Search of Mission: A History of the General Conference Mennonite Women's Organization* (Newton: Faith and Life Press 1980), 38. Redekop, *Work of Their Hands*, chap. 6

80 'Mitteilungen einer Immigrantin,' *Der Bote* 24 (12 Nov. 1947): 3

81 Frances Swyripa, *Wedded to the Cause: Ukrainian-Canadian Women and Ethnic Identity, 1891–1991* (Toronto: University of Toronto Press 1993), chap. 5

82 *25th Anniversary*, 29

83 *Niagara United Mennonite Church*, 86

84 Quoted in Taves, 'Reunification of Russian Mennonites,' 6

85 *25 Jahre: Sargent Avenue Mennonitengemeinde, 1950–1975* (Winnipeg: Sargent Avenue Mennonite Chruch 1975) 17

86 Breton, 'Collective Dimensions,' 6–7

87 Interview 16

88 Fitzpatrick, *Stalin's Peasants*, 224

89 Interview 9. Similarly, Gerhard Fast entered the University of Moscow to study engineering in the mid-1930s but was expelled in 1938 because of his German-Dutch ethnicity. Bruno Fast, 'Recollections of a Refugee,' *Mennonite Brethren Herald* 22, no. 13 (July 1983): 6

90 Debbie Kirkpatrick, 'The Story of Mrs. Suse Rempel and Her Family' (research paper, Mennonite Heritage Centre, Winnpeg, 1979), 44

91 See Regehr, *Mennonites in Canada*, 247.

92 Of the people interviewed for this study, four had achieved graduate degrees and were teaching at, or retired from, universities. Several others had completed their high school in adulthood or had taken university or college courses. Others emphasized the importance of higher education for their children.

93 Klassen, *Going By the Moon and the Stars*, 91

94 Interview 25

Conclusion

1 The Abdi family's story is told by Edward Opaku–Dapaah and Elizabeth McLuhan, 'The Abdi Family Speaks,' in *Safe Haven: The Refugee Experience of Five Families*, ed. Elizabeth McLuhan (Toronto: Multicultural History Society of Ontario 1995), 183–207.

2 The reinforcement of these gender traits by Mennonite theology has been explored by a number of writers and scholars. See, for instance, Tina Hartzler, 'Choosing to Be Honest Rather Than Good,' *Festival Quarterly* 13, no. 3 (fall 1986): 7–9, 18; Magdalene Redekop, 'Through the Mennonite Looking Glass,' in *Why I Am a Mennonite: Essays on Mennonite Identity*, ed. Harry Loewen (Kitchener, ON: Herald Press 1988), 226–53; Elizabeth G. Yoder, ed., *Peace Theology and Violence against Women* (Elkhart, IN: Institute of Mennonite Studies 1992).

3 John B. Toews, *Czars, Soviets, and Mennonites* (Newton, KS: Faith and Life Press 1982), 179. Other sources on Soviet Mennonites in the postwar era include: Victor G. Doerksen, 'Survival and Identity in the Soviet Era,' 289–98,

and Walter Sawatsky, 'From Russian to Soviet Mennonites 1941–1988,' 299–337, in *Mennonites in Russia: Essays in Honour of Gerhard Lohrenz*, ed. John Friesen (Winnipeg: CMBC Publications 1989).

4 See for instance: Toews, *Czars, Soviets and Mennonites*, 179; Justina Neufeld, 'A Family Remembers,' *Mennonite Life* 45, no. 1 (March 1990): 4–7; Heinrich Woelk and Gerhard Woelk, *A Wilderness Journey: Glimpses of the Mennonite Brethren Church in Russia, 1925–1980*, trans. Victor G. Doerksen (Fresno, CA: Center for Mennonite Brethren Studies and Mennonite Brethren Biblical Seminary 1982). Also, the stories in John B. Toews, *Journeys: Mennonite Stories of Faith and Survival in Stalin's Russia* (Winnipeg, MB: Kindred Productions 1998).

Selected Bibliography

A Note on Primary Sources

The primary archival collection utilized for this study was that of the Canadian Mennonite Board of Colonization (CMBC), housed at the Mennonite Heritage Centre, Winnipeg, Manitoba. This collection contains official board minutes; correspondence by CMBC leaders, government officials, and immigrants; and forms and registers related to immigration and settlement. The Mennonite Heritage Centre together with the archival holdings of the Centre for Mennonite Brethren Studies (also in Winnipeg) contain the records of individual Mennonite congregations in Canada, as well as provincial and national Mennonite conference bodies, all of which were consulted to varying degrees. A number of personal collections of Mennonite individuals involved in the relief and immigration process are housed at the two Mennonite archives in Winnipeg, and these proved useful as well.

During 1992–4, I conducted oral interviews with thirty-four individuals in Ontario, Manitoba, Alberta, and British Columbia. All the interviews were tape recorded and remain in my possession. In order to respect the confidentiality desired by most individuals who shared their life story, I have referred to these interviews by number only. A collection of interviews with post–Second World War Mennonite immigrants was gathered by historian Cornelius Krahn in the early 1950s; I made use of a number of the transcripts of these interviews, which are housed at the Mennonite Library and Archives in Newton, Kansas.

In addition to the archival collections and oral interviews, a wide range of primary material exists in Mennonite periodicals and newspapers. I made use of a sampling of this literature, which contains abundant information about and by postwar Mennonite refugees. Specific periodicals and articles are referenced in the notes for each chapter.

Published Sources

Abella, Irving, and Harold Troper. *None Is Too Many: Canada and the Jews of Europe, 1933–1948*. Toronto: Lester and Orpen Dennys 1982

After the Door Has Been Opened: Mental Health Issues Affecting Immigrants and Refugees in Canada. Report of the Canadian Task Force on Mental Health Issues Affecting Immigrants and Refugees. Ottawa: Health and Welfare Canada and Multiculturalism and Citizenship Canada 1988

Anderson, Alan, and Leo Driedger. 'The Mennonite Family: Culture and Kin in Rural Saskatchewan.' In *Canadian Families: Ethnic Variations*, edited by K. Ishwaran, 161–80. Toronto: McGraw-Hill Ryerson 1980

Appavoo, David. 'Ideology, Family, and Group Identity in a Mennonite Community in Southern Ontario.' *Mennonite Quarterly Review* 59, no. 1 (Jan. 1985): 67–93

Avery, Donald H. *Reluctant Host: Canada's Response to Immigrant Workers, 1896–1994*. Toronto: McClelland and Stewart 1995

Barber, Marilyn. 'The Women Ontario Welcomed: Immigrant Domestics for Ontario Homes, 1870–1930.' *Ontario History* 7 (1980): 148–72

– 'The Servant Problem in Manitoba, 1896–1930.' In *First Days, Fighting Days: Women in Manitoba History*, edited by Mary Kinnear, 100–19. Regina: Canadian Plains Research Center 1987

Bartel, Siegfried. *Living with Conviction: German Army Captain Turns to Cultivating Peace*. Winnipeg: CMBC Publications 1994

Bergen, Doris L. 'The Nazi Concept of "Volksdeutsche" and the Exacerbation of Anti-Semitism in Eastern Europe, 1939–1945.' *Journal of Contemporary History* 29 (1994): 569–82

Bergland, Betty. 'Ideology, Ethnicity, and the Gendered Subject: Reading Immigrant Women's Autobiographies.' In *Seeking Common Ground: Multidisciplinary Studies of Immigrant Women in the United States*, edited by Donna Gabaccia. Westport, CT: Praeger 1992

– 'Immigrant History and the Gendered Subject: A Review Essay.' *Ethnic Forum* 8, no. 2 (1988): 24–39

Bertaux, Daniel, and Paul Thompson, eds. *Between Generations: Family Models, Myths, and Memories*. International Yearbook of Oral History and Life Stories Series, vol. 2. Oxford: Oxford University Press 1993

Bethell, Nicholas. *The Last Secret: Forcible Repatriation to Russia, 1944–1947*. London: Deutsch 1974

Blom, Ida. 'The History of Widowhood: A Bibliographic Overview.' *Journal of Family History* 16, no. 2 (1991): 191–210

Boshyk, Yury, ed. *Ukraine during World War II: History and Its Aftermath*. Edmonton: Canadian Institute of Ukrainian Studies 1986

Bradbury, Bettina. 'The Fragmented Family: Family Strategies in the Face of Death, Illness, and Poverty, Montreal, 1860–1885.' In *Childhood and Family in Canadian History*, edited by Joy Parr, 109–28. Toronto: McClelland and Stewart 1982

– 'Surviving as a Widow in Nineteenth-Century Montreal.' *Urban History Review* 17, no. 3 (Feb. 1989): 148–60

– *Working Families: Age, Gender, and Daily Survival in Industrializing Montreal.* Toronto: McClelland and Stewart 1993

Brenneman, Helen Good. *But Not Forsaken: A Vivid Story about the Tragic Experiences of a Russian Mennonite Refugee Family.* Scottdale, PA: Herald Press 1954

Brownmiller, Susan. *Against Our Will: Men, Women, and Rape.* New York: Simon and Schuster 1975

Burnet, Jean, ed. *Looking into My Sister's Eyes: An Exploration in Women's History.* Toronto: Multicultural History Society of Ontario 1986

Burnet, Jean, Danielle Juteau, Enoch Padolsky, Anthony Rasporich, and Antoine Sirois, eds. *Migration and the Transformation of Cultures.* Toronto: Multicultural History Society of Ontario 1992

Calliste, Agnes. 'Race, Gender, and Canadian Immigration Policy: Blacks from the Caribbean, 1900–1932.' *Journal of Canadian Studies* 28, no. 4 (winter 1993–4): 131–48

Chandler, Joan. *Women without Husbands: An Exploration of the Margins of Marriage.* London: Macmillan 1991

Clements, Barbara Evans, Barbara Alpern Engel, and Christine D. Worobec, eds. *Russia's Women: Accommodation, Resistance, Transformation.* Berkeley: University of California Press 1991

Cole, Ellen, Oliva M. Espin, and Esther D. Rothblum, eds. *Refugee Women and Their Mental Health: Shattered Societies, Shattered Lives.* Binghamton, NY: Harrington Park Press 1992

Comacchio, Cynthia R. 'Beneath the "Sentimental Veil": Families and Family History in Canada.' *Labour/Le Travail* 33 (spring 1994): 279–302

Connerton, Paul. *How Societies Remember.* Cambridge: Cambridge University Press 1989

Conquest, Robert. *The Great Terror: A Reassessment.* London: Pimlico 1992

– *The Harvest of Sorrow: Soviet Collectivization and the Terror-Famine.* Edmonton: University of Alberta Press in Association with the Canadian Institute of Ukrainian Studies 1986

Coontz, Stephanie. *The Way We Never Were: American Families and the Nostalgia Trap.* New York: Basic Books 1992

Cruikshank, Julie. *Life Lived Like a Story: Life Stories of Three Yukon Native Elders.* Lincoln: University of Nebraska Press 1990

Dallin, Alexander. *German Rule in Russia, 1941–1945: A Study of Occupation Policies.* 2nd rev. ed. Boulder, CO: Westview Press 1981

Danys, Milda. 'Contract Hiring of Displaced Persons in Canadian Domestic Employment, 1947–1950.' *Lituanus* 29, no. 2 (summer 1983): 40–51

– *DP: Lithuanian Immigration to Canada after the Second World War.* Toronto: Multicultural History Society of Ontario 1986

DeFehr, C.A. *Memories of My Life Recalled for My Family.* Altona, MB: D.W. Friesen 1967

deZayas, Alfred M. *Nemesis at Potsdam: The Expulsion of the Germans from the East.* 3rd ed. Lincoln: University of Nebraska Press 1989

Dick, C.L. *The Mennonite Conference of Alberta: A History of Its Churches and Institutions.* Edmonton: Mennonite Conference of Alberta 1980

Dick, Margaret L. *From Breslau to America.* Wichita, KS: the author 1992

Diefendorf, Barbara B. 'Widowhood and Remarriage in Sixteenth-Century Paris.' *Journal of Family History* 7, no. 4 (winter 1982): 379–95

Dirks, Gerald E. *Canada's Refugee Policy: Indifference or Opportunism?* Montreal: McGill-Queen's University Press 1977

Dueck, Helene. *Durch Trübsal und Not.* Winnipeg: Centre for Mennonite Brethren Studies 1995

Dupré, Louis. *Transcendent Selfhood: The Loss and Rediscovery of the Inner Life.* New York: Seabury 1976

Dyck, Cornelius J. *An Introduction to Mennonite History.* 3rd ed. Scottdale, PA: Herald Press, 1993

Dyck, Cornelius J., ed. *Something Meaningful for God: The Stories of Some Who Served with MCC.* Scottdale, PA: Herald Press 1981

Dyck, Harvey L., trans. and ed. *A Mennonite in Russia: The Diaries of Jacob D. Epp, 1851–1880.* Toronto: University of Toronto Press 1991

Dyck, Peter, and Elfrieda Dyck. *Up from the Rubble: The Epic Rescue of Thousands of War-Ravaged Mennonite Refugees.* Scottdale, PA: Herald Press 1991

Dyck, Sarah, ed. and trans. *The Silence Echoes: Memoirs of Trauma and Tears.* Kitchener: Pandora Press, 1997

Ediger, Katharina. *Under His Wings: Events in the Lives of Elder Alexander Ediger and His Family.* Kitchener: the author 1994

Elliott, Mark R. *Pawns of Yalta: Soviet Refugees and America's Role in Their Repatriation.* Urbana: University of Illinois Press 1982

Epp, Frank H. *Mennonite Exodus: The Rescue and Resettlement of the Russian Mennonites since the Communist Revolution.* Altona, MB: D.W. Friesen 1962

Epp, Frank H., ed. *Partners in Service: The Story of Mennonite Central Committee Canada.* Winnipeg: Mennonite Central Committee Canada 1983

Epp, George K. 'Mennonite Immigration to Canada after World War II.' *Journal of Mennonite Studies* 5 (1987): 108–19

Epp, Marlene. 'Alternative Service and Alternative Gender Roles: Conscientious Objectors in B.C. during World War II.' *BC Studies*, nos. 105/106 (spring/summer 1995): 139–58

– 'Carrying the Banner of Nonconformity: Ontario Mennonite Women and the Dress Question.' *Conrad Grebel Review* 8, no. 3 (fall 1990): 237–57

– 'The Memory of Violence: Soviet and East European Mennonite Refugees and Rape in the Second World War.' *Journal of Women's History* 9, no. 1 (spring 1997): 58–87

– 'The Mennonite Girls' Homes of Winnipeg: A Home Away from Home.' *Journal of Mennonite Studies* 6 (1988): 100–14

– 'Moving Forward, Looking Backward: The "Great Trek" from the Soviet Union, 1943–45.' *Journal of Mennonite Studies* 16 (1998): 59–75

– 'Women in Canadian Mennonite History: Uncovering the "Underside".' *Journal of Mennonite Studies* 5 (1987): 90–107

Epp, Peter. *Ob Tausend Fallen ... Mein Leben im Archipel Gulag*. Weichs: Memra-Verlag 1988

Ewert, David. *A Journey of Faith: An Autobiography*. Winnipeg: Centre for Mennonite Brethren Studies 1993

Farnsworth, Beatrice, and Lynne Viola, eds. *Russian Peasant Women*. New York: Oxford University Press 1992

Fast, Karl. *Gebt der Wahrheit die Ehre! Ein Schicksalsbericht*. 2nd ed. Winnipeg: Canzona Publishing 1989

Fentress, James and Chris Wickham. *Social Memory*. Cambridge, MA: Blackwell 1992

Fitzpatrick, Sheila. *Stalin's Peasants: Resistance and Survival in the Russian Village after Collectivization*. New York: Oxford University Press 1994

Fleischhauer, Ingeborg, and Benjamin Pinkus. *The Soviet Germans: Past and Present*. London: C. Hurst 1986

Foth, Maria. *Beyond the Border: Maria's Miraculous Pilgrimage*. Burlington, ON: G.R. Welch 1981

Fretz, J. Winfield. *Pilgrims in Paraguay*. Scottdale, PA: Herald Press 1953

Freund, Alexander, and Laura Quilici. 'Exploring Myths in Women's Narratives: Italian and German Immigrant Women in Vancouver, 1947–1961.' *BC Studies* nos. 105/106 (spring/summer 1995): 159–82

Friesen, John. *Against the Wind: The Story of Four Mennonite Villages*. Winnipeg: Henderson Books 1994

Friesen, John, ed. *Mennonites in Russia, 1788–1988: Essays in Honour of Gerhard Lohrenz*. Winnipeg: CMBC Publications 1989

Friesen, Katie. *Into the Unknown*. Steinbach, MB: the author 1986

Funk, Abram, ed. *25 Jahre Volendam, 1947–1972*. Paraguay: Kolonie Volendam 1972

Gabaccia, Donna. *From the Other Side: Women, Gender, and Immigrant Life in the U.S., 1820–1990*. Bloomington: Indiana University Press 1994

– 'Immigrant Women: Nowhere at Home?' *Journal of American Ethnic History* 10, no. 4 (summer 1991): 61–87

Gabaccia, Donna, ed. *Seeking Common Ground: Multidisciplinary Studies of Immigrant Women in the United States*. Westport, CT: Praeger 1992

Geiger, Susan. 'What's So Feminist about Doing Women's Oral History?' *Journal of Women's History* 2, no. 1 (spring 1990): 169–82

Gerlach, Horst. 'The Final Years of Mennonites in East and West Prussia, 1943–45.' *Mennonite Quarterly Review* 66 (April/July 1992): 221–46, 391–423

– 'Mennonites, the Molotschna, and the *Volksdeutsche Mittelstelle* in the Second World War.' Translated by John D. Thiesen. *Mennonite Life* 41, no. 3 (Sept. 1986): 4–9

– *Nightmare in Red*. Carol Stream, IL: Creation House c1970

Gittins, Diana. *The Family in Question: Changing Households and Familiar Ideologies*. London: Macmillan 1985

Gleason, Mona. 'Psychology and the Construction of the "Normal" Family in Postwar Canada, 1945–60.' *Canadian Historical Review* 78, no. 3 (Sept. 1997): 442–77

Goering, Gladys V. *Women in Search of Mission: A History of the General Conference Mennonite Women's Organization*. Newton, KS: Faith and Life Press 1980

Goerzen, Anny Penner Klassen, with Anne Klassen Suderman and Susan Thiessen Klassen. *Anny: Sheltered in the Arms of God. A True Story of Survival in Russia*. Fort St James, BC: the author 1988

Gölz, Annalee. 'Family Matters: The Canadian Family and the State in the Postwar Period.' *left history* 1 (fall 1993): 9–49

Grossmann, Atina. 'A Question of Silence: The Rape of German Women by Occupation Soldiers.' *October* 72 (spring 1995): 43–63

– *Reforming Sex: The German Movement for Birth Control and Abortion Reform, 1920–1950*. New York: Oxford University Press 1995.

Guest, Dennis. *The Emergence of Social Security in Canada*. Vancouver: University of British Columbia Press 1980

Hamm, Abram, and Maria Hamm. *Die Wege des Herrn sind Lauter Guete*. Gummersbach: Verlag Friedensstimme 1985

Hareven, Tamara K. 'The History of the Family and the Complexity of Social Change.' *American Historical Review* 96, no. 1 (Feb. 1991): 95–124

Harney, Robert F. 'Men without Women: Italian Migrants in Canada, 1885–1930.' In *The Italian Immigrant Woman in North America*, edited by Betty Boyd Caroli, Robert F. Harney, and Lydio F. Tomasi. Toronto: Multicultural History Society of Ontario 1978

Harris, Ruth. 'The "Child of the Barbarian": Rape, Race and Nationalism in France during the First World War.' *Past and Present* 141 (Nov. 1993): 170–206

Heaton, Tim B., and Marie Cornwall. 'Religious Group Variation in the Socioeconomic Status and Family Behavior of Women.' *Journal for the Scientific Study of Religion* 28, no. 3 (1989): 283–99

Heineman, Elizabeth. 'Complete Families, Half Families, No Familes at All: Female-Headed Households and the Reconstruction of the Family in the Early Federal Republic.' *Central European History* 29, no. 1 (1996): 19–60

Herbert, Ulrich. *Fremdarbeiter: Politik und Praxis des 'Auslaender-Einsatzes' in der Kriegswirtschaft des Dritten Reiches.* Berlin: Verlag J.H.W. Dietz Nachf. 1985

Higonnet, Margaret R., and Patrice L.-R. Higonnet. 'The Double Helix.' In *Behind the Lines: Gender and the Two World Wars*, edited by Margaret Randolph Higonnet, Jane Jenson, and Margaret Collins Weitz, 31–47. New Haven: Yale University Press 1987

Houstoun, Marion F., Roger G. Kramer, and John Mackin Barrett. 'Female Predominance in Immigration to the United States since 1930: A First Look.' *International Migration Review* 18 (winter 1984): 908–63

Huebert, Helmut T. *Hierschau: An Example of Russian Mennonite Life.* Winnipeg: Springfield Publishers 1986

Hufton, Olwen. 'Women without Men: Widows and Spinsters in Britain and France in the Eighteenth Century.' *Journal of Family History* 9, no. 4 (winter 1984): 355–76

Iacovetta, Franca. 'Making "New Canadians": Social Workers, Women, and the Reshaping of Immigrant Families.' In *Gender Conflicts: New Essays in Women's History*, edited by Franca Iacovetta and Mariana Valverde, 261–303. Toronto: University of Toronto Press 1992

– 'Manly Militants, Cohesive Communities, and Defiant Domestics: Writing about Immigrants in Canadian Historical Scholarship.' *Labour/Le Travail* 36 (Fall 1995): 217–52

– 'Remaking Their Lives: Women Immigrants, Survivors, and Refugees.' In *A Diversity of Women: Ontario, 1945–1980*, edited by Joy Parr, 135–67. Toronto: University of Toronto Press 1995

– *Such Hardworking People: Italian Immigrants in Postwar Toronto.* Montreal: McGill-Queen's University Press 1992

Indra, Doreen. 'Ethnic Human Rights and Feminist Theory: Gender Implications for Refugee Studies and Practice.' *Journal of Refugee Studies* 2, no. 2 (1989): 221–42

– 'Gender: A Key Dimension of the Refugee Experience.' *Refuge* 6, no. 3 (Feb. 1987): 3–4

Isajiw, Wsevolod, Yury Boshyk, and Roman Senkus, eds. *The Refugee Experience:*

Ukrainian Displaced Persons after World War II. Edmonton: Canadian Institute of Ukrainian Studies Press 1992

Janzen, Victor. *Vom Dnjepr zum Paraguay Fluss.* Winnipeg: the author 1995

Klassen, Herbert, and Maureen Klassen. *Ambassador to His People: C.F. Klassen and the Russian Mennonite Refugees.* Winnipeg: Kindred Press 1990

Klassen, Pamela E. *Going By the Moon and the Stars: Stories of Two Russian Mennonite Women.* Waterloo: Wilfrid Laurier University Press 1994

– 'Submerged in Love: An Interpretation of the Diary of Lydia Reimer, 1922–24.' *Studies in Religion/Sciences religieuses* 23, no. 4 (1994): 429–39

Klassen, Peter J. *A Homeland for Strangers: An Introduction to Mennonites in Poland and Prussia.* Fresno, CA: Center for Mennonite Brethren Studies 1989

Klassen, Peter P. *Die Mennoniten in Paraguay: Reich Gottes und Reich dieser Welt.* Bolanden-Weierhof, Germany: Mennonitischer Geschichtsverein 1988

Klippenstein, Frieda Esau. '"Doing What We Could": Mennonite Domestic Servants in Winnipeg, 1920s to 1950s.' *Journal of Mennonite Studies* 7 (1989): 145–66

Koch, Gertrud. 'Blood, Sperm, and Tears.' *October* 72 (spring 1995): 27–41

Kolinsky, Eva. *Women in Contemporary Germany: Life, Work and Politics.* rev. ed. Providence, RI: Berg 1993

Knowles, Valerie. *Strangers at Our Gates: Canadian Immigration and Immigration Policy, 1540–1990.* Toronto: Dundurn Press 1992

Krall, Ruth E. 'Christian Ideology, Rape and Women's Postrape Journeys to Healing.' In *Peace Theology and Violence against Women.* Occasional Papers no.16, edited by Elizabeth G. Yoder, 76–92. Elkhart, IN: Institute of Mennonite Studies 1992

Krause, J.C. *Gnadenfeld. Molotschna, Sued-Ruszland, 1835–1943: Erinnerungen aus guter und schwerer Zeit.* Yarrow, BC: the author 1954

Kreider, Robert. *Interviews with Peter J. Dyck and Elfrieda Klassen Dyck: Experiences in Mennonite Central Committee Service in Europe, 1941–1949.* Akron, PA: Mennonite Central Committee 1988

Krueger, Katharine. *Schicksal einer Russlanddeutschen.* Goettigen: Im Graphikum 1991

Latter, Helene. *I Do Remember.* Morden, MB: Walter F. Latter 1988

Lehn, Cornelia. *Frontier Challenge: A Story of the Conference of Mennonites in B.C.* Clearbrook, BC: Conference of Mennonites in British Columbia 1990

Lentin, Ronit, ed. *Gender and Catastrophe.* London: Zed Books, 1997

Leslie, Genevieve. 'Domestic Service in Canada, 1880–1920.' In *Women at Work: Ontario, 1850–1930,* edited by Janice Acton, Penny Goldsmith, and Bonnie Shepard, 71–125. Toronto: Women's Educational Press 1974

Letkemann, Peter. 'Mennonite Victims of the "Great Terror," 1936–1938.' *Journal of Mennonite Studies* 16 (1998): 33–58

Liebman, Stuart, and Annette Michelson. 'After the Fall: Women in the House of the Hangmen.' *October* 72 (spring 1995): 5–14

Liebman, Stuart, and Annette Michelson, eds. 'Berlin 1945: War and Rape – "Liberators Take Liberties".' Special issue, *October* 72 (spring 1995)

Linden, Ruth R. *Making Stories, Making Selves: Feminist Reflections on the Holocaust.* Columbus: Ohio State University Press 1993

Lindström-Best, Varpu. *Defiant Sisters: A Social History of Finnish Immigrant Women in Canada.* Toronto: Multicultural History Society of Ontario 1988

Linz, Susan J., ed. *The Impact of World War II on the Soviet Union.* Totowa, NJ: Rowman and Allanheld 1985

Little, Margaret. 'The Blurring of Boundaries: Private and Public Welfare for Single Mothers in Ontario.' *Studies in Political Economy* 47 (summer 1995): 89–109

Loewen, Harry. '"Can the Son Answer for the Father?" Reflections on the Stalinist Terror.' *Journal of Mennonite Studies* 16 (1998): 76–90

Loewen, Jacob A., and Wesley J. Prieb. 'The Abuse of Power among Mennonites in South Russia, 1789–1919.' *Journal of Mennonite Studies* 14 (1996): 17–44

Loewen, Royden. '"The Children, the Cows, My Dear Man and My Sister": The Transplanted Lives of Mennonite Farm Women, 1874–1900.' *Canadian Historical Review* 73, no. 3 (1992): 344–73.

– *Family, Church, and Market: A Mennonite Community in the Old and the New Worlds, 1850–1930.* Toronto: University of Toronto Press 1993

– 'Rurality, Ethnicity, and Gender Patterns of Cultural Continuity during the "Great Disjuncture" in the R.M. of Hanover, 1945–1961.' *Journal of the Canadian Historical Association* (1993): 161–82

Lohrenz, Gerhard. *The Lost Generation and Other Stories.* Winnipeg: the author 1982

– *The Odyssey of the Bergen Family.* Winnipeg: the author 1978

– *Stories from Mennonite Life.* Winnipeg: the author 1980

Lopata, Helena Z. 'Widowhood in Polonia.' *Polish American Studies* 34 (1977): 7–25

Luciuk, Lubomyr K. 'Unintended Consequences in Refugee Resettlement: Post-War Ukrainian Refugee Immigration to Canada.' *International Migration Review* 20, no. 2 (summer 1986): 467–82

Marrus, Michael R. *The Unwanted: European Refugees in the Twentieth Century.* New York: Oxford University Press 1985

Martin, Susan Forbes. *Refugee Women.* London: Zed Books 1992

Mathies, Gudrun L. (Wohlgemut). 'Refugee Pilgrimage: A Story of God's Care; Lina (Heinrich) Wohlgemut: From Poland to Canada.' *Ontario Mennonite History* 13, no. 1 (March 1995): 8–14

McLuhan, Elizabeth, ed. *Safe Haven: The Refugee Experience of Five Families*. Toronto: Multicultural History Society of Ontario 1995

Melman, Billie. 'Gender, History and Memory: The Invention of Women's Past in the Nineteenth and Early Twentieth Centuries.' *History and Memory* 5, no. 1 (spring/summer 1993): 5–41

'Mennonite Central Committee, 1920–1970.' Special Issue. *Mennonite Quarterly Review* 44, no. 3 (July 1970)

Miller, Donald E., and Lorna Touryan Miller. *Survivors: An Oral History of the Armenian Genocide*. Berkeley: University of California Press 1993

Miron, John R. *Housing in Postwar Canada: Demographic Change, Household Formation, and Housing Demand*. Montreal: McGill-Queen's University Press 1988

Nafziger, Elfrieda Toews. *A Man of His Word: A Biography of John A. Toews*. Hillsboro, KS: Kindred Press 1992

Naimark, Norman M. *The Russians in Germany: A History of the Soviet Zone of Occupation, 1945–1949*. Cambridge: Belknap Press of Harvard University Press 1995

Neufeld, Dietrich. *A Russian Dance of Death: Revolution and Civil War in the Ukraine*, translated and edited by Al Reimer. Winnipeg: Hyperion Press 1977

Neufeld, Jacob A. *Tiefenwege: Erfahrungen und Erlebnisse von Russland-Mennoniten in zwei Jahrzehnten bis 1949*. Virgil, ON: the author 1958

Neufeldt, Colin P. 'Through the Fires of Hell: The Dekulakization and Collectivization of the Soviet Mennonite Community, 1928–1933.' *Journal of Mennonite Studies* 16 (1998): 9–32

Neufeldt, Harvey. 'Creating the Brotherhood: Status and Control in the Yarrow Mennonite Community, 1928–1960.' In *Canadian Papers in Rural History*, vol. 9, edited by Donald H. Akenson, 211–38. Gananoque, ON: Langdale Press 1994

Noivo, Edite. *Inside Ethnic Families: Three Generations of Portuguese-Canadians*. Montreal: McGill-Queen's University Press, 1997

Parr, Joy. 'The Skilled Emigrant and Her Kin: Gender, Culture and Labour Recruitment.' *Canadian Historical Review* 68, no. 4 (Dec. 1987): 529–51

Parr, Joy, ed. *A Diversity of Women: Ontario, 1945–1980*. Toronto: University of Toronto Press 1995

Parr, Joy, and Mark Rosenfeld, eds. *Gender and History in Canada*. Toronto: Copp Clark 1996

Parrino, Maria. 'Breaking the Silence: Autobiographies of Italian Immigrant Women.' *Storia Nord Americana* 5, no. 1 (1988): 137–58

Passerini, Luisa. *Fascism in Popular Memory*. Cambridge: Cambridge University Press 1987

Patai, Daphne, and Sherna Berger Gluck, eds. *Women's Words: The Feminist Practice of Oral History*. New York: Routledge 1991

Peavy, Linda, and Ursula Smith. *The Gold Rush Widows of Little Falls: A Story Drawn from the Letters of Pamelia and James Fergus*. St Paul: Minnesota Historical Society Press 1990

Pedraza, Silvia. 'Women and Migration: The Social Consequences of Gender.' *Annual Review of Sociology* 17 (1991): 303–25

Penner, Horst. *Die ost- und westpreussischen Mennoniten in ihrem religioesen und sozialen Leben in ihren kulturellen und wirtschaftlichen Leistungen*. Kirchheimbolanden: the author 1987

Personal Narratives Group, ed. *Interpreting Women's Lives: Feminist Theory and Personal Narratives*. Bloomington: Indiana University Press 1989

Peters, Gerald, trans. and ed. *Diary of Anna Baerg, 1916–1924*. Winnipeg: CMBC Publications 1985

Peters, Jake. *The Waisenamt: A History of Mennonite Inheritance Custom*. Steinbach, MB: Mennonite Village Museum 1985

Peters, John F. 'Traditional Customs of Remarriage among Some Canadian Mennonite Widow(er)s.' *Journal of Mennonite Studies* 10 (1992): 118–29

Potter-MacKinnon, Janice. *While the Women Only Wept: Loyalist Refugee Women in Eastern Ontario*. Montreal: McGill-Queen's University Press 1993

Radecki, Henry, with Benedykt Heydenkorn. *A Member of a Distinguished Family: The Polish Group in Canada*. Toronto: McClelland and Stewart 1976

Reardon, Betty A. *Sexism and the War System*. New York: Teachers College Press 1985

Redekop, Calvin. *Mennonite Society*. Baltimore: Johns Hopkins University Press 1989

Redekop, Calvin Wall, and Samuel J. Steiner, eds. *Mennonite Identity: Historical and Contemporary Perspectives*. Lanham, MD: University Press of America 1988

Redekop, Gloria Neufeld. 'The Understanding of Woman's Place among Mennonite Brethren in Canada: A Question of Biblical Interpretation.' *Conrad Grebel Review* 8, no. 3 (fall 1990): 259–74

– *The Work of Their Hands: Mennonite Women's Societies in Canada*. Waterloo: Wilfrid Laurier University Press 1996

Redekop, Magdalene. 'Escape from the Bloody Theatre: The Making of Mennonite Stories.' *Journal of Mennonite Studies* 11 (1993): 9–22

– 'Through the Mennonite Looking Glass.' In *Why I Am a Mennonite: Essays on Mennonite Identity*, edited by Harry Loewen, 226–53. Kitchener, ON: Herald Press 1988

Redekop, Paul. 'The Mennonite Family in Tradition and Transition.' *Journal of Mennonite Studies* 4 (1986): 77–93

Regehr, T.D. 'Anatomy of a Mennonite Miracle: The Berlin Rescue of 30–31 January 1947.' *Journal of Mennonite Studies* 9 (1991): 11–33

- 'Of Dutch or German Ancestry? Mennonite Refugees, MCC and the International Refugee Organization.' *Journal of Mennonite Studies* 13 (1995): 7–25
- *Mennonites in Canada, 1939–1970: A People Transformed.* Toronto: University of Toronto Press 1996
- 'Polish and Prussian Mennonite Displaced Persons, 1944–50.' *Mennonite Quarterly Review* 66 (April 1992): 247–66
Regehr, Walter, ed. *25 Jahre Kolonie Neuland Chaco-Paraguay, 1947–1972.* Colonia Neuland, Paraguay: Kolonie Neuland 1972.
Reimer, Al. *My Harp Is Turned to Mourning.* Winnipeg: Hyperion Press 1985
Rimland, Ingrid. *The Wanderers: The Saga of Three Women Who Survived.* St Louis, MO: Concordia 1977
- 'The Wanderers Revisited.' In *Mennonite Images: Historical, Cultural, and Literary Essays Dealing with Mennonite Issues,* edited by Harry Loewen, 267–73. Winnipeg: Hyperion Press 1980
Ryan, Cornelius. *The Last Battle.* New York: Simon and Schuster 1966
Samuel, Raphael, and Paul Thompson, eds. *The Myths We Live By.* London: Routledge 1990
Sander, Helke, and Barbara Johr, eds. *BeFreier und Befreite: Krieg, Vergewaltigungen, Kinder.* Munich: Verlag Antje Kunstmann 1992
Sangster, Joan. 'Doing Two Jobs: The Wage-Earning Mother, 1945–1970.' In *A Diversity of Women: Ontario, 1945–1980,* edited by Joy Parr, 98–134. Toronto: University of Toronto Press 1995
- *Earning Respect: The Lives of Working Women in Small-Town Ontario, 1920–1960.* Toronto: University of Toronto Press 1995
Sauer, Angelika E. 'A Matter of Domestic Policy? Canadian Immigration Policy and the Admission of Germans, 1945–50.' *Canadian Historical Review* 74, no. 2 (June 1993) : 226–63
Scadron, Arlene, ed. *On Their Own: Widows and Widowhood in the American Southwest, 1848–1939.* Urbana: University of Illinois Press 1988
Schieder, Theodor, ed. *Documents on the Expulsion of the Germans from Eastern-Central Europe.* Vol. 1. *The Expulsion of the German Population from the Territories East of the Oder-Neisse-Line.* Bonn: Federal Ministry for Expellees, Refugees and War Victims, n.d.
Schloneger, Florence. *Sara's Trek.* Newton: KS: Faith and Life Press 1981
Schmidt, Agatha Loewen. *Gnadenfeld, Molotschna, 1835–1943.* Kitchener: the author 1989
Schroeder, William, and Helmut T. Huebert, *Mennonite Historical Atlas.* Winnipeg: Springfield Publishers 1990
Scott, Joan W. 'Rewriting History.' In *Behind the Lines: Gender and the Two World*

Wars, edited by Margaret Randolph Higonnet, Jane Jenson, and Margaret Collins Weitz, 19–30. New Haven: Yale University Press 1987

Simon, Rita James, and Caroline B. Brettell, eds. *International Migration: The Female Experience*. Totowa, NJ: Rowman and Allanheld 1986

Smucker, Barbara. *Henry's Red Sea*. Scottdale: PA: Herald Press 1955

'Special Issue on Women Refugees.' *Refuge* 14, nos. 7/8 (Dec. 1994/Jan. 1995)

Stiglmayer, Alexandra, ed. *Mass Rape: The War against Women in Bosnia-Herzegovina*. Lincoln: University of Nebraska Press 1994

Stola, Dariusz. 'Forced Migrations in Central European History.' *International Migration Review* 26, no. 2 (summer 1992): 324–41

Strong-Boag, Veronica. 'Home Dreams: Women and the Suburban Experiment in Canada, 1945–60.' *Canadian Historical Review* 72, no. 4 (Dec. 1991): 471–504

Swyripa, Frances. *Wedded to the Cause: Ukrainian-Canadian Women and Ethnic Identity, 1891–1991*. Toronto: University of Toronto Press 1993

Taves, Krista M. 'The Reunification of Russian Mennonites in Post-World War II Canada.' *Ontario Mennonite History* 13, no. 1 (March 1995): 1–7

Todd, Barbara J. 'The Remarrying Widow: A Stereotype Reconsidered.' In *Women in English Society, 1500–1800*, edited by Mary Prior, 54–92. London: Methuen 1985

Toews, Aaron A. *Mennonite Martyrs: People Who Suffered for Their Faith, 1920–1940*. Translated by John B. Toews. Winnipeg: Kindred Press 1990

Toews, C.P., Heinrich Friesen, and Arnold Dyck. *The Kuban Settlement*. Translated by Herbert Giesbrecht. Winnipeg: CMBC Publications and Manitoba Mennonite Historical Society 1989

Toews, John B. 'Abram's List.' *Journal of the American Historical Society of Germans from Russia* 17, no. 4 (Winter 1994): 26–39

– 'Childbirth, Disease, and Death among the Mennonites in Nineteenth-Century Russia.' *Mennonite Quarterly Review* 60, no. 3 (July 1986): 450–68

– *Czars, Soviets and Mennonites*. Newton, KS: Faith and Life Press 1982

– *Journeys: Mennonite Stories of Faith and Survival in Stalin's Russia*. Winnipeg: Kindred Productions 1998

– *With Courage to Spare: The Life of B.B. Janz, 1877–1964*. Hillsboro, KS: Board of Christian Literature of the General Conference of Mennonite Brethren Churches 1978

Toews, John B., trans. and ed. *Letters from Susan: A Woman's View of the Russian Mennonite Experience (1928–1941)*. North Newton, KS: Bethel College 1988

Toews, Paul, ed. *Bridging Troubled Waters: Mennonite Brethren at Mid-Twentieth Century*. Winnipeg: Kindred Productions 1995

Toews, Susanna. *Trek to Freedom: The Escape of Two Sisters from South Russia dur-*

ing World War II. Translated by Helen Megli. Winkler, MB: Heritage Valley Publications 1976

Tolstoy, Nikolai. *Victims of Yalta*. London: Hodder and Stoughton 1977

Tröger, Annemarie. 'Between Rape and Prostitution: Survival Strategies and Chances of Emancipation for Berlin Women after World War II.' In *Women in Culture and Politics: A Century of Change*, edited by Judith Friedlander, Blanche Wiesen Cook, Alice Kessler-Harris, and Carroll Smith-Rosenberg, 97–117. Bloomington: Indiana University Press 1986

– 'German Women's Memories of World War II.' In *Behind the Lines: Gender and the Two World Wars*, edited by Margaret Randolph Higonnet, Jane Jenson, and Margaret Collins Weitz, 285–99. New Haven: Yale University Press 1987

Unruh, John C. *In the Name of Christ: A History of the Mennonite Central Committee and Its Service, 1920–1951*. Scottdale, PA: Herald Press 1952

Urry, James. *None But Saints: The Transformation of Mennonite Life in Russia, 1789–1889*. Winnipeg: Hyperion Press 1989

Weinberg, Sydney Stahl. 'The Treatment of Women in Immigration History: A Call for Change.' With comments by Donna Gabaccia, Hsia R. Diner, and Maxine Schwartz Seller. *Journal of American Ethnic History* 11, no. 4 (summer 1992): 25–69

Whitaker, Reg. *Canadian Immigration Policy since Confederation*. Ottawa: Canadian Historical Association 1991

Wiebe, Katie Funk. 'Women in the Mennonite Brethren Church.' In *Your Daughters Shall Prophesy: Women in Ministry in the Church*, edited by John E. Toews, Valerie Rempel, Katie Funk Wiebe. Winnipeg: Kindred Press 1992

Wiebe, Rudy. 'Flowers for Approaching the Fire: A Meditation on *The Bloody Theatre, or Martyrs Mirror.*' *Conrad Grebel Review* 16, no. 2 (spring 1998): 110–24

Wiens, Elisabeth. 'Flucht vom Weichseltal 1945.' *Mennonitische Geschichtsblaetter* 38 (1981): 7–22

– *Schicksalsjahr 1945: Erlebnisse nach Tagebuchnotizen*. Niagara-on-the-Lake, ON: the author 1993.

Winter, Henry H. *A Shepherd of the Oppressed: Heinrich Winter, the Last Aeltester of Chortitza*. Leamington, ON: the author 1990

Woelk, Heinrich, and Gerhard Woelk, *A Wilderness Journey: Glimpses of the Mennonite Brethren Church in Russia, 1925–1980*. Translated by Victor Doerksen. Fresno, CA: Center for Mennonite Brethren Studies 1982

Wyman, Mark. *DP: Europe's Displaced Persons, 1945–1951*. Philadelphia: Balch Institute Press 1989

Wyntjes, Sherrin Marshall. 'Survivors and Status: Widowhood and Family in the

Early Modern Netherlands.' *Journal of Family History* 7, no. 4 (winter 1982): 396–405

Yans-McLaughlin, Virginia, ed. *Immigration Reconsidered: History, Sociology and Politics.* New York: Oxford University Press 1990

Yoder, Elizabeth G., ed. *Peace Theology and Violence against Women.* Elkhart, IN: Institute of Mennonite Studies 1992

Illustration Credits

Archives of the Mennonite Church, Mennonite Central Committee Photograph Collection: preparing vegetables for noonday meal; working at the home for the aged

Centre for Mennonite Brethren Studies: Refugee children loaded on a boxcar; refugee women gathering fuel; Elfrieda Klassen Dyck

Otto Klassen: Work crews along the Dnieper River; westward trek from Ukraine; sleeping child; officers survey massacre; family and newly built home; woman preparing a meal on her mud stove

Mennonite Heritage Centre: Molotschna settlement; taking cows to drink; first baptismal group

Index

STUDIES IN GENDER AND HISTORY

General editors: Franca Iacovetta and Karen Dubinsky